£80.00

Post-Conflict Heritage, Postcolonial Tourism

Angkor, Cambodia's only World Heritage Site, is enduring one of the most crucial, turbulent periods in its 1200-year history. Given Cambodia's need to restore its shattered social and physical infrastructures after decades of violent conflict, and with tourism to Angkor increasing by a staggering 10,000 percent in just over a decade, the site has become an intense focal point of competing agendas. Angkor's immense historical importance, along with its global prestige, has led to an unprecedented influx of aid, with over 20 countries together donating millions of dollars for conservation and research. For the Royal Government, however, Angkor has become a 'cash cow' of development.

Post-Conflict Heritage, Postcolonial Tourism critically examines this situation and locates Angkor within the broader contexts of post-conflict reconstruction, nation building, and socio-economic rehabilitation. Based on two years of field-work, the book explores culture, development, the politics of space, and the relationship between consumption, memory and identity to reveal the aspirations and tensions, anxieties and paradoxical agendas, which form around a heritage tourism landscape in a post-conflict, postcolonial society.

With the situation in Cambodia examined as a stark example of a phenomenon common to many countries attempting to recover after periods of war or political turmoil, *Post-Conflict Heritage, Postcolonial Tourism* will be of particular interest to students and scholars working in the fields of Asian studies, tourism, heritage, development, and cultural and postcolonial studies.

Tim Winter is based at the University of Sydney researching heritage and tourism in Asia. Having published widely on Angkor, he is editor of *Expressions of Cambodia: the politics of tradition, identity and change* (Routledge 2006) and *Asia on Tour: exploring the rise of Asian Tourism* (Routledge, 2008). He is also editor of the ICOMOS journal *Historic Environment*.
Visit www.postconflictheritage.com

Asia's Transformations
Edited by Mark Selden
Binghamton and Cornell Universities, USA

The books in this series explore the political, social, economic and cultural consequences of Asia's transformations in the twentieth and twenty-first centuries.
The series emphasizes the tumultuous interplay of local, national, regional and
global forces as Asia bids to become the hub of the world economy. While focusing on the contemporary, it also looks back to analyse the antecedents of Asia's
contested rise.

This series comprises several strands:

Asia's Transformations aims to address the needs of students and teachers, and
the titles will be published in hardback and paperback. Titles include:

Debating Human Rights
Critical essays from the United States and Asia
Edited by Peter Van Ness

Hong Kong's History
State and society under colonial rule
Edited by Tak-Wing Ngo

Japan's Comfort Women
Sexual slavery and prostitution during World War II and the US occupation
Yuki Tanaka

Opium, Empire and the Global Political Economy
Carl A. Trocki

Chinese Society
Change, conflict and resistance
Edited by Elizabeth J. Perry and Mark Selden

Mao's Children in the New China
Voices from the Red Guard generation
Yarong Jiang and David Ashley

Remaking the Chinese State
Strategies, society and security
Edited by Chien-min Chao and Bruce J. Dickson

Korean Society
Civil society, democracy and the state
Edited by Charles K. Armstrong

The Making of Modern Korea
Adrian Buzo

The Resurgence of East Asia
500, 150 and 50 Year perspectives
Edited by Giovanni Arrighi, Takeshi Hamashita and Mark Selden

Chinese Society, second edition
Change, conflict and resistance
Edited by Elizabeth J. Perry and Mark Selden

Ethnicity in Asia
Edited by Colin Mackerras

The Battle for Asia
From decolonization to globalization
Mark T. Berger

State and Society in 21ˢᵗ Century China
Edited by Peter Hays Gries and Stanley Rosen

Japan's Quiet Transformation
Social change and civil society in the 21ˢᵗ century
Jeff Kingston

Confronting the Bush Doctrine
Critical views from the Asia-Pacific
Edited by Mel Gurtov and Peter Van Ness

China in War and Revolution, 1895–1949
Peter Zarrow

The Future of US–Korean Relations
The imbalance of power
Edited by John Feffer

Working in China
Ethnographies of labor and workplace transformations
Edited by Ching Kwan Lee

Korean Society, second edition
Civil society, democracy and the state
Edited by Charles K. Armstrong

Singapore
The State and the Culture of Excess
Souchou Yao

Pan-Asianism in Modern Japanese History
Colonialism, regionalism and borders
Edited by Sven Saaler and J. Victor Koschmann

The Making of Modern Korea, 2nd Edition
Adrian Buzo

Asia's Great Cities
Each volume aims to capture the heartbeat of the contemporary city from multiple perspectives emblematic of the authors' own deep familiarity with the distinctive faces of the city, its history, society, culture, politics and economics, and its evolving position in national, regional and global frameworks. While most volumes emphasize urban developments since the Second World War, some pay close attention to the legacy of the longue durée in shaping the contemporary. Thematic and comparative volumes address such themes as urbanization, economic and financial linkages, architecture and space, wealth and power, gendered relationships, planning and anarchy, and ethnographies in national and regional perspective. Titles include:

Bangkok
Place, practice and representation
Marc Askew

Beijing in the Modern World
David Strand and Madeline Yue Dong

Shanghai
Global city
Jeff Wasserstrom

Hong Kong
Global city
Stephen Chiu and Tai-Lok Lui

Representing Calcutta
Modernity, nationalism and the colonial uncanny
Swati Chattopadhyay

Singapore
Wealth, power and the culture of control
Carl A. Trocki

Asia.com is a series which focuses on the ways in which new information and communication technologies are influencing politics, society and culture in Asia. Titles include:

Japanese Cybercultures
Edited by Mark McLelland and Nanette Gottlieb

Asia.com
Asia encounters the Internet
Edited by K. C. Ho, Randolph Kluver and Kenneth C. C. Yang

The Internet in Indonesia's New Democracy
David T. Hill & Krishna Sen

Chinese Cyberspaces
Technological changes and political effects
Edited by Jens Damm and Simona Thomas

Literature and Society is a series that seeks to demonstrate the ways in which Asian Literature is influenced by the politics, society and culture in which it is produced. Titles include:

The Body in Postwar Japanese Fiction
Edited by Douglas N. Slaymaker

Chinese Women Writers and the Feminist Imagination, 1905–1948
Haiping Yan

Routledge Studies in Asia's Transformations is a forum for innovative new research intended for a high-level specialist readership, and the titles will be available in hardback only. Titles include:

1. **The American Occupation of Japan and Okinawa***
   Literature and memory
   Michael Molasky

2. **Koreans in Japan***
   Critical voices from the margin
   Edited by Sonia Ryang

3. **Internationalizing the Pacific**
   The United States, Japan and the Institute of Pacific Relations in war and peace, 1919–1945
   Tomoko Akami

4. **Imperialism in South East Asia**
   'A fleeting, passing phase'
   Nicholas Tarling

5. **Chinese Media, Global Contexts**
   Edited by Chin-Chuan Lee

6. **Remaking Citizenship in Hong Kong**
   Community, nation and the global city
   Edited by Agnes S. Ku and Ngai Pun

7. **Japanese Industrial Governance**
   Protectionism and the licensing state
   Yul Sohn

8. **Developmental Dilemmas**
   Land reform and institutional change in China
   Edited by Peter Ho

9. **Genders, Transgenders and Sexualities in Japan**
   Edited by Mark McLelland and Romit Dasgupta

10. **Fertility, Family Planning and Population Policy in China**
    Edited by Dudley L. Poston, Che-Fu Lee, Chiung-Fang Chang, Sherry L. McKibben and Carol S. Walther

11. **Japanese Diasporas**
   Unsung pasts, conflicting presents and uncertain futures
   Edited by Nobuko Adachi

12. **How China Works**
   Perspectives on the twentieth-century industrial workplace
   Edited by Jacob Eyferth

13. **Remolding and Resistance among Writers of the Chinese Prison Camp**
   Disciplined and published
   Edited by Philip F. Williams and Yenna Wu

14. **Popular Culture, Globalization and Japan**
   Edited by Matthew Allen and Rumi Sakamoto

15. **medi@sia**
   Global mediation in and out of context
   Edited by Todd Joseph Miles Holden and Timothy J. Scrase

16. **Vientiane**
   Transformations of a Lao landscape
   Marc Askew, William S. Logan and Colin Long

17. **State Formation and Radical Democracy in India**
   Manali Desai

18. **Democracy in Occupied Japan**
   The U.S. occupation and Japanese politics and society
   Edited by Mark E. Caprio and Yoneyuki Sugita

19. **Globalization, Culture and Society in Laos**
   Boike Rehbein

20. **Transcultural Japan**
   At the borderlands of race, gender, and identity
   Edited by David Blake Willis and Stephen Murphy-Shigematsu

21. **Post-Conflict Heritage, Postcolonial Tourism**
   Culture, politics and development at Angkor
   Tim Winter

*Now available in paperback

Critical Asian Scholarship is a series intended to showcase the most important individual contributions to scholarship in Asian Studies. Each of the volumes presents a leading Asian scholar addressing themes that are central to his or her most significant and lasting contribution to Asian studies. The series is committed to the rich variety of research and writing on Asia, and is not restricted to any particular discipline, theoretical approach or geographical expertise.

Southeast Asia
A testament
George McT. Kahin

Women and the Family in Chinese History
Patricia Buckley Ebrey

China Unbound
Evolving perspectives on the Chinese past
Paul A. Cohen

China's Past, China's Future
Energy, food, environment
Vaclav Smil

The Chinese State in Ming Society
Timothy Brook

Education and Reform in China
Emily Hannum and Albert Park

Post-Conflict Heritage, Postcolonial Tourism

Culture, politics and development at Angkor

Tim Winter

Routledge
Taylor & Francis Group

LONDON AND NEW YORK

First published 2007
by Routledge
2 Park Square, Milton Park, Abingdon, Oxon OX14 5RN

Simultaneously published in the USA and Canada
by Routledge
29 West 35th Street, New York, NY 10001

*Routledge is an imprint of the Taylor & Francis Group, an informa
business*

© 2007 Tim Winter

Reprinted 2008

Typeset in Times New Roman by Keyword Group Ltd
Printed and bound in Great Britain by MPG Books Ltd, Bodmin, Cornwall

British Library Cataloguing in Publication Data
A catalogue record for this book is available from the British Library

Library of Congress Cataloging in Publication Data
A catalog record for this book has been requested

ISBN10: 0-415-43095-X (hbk)
ISBN10: 0-203-94638-3 (ebk)

ISBN13: 978-0-415-43095-1 (hbk)
ISBN13: 978-0-203-94638-1 (ebk)

To an enduring spirit, and the faith inherited...

Contents

List of figures   xv
List of tables   xvii
Acknowledgments   xix
Abbreviations   xxi

1 From a time of conflict to conflicting times   1

2 'Lost civilization' to free-market commerce: the modern
   social life of Angkor   25

3 World heritage Angkor   47

4 Remapping Angkor: from landscape to touristscape(s)   67

5 Angkor in the frame   90

6 Collapsing policies and ruined dreams   116

7 Conclusion – in (the) place of modernity appears the illusion
   of history   139

Notes   150
Bibliography   157
Index   168

Figures

A   Map of Cambodia   xxiii
B   Map of Angkor   xxiv
1.1   APSARA sign warning residents of illegal construction   12
1.2   Sign – We No Longer Need Weapons   12
2.1   Angkorean montage   46
3.1   Map of ZEMP scheme   49
3.2   Cambodian visitors to monastery in Bakong Complex   61
4.1   Advertisement for Thai Air   87
5.1   Advertisement for Mekong World Heritage Tour   96
5.2   Afternoon picnicking at Angkor Wat   112
6.1   Doorway of Ta Prohm   120
6.2   Tree roots at Ta Prohm   122
6.3   Open-top driving during Khmer New Year   129

Tables

3.1 Major international projects coordinated by ICC 1993–1998   52
4.1 Growth trajectories: Southeast Asia in global perspective   83

Acknowledgments

Undertaking a project like this is an endeavor of constant surprises, people are willing to help, spare their time, refuse payment, encourage, offer their expertise, share a problem, or indeed, just listen. Without such kindness and generosity this book would never have been possible.

Over the course of two, one-year periods spent in Cambodia, the task of conducting fieldwork was greatly eased by the help of many organizations and individuals. In particular I would like to thank Chau Sun Kerya and Ang Choulean (APSARA), Jacques Gaucher and Christophe Pottier (EFEO), Tamara Teneishvili and Etienne Clément (UNESCO), Alice Harvey and John Sanday (WMF), Namiko Yamauchi (JSA), and various staff working at the Royal Government's Ministry of Tourism and Ministry of Culture, the National Archives of Cambodia, the Angkor Participatory Development Organization, United Nations Development Programme and Asian Development Bank (Phnom Penh), and the Cambodia Development Resource Institute for their time and assistance. The collection of tourist interview data was only made possible by the extremely generous hospitality of Weng Aow, Geert Caboor, Craig Hodges, David Morrow, and Masaki Nakamoto. I am indebted to Keiko Miura, Mandy Summerscales, and Enora Le Goff for their assistance in gathering interview data from Japanese and French tourists.

My understanding of Cambodia was greatly enhanced by many enlightening conversations with members of the research community there. Among those I would like to acknowledge Penny Edwards, Roland Fletcher, Fabienne Luco, Tara Mar, John Miksic, Keiko Miura, Ingrid Muan, Thina Ollier, Philippe Peycam, Robert Turnbull, Michael Vickery, John Weeks, and Bernard Wouters. My time there was also greatly enhanced by the friendship and humor offered by Khin Po Thai. The clarity of data on domestic tourism in this book bears testimony to Thai's excellent research and interpretation skills. Anthony Alderson and Phillip Kao offered ongoing support and helpful suggestions, and Lim Savuth, Heng Neang, and Toby Anderson also provided countless laughs through their friendship and hospitality. I am also greatly indebted to the 220 or so tourists that gave up their evenings, afternoons, and even breakfasts to be interviewed for this book.

In the UK, Virinder Kalra greatly helped during the closing stages of the PhD, and special thanks are given to Sallie Westwood, whose continual support and belief in the project never ceased to amaze me. Alan Metcalfe, Will Gibson, and Jacob Ramsay helped me through the struggle of writing text, and their thoughts and critique helped me clarify ideas and arguments. Not being a historian I appreciate greatly the time spent by Penny Edwards, David Chandler, and Mark Selden reading various chapters from the final draft. I also wish to thank Stephanie Rogers, Hayley Norton, and the whole editorial team at Routledge for their invaluable support and patience. I'm very grateful to Kath Sund and Ralph Gray for producing the two Maps at the front of the book. And special thanks are owed, once again, to Laavanya Kathiravelu for editing the final manuscript. Having spent far too long working on two books on Cambodia, she really must now become an expert on Indian modernity and Dubai.

This project would never have progressed as far as it has without the generous support of various institutions. I would like to thank the Economic and Social Research Council and the University of Manchester for supporting my PhD; Jonathan Rigg and the British Academy for supporting my Postdoctoral research grant; the Center for Khmer Studies, Siem Reap, and the Asia Research Institute, Singapore for a two-year fellowship to write this book up.

Special thanks and love, as always, go to my mum. Without her support this project would never have evolved from its initial 'crackpot idea' stage. Finally, I would like to acknowledge the love and support of those closest to me during the past nine years. They know, only too well, that Angkor has been a struggle.

Abbreviations

ACO	Angkor Conservation Office
ADB	Asian Development Bank
AFD	Agence Française de Développement
APSARA	Authority for the Protection and Safeguarding of the Angkor Region – (Autorité pour la sauvegarde et l'aménagement de la region d'Angkor)
ASEAN	Association of Southeast Asian Nations
BEFEO	Bulletin d'Ecole Française d'Extrême Orient
CARERE	Cambodia Area Rehabilitation and Regeneration Project
CCP	Chinese Communist Party
CGDK	Coalition Government of Democratic Kampuchea
CMAC	Cambodian Mine Action Center
CPK	Communist Party of Kampuchea
CPP	Cambodian Peoples' Party
CSA	Chinese Team for Safeguarding Angkor
EFEO	École française d'Extrême Orient
EMR	Extended Metropolitan Region
DK	Democratic Kampuchea
FUNCINPEC	Front Uni National pour un Cambodge Indépendant, Neutre, Pacifique, et Coopératif
GACP	German Apsara Conservation Project
ICC	International Coordinating Committee for the Safeguarding and Development of Angkor
ICCROM	International Centre for the Study of the Preservation and Restoration of Cultural Property
ICOMOS	International Council on Monuments and Sites
ICORC	International Committee on the Reconstruction of Cambodia
IGeS	Ingegneria Geotechnica e Strutturale
ILO	International Labour Organization
IMF	International Monetary Fund
JICA	Japanese International Co-operation Agency
JSA	Japanese Government Team for Safeguarding Angkor
MOD	Ministry of Development

MOT	Ministry of Tourism
NGO	Non-Governmental Organization
NPRD	National Program to Rehabilitate and Develop Cambodia
PDK	Party of Democratic Kampuchea
PPA	Paris Peace Accords
PRK	People's Republic of Kampuchea
RGC	Royal Government of Cambodia
SCNC	Supreme Council on National Culture
SNC	Supreme National Council
SOC	State of Cambodia
UN	United Nations
UNTAC	United Nations Transitional Authority in Cambodia
UNDP	United Nations Development Programme
UNESCO	United Nations Educational, Scientific and Cultural Organization
UNTAC	United Nations Transitional Authority in Cambodia
UNV	United Nations Volunteers
WMF	World Monuments Fund
WTO	World Tourism Organization
ZEMP	Zoning and Environment Management Plan

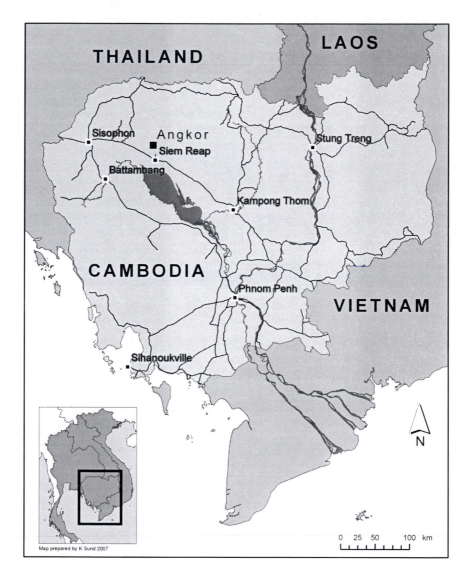

Figure A Map of Cambodia. (Copyright Kathyrn Sund.)

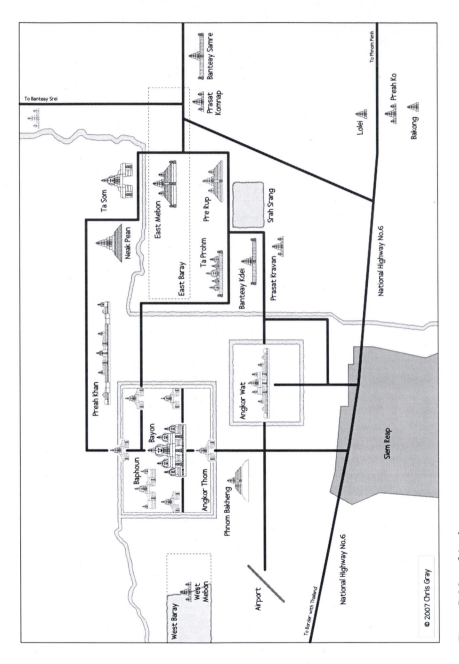

Figure B Map of Angkor.

© 2007 Chris Gray

All profound changes in consciousness, by their very nature, bring with them uncharacteristic amnesias. Out of such oblivions, in specific historical circumstances, spring narratives.

Benedict Anderson

From the moment it entered global consciousness Cambodia was spectacle.

Anthony Barnett

Landscape is a signifying system through which the social is reproduced and transformed, explored and structured.

Chris Tilley

In Angkor – a geographical region, an archaeological site and a cultural concept – lies much of Cambodia's future.

UNESCO

George (*75, American, trip to Thailand and Cambodia for 7 days*): Oh I came to see Angkor, it was nothing to do with Cambodia. It was like Machu Picchu or Timbuktu, it's one of those places everyone's heard about but never been, that's the attraction. To go to Thailand, yeah, but to Angkor Wat? That's the frosting on the cake, out of the jungle, ancient civilization, just how many of our friends have been here? Not many.

Michael (*40, British, traveling across Asia for six months*): We saw a program on Angkor just before we went away and the image was predominantly of you as the explorer, the archaeologist going through these completely unexplored temples, these magical mystical temples, of you exploring something that hasn't been discovered before … you have this idea that it was not 'touristy' at all. You arrive at this temple, you're Indiana Jones exploring this place.

Chum (*40s, Cambodian, Samroun district, day visitor*): I am very happy to see these temples restored. It keeps it for our next generation, it will help stop them being damaged by touching. People touching does not make me angry, but I know it is not good for the country, we may lose our heritage. I want to see these temples restored for my children to see.

Jennifer (*64, American, on 7 day tour of Thailand and Cambodia*): For me it is all ruins and the world's largest monastery, but I hope we can see them, are they not all covered up in vines? I hope you can see something and that it's not all covered in vines. I hope we can see the buildings.

Barry (*33, Australian, visiting Southeast Asia for 1 month*): We knew it was mystical, that it was hard to get to. I had the idea that all of Cambodia was dense jungle, and that would be from American war movies.

Tasos (*28, Greek, living in Singapore, in Cambodia for 3 days*): Angkor is a place that is a very, very vivid remnant of the past. It puts you in another place, another time.

Meng (*30s, Cambodian Resident of Siem Reap*): Angkor Wat is a symbol and creation of Khmer culture, a symbol of national culture. That is why it is important for me, and why it is important for me to come here.

Barton (*30s, Canadian, lives in Singapore, in Cambodia for 3 days*): Cambodia is all about landmines, Pol Pot and that America dropped millions of bombs on the country. Do I feel guilt as a North American, partly, but more like compassion really.

1 From a time of conflict to conflicting times

> Today, all around the country you see mass graves and ruined structures; the latter are the result not of neglect but of a conscious, coordinated campaign by the Khmer Rouge to smash the country's pre-revolutionary culture. And you see underpopulated towns and cities whose inhabitants are only slowly emerging from a nightmare that claimed the lives of their parents, spouses, siblings and children.[1]

Taken from the opening page of the Introduction to the 1992 *Cambodia Lonely Planet*, this excerpt provides some indication of what a visitor to Cambodia might find. These few lines also reveal why the publisher of what has become the bible of contemporary travel waited until then to publish a guide dedicated to the country. Indeed, in many respects, the publication of this first edition marked the beginning of Cambodia's return as a major destination of international tourism; a turbulent journey which would bring numerous contradictions, paradoxes and dilemmas. By the late 1960s Cambodia had become increasingly familiar with the challenges and opportunities presented by tourism. Two and a half decades of war and intense social turmoil virtually erased that familiarity. In the early 1990s the country would be starting again, and, as such, totally unprepared for the frenzy of international attention – and millions of visitors – which would arrive over the coming years.

Despite having so much of its physical infrastructure destroyed by decades of armed conflict, as well as its social institutions shattered by devastating periods of genocide and foreign occupation, Cambodia was about to witness an explosion in tourism unparalleled in any other country in recent times. Far from national in scope, this infant industry would focus overwhelmingly on the spectacular temple complex of Angkor. After decades of trauma, and with the country heavily dependent on international aid, reconciliation, cultural rejuvenation and economic rehabilitation were urgent and simultaneous demands. Located at the heart of this matrix, Angkor would witness an intense and fractious convergence between agendas of cultural preservation and socio-economic development. The situation was especially severe due to the country's need to restore a national identity severely damaged by prolonged conflict, the immense scale of the past to which that identity adheres and the dependence of the state on the revenue of tourism.

As a result, Angkor is enduring one of the most crucial, turbulent periods in its 1200-year history. Its immense historical importance, along with its global prestige, has led to an influx of international assistance, with more than twenty countries – including France, Japan, China, India, America, Germany, Italy, and Australia – donating millions of dollars to help restore and safeguard the temples. While such efforts have prioritized architectural restoration and archaeological research, the number of international tourists visiting the site has risen by a staggering 10,000 percent in just over a decade. Not surprisingly, the Royal Government has paid far greater attention to this growth in tourism, with Angkor now regarded as a 'cash cow' of much needed socio-economic development and wealth generation for a country plagued by shattered physical and social infrastructures. In such a context, culture, history, and local communities have become entwined in an elaborate set of political, economic, and social relations.

This book takes a critical look at this evolving situation. It explores conceptions of culture and development, the politics of space, and the relationship between consumption, memory and identity to illustrate the intense battleground which has formed around Angkor since it became a World Heritage Site in 1992. I locate heritage and tourism within their broader political and socio-economic contexts, both historical and contemporary, to reveal the aspirations and tensions, anxieties and paradoxical agendas, which have emerged due to the lure of the tourist dollar and the need to prevent the rampant destruction that the dollar and its bearers might bring. The situation in Cambodia today is a stark example of a phenomenon common to many countries attempting to recover after periods of conflict or political turmoil. Heritage and cultural tourism are widely regarded by host governments and international bodies like the United Nations Educational, Scientific and Cultural Organization (UNESCO) or the World Tourism Organization (WTO) as effective tools for protecting past histories, whilst simultaneously providing the economic fuel for societal modernization (Meethan 2001). In essence, tourism looks in both directions: it restores and promotes the past while promising future prosperity.

By addressing such issues at Angkor the book sets out to place cultural heritage and tourism in the foreground of debates concerning post-conflict nation building, postcolonial cultural politics, and the socio-spatial changes brought about by contemporary globalization. The immense scale and complexity of the Angkor region also brings into sharp focus the challenges facing countless heritage landscapes around the world today as they attempt to marry a series of interconnected agendas: development with conservation; national sovereignty with global patrimony; modernization with tradition; responsible governance with democratic ownership; and cultural values with economic value. A recurrent theme of academic studies on tourism and heritage has been the analytically elusive relationship between the discursive nature of the tourism industry, the ways in which tourists actually encounter landscapes, and how such processes come to shape the development of destinations. Recent years have seen increasingly sophisticated accounts in this area, and by exploring consumption in terms of various symbolic economies and the materialities of touristic performances, this book seeks to add clarity to these debates.

I argue that scholars of tourism and heritage need to pay greater attention to the cultural politics of development and postcolonial theory than they have done previously. An analysis of Cambodia, I believe, provides valuable insights for countries such as Iraq, Afghanistan or Rwanda which face similar challenges of marrying agendas of cultural restitution and modernization in their quest to recover from eras of war and social instability. Finally, this text joins the literature on contemporary Southeast Asia, a field which includes a limited number of works on Cambodia. Since the late 1970s two antithetical histories have received much attention: the ancient glories of Angkorean splendor and the horrors of the modern Khmer Rouge regime. By focusing on issues such as cultural politics and regional re-integration, it is hoped this book can offer a perspective that challenges some of the misconceptions, even clichés, about the country which continue to linger.

Years of turmoil

Situated at the heart of mainland Southeast Asia, Cambodia covers an area of just over 180,000 square kilometers. It is bordered by Thailand to the west and northwest, by Vietnam to the east and southeast, by Lao People's Democratic Republic to the north, and by the Gulf of Thailand to the south. Largely made up of plains, the country's topography also includes low mountain ranges in the southwest and north, and Southeast Asia's largest freshwater lake, the Tonle Sap. At the beginning of the 1990s Cambodia was a 'transitional society' in every sense, to use Curtis's terms (1998). The country would move 'from a centrally planned economic system to a market oriented one ... from a war economy to a peace economy, and from a poor and underdeveloped economy to a more prosperous and developed one' (Tith 1998: 102).

Cambodia's turmoil began in the late 1960s through its involvement in the Vietnam–America war, in what Shawcross (1993) famously dubbed as the conflict's 'Sideshow'. As North Vietnamese communist forces moved southwest into Cambodia the US responded by launching a series of devastating bombing campaigns that penetrated further and further into the country. Frustrated by Norodom Sihanouk's alliances with Beijing and Moscow, Washington supported the overthrow of Cambodia's Prime Minister by military coup in 1970. As eastern provinces increasingly fell under communist control the country became further embroiled in the conflict (Kiernan 2004). The death toll grew to the hundreds of thousands, with a similar number of internally displaced refugees fleeing to escape the conflict. For those Cambodians with the political and/or financial means to leave, many sought refuge in France, and to a lesser extent the US. Global media coverage produced both expressions of sympathy for the Cambodian people, as well as visions of the country as the political 'other' of western democracy and capitalism – an image which would be subsequently reinforced by the isolationist policies of the Khmer Rouge regime.

On 17 April 1975, paralyzed by years of US bombing and domestic turmoil, Cambodia experienced the start of one of the most radical and brutal social experiments ever inflicted upon a nation. Saloth Sar, latterly known as Pol Pot, promised to 'liberate' the country from the tyranny of both Vietnamese and American intervention. Through his revolutionist ideology Pol Pot would set about replacing previous post-independence modernization programs – seen as corrupt, elitist and urban-centric – with an agrarian-based economy. Within a matter of weeks all major cities and towns were evacuated, with their residents forced to become agricultural workers in the countryside. Although bearing a number of similarities with Maoist and Marxist-Leninist doctrines, Pol Pot's utopian vision recognized no precedents. As Chandler (1996a) asserts, it was revolutionary in every sense. According to Kiernan (1996) the issue of race would be central to the regime. In the quest for Khmer purity, the removal of 'those of foreign origin, education, or employment' resulted in the execution of tens of thousands of non-Khmers (ibid: 27).

Anonymous at first, it was not until September 1976 that the Communist Party of Kampuchea (CPK) declared themselves as leaders of a new Democratic Kampuchea (DK). By then however, a fresh constitution had already been promulgated abolishing all religious practices, private property and even the most basic human rights (Chandler 1996a). The imposed ideology of collectivist production and consumption rapidly began to unravel, and with failing harvests and increasing foreign hostilities came ever greater levels of brutality. By 1977 killings across the country were vast and largely indiscriminate. Fears of potential 'pollution' from contact with the neighboring Vietnamese meant the country's eastern provinces suffered the highest numbers of murders (Etchison 2005).[2] In Phnom Penh, an infamous facility with the code name S-21, now known as Tuol Sleng, incarcerated, tortured and sentenced to death over 14,000 victims accused of threatening the security of the party centre (Chandler 2000).

Lasting until early 1979, this horrific episode in Cambodia's history finally ended with the arrival of over 100,000 Vietnamese troops. On January 7, 1979 Phnom Penh was once again liberated as Pol Pot fled westwards by helicopter. While the Khmer Rouge regrouped as a jungle guerrilla army in Thailand, a new government formed in Phnom Penh calling itself the People's Republic of Kampuchea (PRK). This experiment lasting just under four years in which it is now estimated over one and a half million people died, or one in seven of the population, had finally come to an end.

In addition to new hope, 1980 brought an improved harvest and the reintroduction of money. In a complex political landscape however, various power struggles were being waged across the country, with Hanoi pulling the strings of the PRK government in Phnom Penh (Chandler 1996b). Factions fiercely dedicated to communist ideals were embattled with parties led by former Khmer Rouge defectors, as well as an anti-Vietnamese coalition which somewhat farcically realigned Sihanouk with an unrepentant Pol Pot.

As the 1980s progressed a political and military stalemate would set in with Hanoi and Moscow locked against the Chinese and Western supporters of the

Cambodian resistance (Gottesman 2003). With virtually no humanitarian aid reaching an impoverished population, Cambodia was essentially locked into a struggle which had 'become simultaneously a civil war, a regional war, and a great-power proxy war' (Brown and Timberman 1998: 16). In such circumstances, a gratitude for liberation initially held by many Cambodians was gradually replaced by a resentment towards the Vietnamese as an occupying power.

In 1989, starved of funds by the collapse of the Soviet Union, Vietnamese troops were forced to withdraw from the country. Despite the ongoing presence of numerous factions, the State of Cambodia (SOC) party administered about 90 per-cent of the territory, enabling it to restore Buddhism as the state religion, as well as introduce a new national anthem, flag, and constitution for the country. The ongoing re-population of Phnom Penh after the enforced evacuations of 1975 was largely driven by the desperate situation in the countryside, with physical and mental illnesses, black markets, smuggling and widespread poverty all remaining prevalent (Chandler 1996a). Headquartered along the Thai border in the mountain-ous southwest of the country, and funded by cross-border gem and timber trading, the Khmer Rouge – now known as the Party of Democratic Kampuchea (PDK) – continued to be the most powerful group fighting the SOC.[3]

Nonetheless, the end of the cold war provided the opportunity for unlocking Cambodia's political stalemate. In 1991, the Paris Peace Accords (PPA) attempted to broker a resolution to decades of civil conflict through the creation of a tempo-rary coalition prior to forthcoming elections. To oversee this transition the United Nations implemented its largest and most expensive peacekeeping operation to date, involving around 40,000 personnel, at a cost of over $2 billion. The United Nations Transitional Authority in Cambodia, or UNTAC as it became known, was charged with the task of creating an environment of conciliation and compro-mise, essential for open and fair elections. UNTAC's meticulous planning ensured 95 percent of those deemed eligible to vote were registered for the 1993 elections (Brown and Timberman 1998: 19).

Although passing off peacefully, the election could only produce a compromise dual government, made up of the royalist *Front Uni National pour un Cambodge Indépendant, Neutre, Pacifique, et Coopératif* (FUNCINPEC) party, led by Norodom Ranariddh, and the Cambodian People's Party (CPP), led by the former Khmer Rouge defector Hun Sen. In the ensuing power struggle, FUNCINPEC had little control over the military forces, police or civil administration. Some-what predictably, this fragile democracy would unravel some years later with the ousting of Ranariddh by a violent CPP coup in 1997.

Rebuilding Cambodia

Together with $880 million of aid pledged during the inaugural meeting of the International Committee on the Reconstruction of Cambodia (ICORC), the UNTAC-sponsored elections represented an attempt to kick-start major reforms and a process of transition. In 1993, with 85 percent of the population living in rural communities, agriculture accounted for more than 50 percent of the country's gross domestic product (GDP) (Quintyn & Zamaróczy 1998). Export manufacturing industries were virtually nonexistent and the limited economic growth at that time was principally fuelled by UNTAC's effects on the service and construction industries, the vast majority of which centered on Phnom Penh (Shawcross 1994, Ledgerwood 1998). Nonetheless, the prospect of macro-economic stability – something Cambodia had been denied for over two and a half decades – provided the country with the opportunity to make far reaching, and desperately needed, reforms in 'the context of one of the lowest levels of per capita income in the world'. (Ministry of Planning 2003: 5).

Writing in 1994, Shawcross described Cambodia at that time as 'still a semi-feudal country, a place of bargaining, survival, and lawlessness ... [with] ... no independent legal system, no central authority, no tolerance, no concept of human rights or of loyal opposition' (1994: 2). He also argued that the military and a disproportionately high civil service, a legacy of the command economy established in the 1980s, required major reforms at every level. The Cambodian army, for example, bulged with 2000 generals and 10,000 colonels (Shawcross 1994: 90). The demobilization of these forces, whether they be real or corruption-driven fictitious creations, would be vital to the reconciliation process.

Throughout the 1980s the Soviet Union had funded much of the country's state expenditures. Major reform came in 1994 with the implementation of an International Monetary Fund (IMF) and World Bank three-year structural adjustment program. Cambodia's re-emergence onto the international stage after nearly two decades of isolation would be driven by market liberalization and its geo-political realignment towards a western international donor audience (Hughes 2003). Indeed, the reconstruction of Cambodia's physical and social infrastructure was dependent upon a huge influx of foreign aid. In lieu of an effective state, a broader civil society was installed comprised of bi-lateral donors, multi-lateral banks, and numerous non-governmental organizations. In addition to the US$2.2 billion provided by the international community for the UNTAC operation, a further US$2.3 billion was pledged for the period of 1992–5 alone (with around 61 percent of that total, US$1.39 billion, actually being disbursed).[4]

Efforts to shift from a socialist-style authoritarianism to multi-party democracy in a few short years would, however, be greatly hindered by the absence of any recognizable legal infrastructure. In a country without lawyers or an independent judiciary abuses by the executive branch of government were widespread (Donovan 1993). Not surprisingly, systemic corruption spiraled with the swift transition to a dollar economy and the presence of a multi-billion dollar aid industry (Kamm 1998).

Private appropriation of public office had a major impact on efforts to rebuild Cambodia's shattered physical infrastructure. While the value of real estate in Phnom Penh rocketed, hospitals, universities, schools, airports, water and power supplies all desperately needed reconstructing, a task made considerably worse by the isolation of many provinces from Phnom Penh. Throughout the country hospitals were inundated with patients suffering from a multitude of physical and psychological disorders including malaria, dengue fever or post-war trauma, but had no doctors to treat them; and schools located in communities where 50 percent of the population were under the age of 15 and essentially illiterate, were deprived of any teachers to educate. Migration, both in and out of the country, continued apace. While a number of those who had fled the country in the early 1970s returned to resurrect political or business interests, many skilled and wealthy individuals sought a better life elsewhere. One of the most pernicious legacies of the conflict was the silent threat posed by millions of landmines. In December 1993 only 19,000 of an estimated 10 million mines scattered across the countryside had been cleared (Shawcross 1994: 80). With around 300 Cambodians either killed or maimed each month during this period, their effect on agricultural production and rural communities was devastating (Chandler 1998).

In 1994 the first full-scale national development program was launched. The National Program to Rehabilitate and Develop Cambodia (NPRD) outlined six specific aims, which together encompassed the areas of law, education, healthcare, economic stability, rural development, and the sustainable use of natural resources. Given the immense political and socio-economic challenges facing the country, it was understandable that rehabilitation and development were defined in such physical and structural terms. Within this paradigm however, little attention was given to the more nebulous, and perhaps seemingly less urgent, need for the rehabilitation of the country's cultural and intellectual life.

Not least because of Pol Pot's brutal attempts to erase much of Cambodia's past, recent decades left a deep-seated anxiety over what actually constituted Cambodian, or Khmer, culture, identity and history. Long associations between ethnicity, conflict and aggressive nationalisms within the region also meant losing many of the socio-cultural markers defining 'Khmer' would be politically charged. Understood in its broadest sense, rehabilitation would therefore involve an intense desire to recover the past, and, unsurprisingly, reclaim former glories. In this respect Cambodia at that time can be characterized as an extreme example of the duality familiar to modernity, whereby the desire to embrace the future is accompanied by nostalgic gazes towards forgotten pasts. As we have already seen, in the early 1990s Cambodia was replacing an imposed socialist ideology with free market capitalism. The future was about regional re-integration and embracing the multitude of cultural and economic flows that process would bring. Contemporaneously however, there was an intense looking back beyond the turmoil of two decades; a gaze dominated by a desire to reclaim those elements of Khmer society and culture which had been lost, or were often perceived to be lost. Despite suffering vandalism, theft and a limited amount of structural damage, Angkor had come through relatively unscathed. It was widely accepted that the same could not be said for the other facets of Cambodia's cultural landscape, such as the performance or literary arts, which suffered profoundly. The restoration of ancient temples would thus be deeply imbued with a sense of reconnecting contemporary society with its ancient past, and as such, restoring national pride, strength and identity. Encapsulated within a discourse of genocidal 'erasure', the landscape of Cambodian culture was now seen by many as a *tabula rasa*, and as such open to political manipulation. Crucially, and as this book will extensively illustrate, the political matrix of an internally embattled state buttressed by networks of international aid and trans-national capitalism would hold major implications for how the restoration of Cambodia's past would unfold over the coming years.

An additional factor shaping this milieu was the virtual absence of a Cambodian intellectual elite. Although a small number of academics and scholars returned to the country after the Paris Peace Accords, there was virtually no 'public sphere' for them to contribute to, or dialogue with. In his study of Cambodian Buddhism Harris illustrates how the religion came 'close to extinction' under the Pol Pot regime, with 'little more than a handful' of influential monks surviving the period (2005: 229). His account also reveals that, despite being reinstated as the state religion in the September 1993 constitution, Buddhist monks continued to suffer violence and political marginalization in their quest to restore their institutional structures.

After 23 years of civil war and decline, trust and confidence in the country's institutions had to be re-built. Politics had to be transformed from jungle conflict and guerrilla tactics into non-violent discussion. Abject poverty needed to be replaced with sustained and stable economic growth. And a sense of cultural and political sovereignty needed to be reclaimed – an immense challenge in itself given the lack of skilled human resources and influx of foreign aid and intervention at that time. Embarking upon such roads, early 1990s Cambodia was now a place of optimism, hope, and progress. One of the sites where these aspirations and various challenges converged most intensely was the templed landscape of Angkor.

In December 1992 Angkor was listed as a UNESCO World Heritage Site. In recognition of Cambodia's plight, the site was also added to the List of World Heritage in Danger. The recent past had left the country with a vacuum of expertise in monumental conservation, archaeology, and tourism development. In response to this situation, UNESCO assisted in the establishment of a cultural heritage management policy for the country. This resulted in the creation of the Supreme Council on National Culture (SCNC), and the complementary International Coordinating Committee for the Safeguarding and Development of Angkor (ICC).

The return of peace meant the site emerged as one of the most important assets for a government desperately needing to undertake a nationwide, sustained program of socio-economic development. Typically described as one of the 'cultural highlights' of Southeast Asia, the temples of Angkor were the principle, if not sole, attraction Cambodia could offer in a highly competitive regional tourism industry. In 1993 around 9000 international tourists visited the site. Just over a decade later this figure would rise to over 900,000, an increase of over 10,000 percent. Yet, in that same period, the tourist numbers visiting the northeast of the country rose only by a few thousand. Moreover, Khmer Rouge strongholds, together with widespread unexploded ordinance and shattered social and physical infrastructures would all ensure a number of provinces in the west and north remained inaccessible until the beginning of the twenty-first century.

'Call this a holiday?'; a rough guide to Angkor

Covering an area of just over 400 square kilometers in the northwest of the country, the World Heritage Site of Angkor is comprised of four main elements: tropical forest, areas of cultivated land, a number of rural communities, and some of the most spectacular architectural structures ever created. Dozens of elaborately carved temples are testimony to what was historically Southeast Asia's most powerful and expansive kingdom (see Figure B) – a territory which, at its height, stretched from central Laos in the north to central Thailand in the south, and from the Mekong delta in the west to the borders of Pagan in the east.

In Angkor Wat, the Angkorean period has also given us the largest religious building on the planet. Unlike the Egyptian pyramids, Khmer architecture combined immense scale with intricate ornamental detail. As a result, itineraries incorporating Angkor Wat and the site's other temple complexes of Ta Prohm, Preah Khan, Bayon, Banteay Kdei, Banteay Srei, Ta Keo, Ta Som, Neak Pean and the Roulos group to name a few, come with the risk of 'temple fatigue'. Eyes inevitably glaze over from the thousands upon thousands of intricately carved deities; ears eventually close to the seemingly endless tales of myths, legends and the unpronounceable names of rulers; and legs invariably give way from the struggle of dozens of incomprehensibly steep staircases baked by the tropical sun.

To give clients a respite from their bodily fatigue and the sensory overload of temple-filled itineraries, local tour guides often arrange for visits to some of the region's other major features, including the great lake Tonle Sap and nearby Kulen mountains: both of which are pivotal in the story of Angkor's history. With water came an abundant supply of fish and a vast flood plain for rice cultivation, whereas the nearby mountains to the north provided the stone required for construction. Nestled in between these two essential resources, Angkor stretched and shifted across the region's flat plains.

The immense amount of architecture available to scholars and researchers of the modern era has meant stone has been consistently regarded as the key for unlocking the secrets of Cambodia's past. Since the beginning of the twentieth century Cambodian historiography has been principally oriented around, and framed by, the temples of Angkor and beyond, and the stories of their creators. Piecing together such histories has made a vital contribution to our understanding of Southeast Asian history and provided a rich tapestry of knowledge concerning the Angkorean period and the centuries either side. Decades of laborious and rigorous scholarship in the fields of epigraphy, archaeology and architectural conservation have given us a detailed – yet still far from exhaustive – account of Angkor's rulers, their shifting religious affiliations, major battles and population changes. The account of the Chinese envoy Zhou Daguan, who visited Angkor in 1296, also depicted some of the details and richness of everyday life. Chapter 2 examines this historiography in greater detail, arguing that a dependence on stone has, however, also created major historical black holes, over-simplifications and various unresolved points of conjecture.

It is commonly accepted today that the Angkorean period lasted from 802 to 1431 CE. Prior to this period the region was made up of various, non-centralized chiefdoms. Battles and subjugation, alliances and break-aways, were the defining features of an era which also included extensive cultural and political influences from India. The ubiquitous imagery of Shiva, Vishnu and Buddha, along with the widespread use of Sanskrit, led early scholars to explain the origins of Angkor principally in terms of an earlier 'Indianisation process' (Vickery 1998). More recently, however, greater attention has been given to an emergent polity and the formation of a more unified 'state' under the rule of Jayavarman II, who, on his ascension to the throne proclaimed himself as the first 'universal monarch'. Jayavarman's consecration as the first 'king of kings in a highly charged ceremony' also involved the creation of a royal court symbolizing both the centre of a kingdom and an earthly representation of heaven (Higham 2001: 53). Although a number of Angkorean kings built little or nothing, this architectural statement would be reproduced over and over on an increasingly grandiose scale. With each new king the construction of temple complexes in honor of the ruling monarch became more ambitious, time consuming and dependent upon ever greater amounts of labor. It was an architectural program that would culminate in Jayavarman VII's highly extravagant thirteenth-century Angkor Thom city complex, the ruins of which dominate the landscape today. The demands of such an extensive construction schedule have been cited by a number of historians as a major contributory factor to Angkor's eventual 'decline' around the mid-fifteenth century (Jacques & Freeman 1997).

After the sacking of the capital by the Siamese c1431, and with regional power shifting towards Siam, Angkor's much reduced population distilled into a collection of rural villages focused around Theravada Buddhist monastic communities. No longer the seat of Southeast Asia's greatest military power, Angkor's architectural landscape steadily succumbed to the tropical climate and surrounding forest. The cumulative effect of intense heat, rain and pernicious vegetation over a number of centuries not only savagely attacked Angkor's stone temples but also destroyed any wooden structures not maintained by the few villages living nearby.

The degree to which Angkor was 'abandoned' in the mid-fifteenth century, as is commonly asserted, remains an area of intense scholarly debate. Over recent decades a number of researchers have focused on religious shifts or the production of rice and associated issue of irrigation to help explain why the population migrated south in a more piecemeal manner. However, as Higham (2001: 160) neatly summarizes, scholarship on Angkor's irrigation network falls into two distinct camps. Eminent researchers like Bernard-Philippe Groslier and Jacques Dumarçay argued that the city's success as a hydraulic society stemmed from its elaborate water infrastructure of rivers, canals and two vast reservoirs, or *barays*. This approach provided the foundations for a more recent study conducted by the University of Sydney, which examines whether the decision to abandon the region was based upon the catastrophic failure of the canal and reservoir system.[5] The other camp, to which it appears Higham subscribes, argues that despite containing millions of cubic meters of water, the *barays* were totally inadequate for extensive rice cultivation. Instead, it is suggested an explanation for these expanses of water lies in their symbolic value as earthly representations of the oceans surrounding Mount Meru.

One additional insight which has emerged from research into this question is the extent to which Angkor extended as a low-density, residential landscape. Through the use of NASA satellite imagery it is now understood that the greater Angkor region potentially stretched over an area as large as 1000 square kilometers, rather than the 400 enlisted as a World Heritage Site (Pottier 1999). A greater understanding of the scale of the settlement might also help fill the fundamental knowledge gaps which still remain concerning Angkor's economy, social structures, and vernacular history (Acker 1998). Similarly, little is known about the territorial extent of the Angkorean kingdom. Inscriptions from temples located in modern-day Laos and Thailand have provided a rudimentary understanding of the reach of Khmer influence at different times, but years of further research at numerous other temple sites across the region are still required in order to flesh out the details of this basic picture.

Contested spaces: the politics of heritage

For those tourists visiting Angkor in the mid-1990s the short journey from Siem Reap was punctuated by a brief stop at a small road-side hut to purchase an entrance ticket. Constructed from concrete and iron bars, and barely big enough to seat its two occupants, the hut marked the boundary of the park. A small, round concrete 'Welcome to Angkor' sign 50 meters further down the road modestly confirmed to the visitor – who perhaps traveled several thousand miles and waited many years for this moment – that he or she had finally arrived at Southeast Asia's largest and most elaborate cultural heritage site.

A decade later this same boundary would be marked by a multi-laned, drive-in ticket booth and a line of road-side signage advertising evening performances, souvenir shops, and one-hour photographic processing. The more observant visitor might also notice two large signs designed for a Cambodian audience. One, entirely made up of text, warns those living inside the Angkor park about the strict regulations on the construction of residential houses, restaurants and other buildings (Figure 1.1). If planning permission has not been obtained from the local Authority for the Protection and Safeguarding of the Angkor Region (APSARA) any modern buildings will be demolished. The sign informs residents that they must uphold the 'traditional' feel of the park. A few hundred meters away, the artwork of another roadside sign persuades residents of the bonds between peace, reconciliation, and modernization (Figure 1.2). The message of interconnected transitions is clear: replace guns with communal harmony, rural poverty with (sub)urban prosperity, and misery with happiness.

In their conflicting messages these two signs vividly capture the divergent, and often contradictory, discourses the park's residents have had to negotiate in that intervening decade. In a post-conflict era a stable growth in trade and commerce

Figure 1.1 APSARA sign warning residents of illegal construction. (Photo by Tim Winter.)

Figure 1.2 Sign – We No Longer Need Weapons. (Photo by Tim Winter.)

has created new forms of wealth and disposable income. Not surprisingly, the aspirations of rural communities have shifted towards pathways of modernization and the signifiers of material development. And yet, in the first sign these values and goals are seemingly refuted, even denied, by a world heritage legislation that prioritizes the 'traditional', and a landscape aesthetic which carefully monitors and defines the validity of any 'modern' intrusions. Seen together, these two signs, by virtue of their co-existence, point towards contestation, intersecting ideologies, and a politics of space and culture. This book sets out to read these signs in such terms and explore the myriad issues, processes and forces they simultaneously reveal and hide. It is also an approach that brings Angkor into the fold of a literature that examines the political and inherently contested nature of heritage tourism landscapes.

As Macdonald points out, recent studies of heritage landscapes – and the heritage industry in general – have now brought 'questions of the implications of materiality, and of the mutual enmeshing of the material and social to the fore' (2006: 11). By implication, greater attention has been given to forms of contestation between groups seeking differing claims of identity from the past. While organizations like UNESCO have attempted to advance a language of cultural difference within a shared inheritance of globally 'unique' sites, a framework of 'world heritage' has invariably led to a battleground between nationalistic agendas and the sub-national interests of minority groups. Observers of this ever-expanding industry have therefore questioned the feasibility of bridging these gaps and using heritage as a way of promoting ideas of a global citizenship or cosmopolitanism (Turtinen 2000, Meethan 2001).

In reflecting upon the concept of world heritage further, authors such as Smith (2004) and Shepherd (2006) have examined landmark international agreements such as the 1964 Venice Charter and 1972 World Heritage Charter as instruments of objectivity, rigor, and depoliticized governance. As Smith suggests, within such frameworks material objects are entrusted to a small number of 'intellectuals associated with their collection, curation and interpretation' (2004: 86). Paralleling such observations, Turtinen also summarizes World Heritage as 'an institutional system of formalised routines, beliefs and practices, in a centre/periphery relationship ... created through highly standardised, transnational processes and procedures based on expertise' (2000: 3).

By examining Stonehenge through a similar analytical lens, Bender (1999) constructs a 'multi-vocal' text to draw our attention to the value systems marginalized by certain institutionalized knowledges, such as those presented by English Heritage, which attempt to narrate a 'standard' account of history, and thus, by implication, secure ownership over the land. She states:

> More often than not, those involved in the conservation, preservation and mummification of landscape create normative landscapes, as though there was only one way of telling or experiencing. They attempt to 'freeze' the landscape as a palimpsest of past activity ... freezing time allows the landscape

or monuments in it to be packaged, presented and turned into museum exhibits.

(Bender 1999: 26)

Implicit here is a concern for a particular value system that promotes a series of naturalized world views cultivated by experts. From the late 1980s onwards parallel observations were made by Shanks and Tilley (1987), Thomas (1996) and Leone et al. (1987), who, in harmony, argued that the task of reading landscapes as socio-political constructions needed to begin with a process of self-reflexive, critical analysis, whereby the field of archaeology itself is treated as an authoritative form of knowledge production. To understand the power/knowledge relationships inherent to the field it is necessary to examine the institutional contexts from which interpretations and pronouncements are made. In considering the particularities of Asia, authors like Taylor (2004), Chen (1998), and Logan (2001) have reflected upon the degree to which fields like archaeology and conservation remain imperialist technologies within Eurocentric world heritage paradigms. To support such arguments Logan also considers how bodies like UNESCO, International Council on Monuments and Sites (ICOMOS), or the International Centre for the Study of the Preservation and Restoration of Cultural Property (ICCROM) impose certain 'best practices' and 'good behaviours' on their member states. The recently developed China Principles and Hoi An Protocols for Best Conservation Practice in Asia are two attempts to move away from the 1964 Venice Charter and deliver heritage policies more sympathetic to the cultural and historical contexts of Asia. As we shall see however, such initiatives have yet to gain any traction in countries like Cambodia, where a language of heritage continues to reflect and reinforce Eurocentric understandings of culture and landscape.

For Smith (2004) these issues are best addressed at the conceptual level. Building on the earlier arguments of Hodder (1992), Kohl and Fawcett (1995), and Tilley (1999), she discusses the now familiar distinction between processual and post-processual forms of archaeology to argue that despite the latter's concern for discourse and ideology, multi-vocality and self-reflexivity, scientifically-driven, positivist approaches remain popular both within the field and its associated discipline of Cultural Resource Management (CRM). Smith extensively illustrates how these fields continue to seek a meta-professional authority through a 'logical positivism [that] stresses objectivity and ensures technical rigor' (2004: 20). CRM – the arena in which archaeology and its theory are practiced beyond their academic contexts – further de-politicizes discussions by focusing attention on two key areas. First, debates over 'ownership' of heritage sites and their objects primarily address questions of access and possession. From this, a secondary level of discussion arises concentrating on the logistics of site management. In essence then culture and cultural heritage are enveloped within science-based and managerial paradigms.

As we shall see in the coming chapters in the context of CRM heritage becomes a 'resource' requiring protection, cataloguing and objective interpretation. More specifically, CRM 'provides the institutions, policies and legislative frameworks that effectively mobilize archaeology as a technology of government' (ibid: 11). Invariably, and with Angkor being no exception, maps have become powerful tools for justifying management rights and even claims of ownership. Inherently spatial, CRM, archaeology and cultural heritage consistently deploy cartography not only to 'codify, to legitimate and to promote [their] world views', but also, and as Harley reminds us, to produce silences and absences (1988: 429). Accordingly, the review of UNESCO's zoning scheme presented in Chapter 3 illustrates how a desire to formalize and define resists pluralism and thus, by implication, excludes those views and parties that fall outside the dominant paradigm.

Studies by Ashworth (1994), Macnaghten and Urry (1998), Bender (1999) and Waterton (2005) have also demonstrated how scientifically oriented frameworks of cultural heritage and CRM tend to inadequately address questions of social justice and indigenous values. A number of authors, including Smith (2004), have therefore argued that CRM needs to move beyond the polarized and oppositional stances of its processual and post-processual traditions and develop more humanist, democratic, and inclusive approaches. However, while these authors commonly draw upon examples from Europe, North America or Australia to support their arguments, we will see over the coming chapters that the challenges they pose take on an altogether different face in countries torn apart by war and violent internal conflict, like Cambodia.

The critiques offered by the above authors remind us of the importance of understanding the interaction between heritage landscapes and their residential communities. In the case of Angkor, a growth in tourism has generated a sharp growth in the number of people living within the park's perimeters. According to World Bank estimates, this population exceeded 150,000 in 2003, up from 50,000 a decade earlier.[6] Detailed anthropological accounts of the values these residents ascribe to Angkor as a lived space, a place of oral traditions and evolving religious practices has been offered by Miura (2004) and Luco (2006). To complement the insights these recent studies offer, the discussion of Angkor as a form of 'living heritage' presented here steers in a somewhat different direction, focusing specifically on tourism and on those who visit the site as tourists.

Cultural economies of tourism

As we saw from the opening words of this Introduction, the first *Lonely Planet* on Cambodia was published in 1992. More than merely 'bibles' for independent travelers, *Lonely Planet* guides, with their recommendations and 'not to miss highlights', invariably make a significant impact on the physical development of emerging tourist destinations like Angkor, Siem Reap. To this end, I have argued elsewhere that descriptions of landmines, jungle hidden ruins and dangerous war-torn cities presented in guidebooks and other media have played a pivotal role in defining the geographical and cultural boundaries of Cambodia's post-conflict tourism industry (Winter 2006). This book builds on these themes and expands their analytical frame to look at Angkor as an emergent tourist space. The following chapters situate media representations alongside discussions of infrastructure resources, airline routes, the logistics of tour itineraries and the consumption practices of both domestic and international tourists. In other words, the development of Angkor's tourism industry is approached as a series of cultural economies, each of which is constituted through an interweaving of the symbolic with the real, the discursive with the non-discursive, and the local with the transnational.

Within the literature on tourism of late there has been a growing unease that the conceptual categories of the 'tourist' and 'place' have created intellectual straightjackets for the field (Coleman and Crang 2002, Terkenli 2002, Roy 2004). Countless studies dedicated to understanding the motivations and desires of tourists have been paralleled by, and yet often separated from, other accounts of how tourism commodifies and transforms 'host' people, places and cultures. In an attempt to overcome this analytical separation a number of authors have turned to a language of performance (Kirshenblatt-Gimblett 1998, Coleman & Crang 2002, Lasansky & McLaren 2004). A shift towards understanding tourism in terms of performativity views the production and consumption of tourist spaces as contingent and mutually constitutive processes. Places are no longer regarded as the static recipients of 'guests' that come and go. Instead there is an awareness of how people and places are concurrently mobilized through the economies and cultures of tourism.

It has long been acknowledged that international tourism provides an effective medium for performing a national 'brand' on the international stage. Richter (1993), Peleggi (1996), and Picard and Wood (1997) have all demonstrated how coherent, state-endorsed images of the nation projected externally also become important mechanisms for nation building or the ethnic profiling of a population. Perhaps the most detailed study in this field has been Dahles' account of cultural tourism in Indonesia; a language seized upon by the New Order government to enhance its political legitimacy and boost economic growth. Dahles concludes that a seemingly innocuous policy of promoting a tapestry of ethnic diversity for an international tourist audience provides a mask for the state's broader ideological interests. Summarizing this argument she states:

> In Indonesia culture and art have become an arena in which seemingly 'unpolitical' visions of national identity are stated. Applying a strategy of 'culturalization' of identity, the government is not only accommodating differences but actually producing them … the concept of culture has gone through a process of aestheticization, stylization, relativization, and standardization. This is not a harmless exercise in semantic associations but a strategy of domination.
>
> (2001: 16)

Clearly for Dahles the transformation of a localized Javanese culture is primarily driven by state policies. Although recognizing that this cultural, political twinning gains momentum through the prospect of financial gain her account speaks less about the power of capital in transforming those places designated for tourism.

To address such questions, authors like Harrison (1992), Wood (1993), and Jackson (2004) have all insightfully demonstrated how developing country government programs to promote places of tourism invariably lead to tensions between the state and localized communities, as disproportionate levels of wealth are accrued by a small elite within a situation of imbalanced modernization. The analysis presented in the following chapters draws these various political and economic threads together.

In a departure from state-centered approaches to unequal patterns of development authors like Sassen (2002), Urry (2000), Appadurai (1990), and Castells (1996, 2000) have foregrounded the idea of regional and global networks. Together they argue that as we embark upon the twenty-first century, processes of socio-spatial change are defined by the flows of people, capital, information and objects within a new social morphology of networks. As Castells states there is a 'performance of activities throughout the social structure. This material basis, built in networks, earmarks dominant social processes, thus shaping the social structure itself' (1996: 471). Evans and Spaul adopt this mode of analysis to interpret the socio-cultural impact of tourism. However, rather than using the familiar examples of 'global cities' like New York, Tokyo or London, they demonstrate how quiet, unpopulated forests in England are encoded with new meanings as they are absorbed into an arena of tourism and leisure. The introduction of stylized signposts, boundary fences and architecturally sympathetic visitor centers tangibly signify the presence of new managerial practices and networks of governance oriented towards consumption. In offering a theoretical interlude to their account the authors declare that:

> Heritage and tourism landscape are no longer in 'place' in the sense that they once were – living embodiments of rooted communities – but have drifted into the 'space' of tourist attractions: alienable parcels of countryside integrated into a social network, created by mobile populations in search of leisure activity.
>
> (2004: 213)

The empirical example given by Evans and Spaul indicates how the metaphor of the network points towards infinite possibilities for systemic interconnectivity. Nomadic capitalism, after all, is said to recognize no boundaries and connects the world through a seemingly endless infrastructure of nodes and scapes. To better understand the broad dynamics by which tourism expands its frontiers and conquers new territories Urry's distinction between scapes and flows is instructive here. Adopting the conceptual language of Arjun Appadurai, Urry suggests scapes are 'the networks of machines, technologies, organizations, texts and actors that constitute various interconnected nodes' (2000: 35). By contrast, flows consist of 'peoples, images, information, money and waste, that move within and especially across national borders' (2000: 36). At the core of his distinction is the greater degree of structure associated with scapes. In developing this idea further in his book *Global Complexity*, Urry argues flows – this time discussed as 'global fluids' – 'result from people acting upon the basis of local information but where these local actions are, through countless iteration, captured, moved, represented, marketed and generalized within multiple global waves' (2003: 60).

In offering such an account, Urry recognizes that, far from being mutually exclusive, scapes and flows continually intersect, with the former providing a partial structure – a global order – within which fluidity can emerge and thrive. Indeed, to mobilize the flow of 'people, capital, images and culture', which Meethan (2001: 4) argues defines today's global tourism industry, an international network of corporations, legislation and trustworthy brands that 'roam[s] … across the surface of the earth' (Urry 2003: 57) delivering predictability and reliability is required.

But equally, unpredictability and an instability of knowledge are crucial factors in the territorial expansion of tourism. Given that crossing frontiers, and entering unknown lands provide much of the impetus to travel, Singh reminds us 'tourism has to search for new horizons of experiences that are bizarre and pregnant with curiosity' (2004: 2). For both the industry and tourists alike, there is a shared desire to move beyond existing frontiers, explore un-chartered territories, to break out of existing circuits. And yet, as we shall see in Chapter 4, a lack of regional airports, hotels and other facilities has both hindered and fostered particular tourist flows within and across Cambodia. In the case of the cruise ship market, the lack of a deep water port in the south has stifled growth in this luxury sector. Whereas for the independent traveler and backpacker markets, the under-developed and unfamiliar nature of Cambodia's tourism scapes represents an opportunity to explore and get off 'the well trodden path' of tourism (Winter 2006). The case of post-conflict Cambodia illustrates how the networks of tourism fray and fragment at the edges, and have their fluidity ruptured by obstacles and an absence of nodes.

For countries engaged in the early stages of tourism, development scapes and flows typically emerge in dialogue, and as one creates the other the voids in the network are filled and its frontiers expanded. But to suggest that development follows a linear, upward path would ignore the economic and political forces within the network that work to retain particular clusters of power and a rigidity of structure. Angkor's rise as a key heritage destination of Southeast Asia has brought it into a new arena of socio-political relations. Rather than viewing the site as the central hub of a wheel, the metaphor of the network enables us to understand Angkor as a single node within a de-centered web of connections. Tourism places come into being through the socio-political and economic developments taking place elsewhere in the system. In other words, Angkor's development has been shaped by power imbalances between nodes and the core, periphery dynamics they help create. As we shall learn, with Cambodia's airports unable to accept long haul aircraft, the expansion of the country's tourism industry has, in part, been determined by decisions made in the regional hubs of Bangkok, Singapore or Hong Kong. Moreover, for tour operators looking to integrate Angkor within their existing regional networks of hospitality, promoting Cambodia beyond temples remains a risky and unprofitable exercise.

A crucial component in the mobilization of places as new tourist destinations is the circulation of images and knowledges. Chapter 5 explores this theme in detail, demonstrating that international tourism in Southeast Asia involves 'the partial erosion of spatially bounded social worlds and the growing role of the imagination of place from a distance' (Gupta and Ferguson 1997: 39). For Cartier such cultural processes represent a symbolic order of seduction. Through an approach that emphasizes 'geographical imaginaries, how people think about destinations' she argues we, as tourists, are drawn to edges: to the beach, the cliff top, or the side of the pool (2005: 2). Moreover, she suggests: 'Secret and enigmatic places are seductive too: archaeological landscapes from the edges of history, the Egyptian pyramids, Mayan capitals, the mounds of imperial graves that mark China's millennial history, still unopened, too many to excavate' (ibid: 7).

Cartier's insightful account acknowledges both discursive and non-discursive practices. Indeed, in stressing that seduction works at both the symbolic level and through the realization of 'emplaced possibilities' her account forms part of a recent turn towards understanding touristic consumption as a process Crouch (2005) has termed 'embodied semiotics'. The late twentieth-century shift towards the subjective nature of place, as noted earlier, has informed more detailed accounts of touristic consumption as a multi-sensory, embodied process. Urry, for example, departed from his ocular-centric 'Tourist Gaze' (1990) to consider why the heritage and tourism industries deploy sounds, smells and textures to signify particular places or memories (1995, 1997). In his detailed account of the Taj Mahal, Edensor (1998, 2001) revisits Goffman's theatrical metaphor to interpret consumption as a series of spatially scripted performances. According to Edensor, the Taj serves as a highly symbolic stage enabling tourists to act out a variety of identity constructions. Similarly, Yalouri (2001) draws upon Bourdieu's notion of habitus to interpret visits to the Acropolis as spatialized cultural productions, known and enacted through the body.

Yalouri's analysis also illustrates a move towards understanding the relationship between identity, place, and history in terms of memory. Rather than viewing history as held within the landscape or building itself, the idea of memory switches attention to the ways places and histories are actively created and recreated in multiple ways on an ongoing basis (Connerton 1995, McCrone 1998). Once framed in such terms landscapes emerge as *lieux de mémoire* (Nora 1998) – spaces through which multiple pasts are simultaneously remembered and forgotten in subjective ways. As Yalouri points out however, given the multiple audiences drawn to the Acropolis, memory and its narration inevitably remains contested and unstable. Recognizing that consumption acts as a '"vehicle of agency" which informs the way Greeks understand their national identity' (2001: 17), she also demonstrates how the site is infused with localized sacred values which resist other more secular ideas of modernity and globalization.[7] In this respect, together with Edensor's (1998) account of the Taj Mahal, Yalouri reveals the complex political web arising from a framework of heritage attempting to encapsulate intersecting local, national, and global memories of place. Along with the contributions of Bender (1999) and Tilley (1999) noted earlier, Yalouri and Edensor have also contributed to our understanding of consumption as a process of appropriation and created meanings.

Pursuing such themes further, this study contrasts the representations offered by an international heritage community and Angkor's local authorities with the practices and narratives of both domestic and international visitors. Touristic consumption is seen as an ensemble of spatial enunciations, to use De Certeau's terms, where place becomes meaningful through its 'kinaesthetic appropriation' (1984: 98). Rejecting the idea that landscapes are consumed through pre-figured or pre-scripted performances, this approach follow's Crouch's assertion that tourists 'figure and refigure knowledge of material and metaphorical spaces … .[by] … trying out, coping, negotiating, and contesting' (1999: 3). Crucially however, and as Crouch points out, such processes involve an interweaving of spaces that 'maybe material, concrete and surround our own bodies … [but] … may also be metaphorical and even imaginative' (ibid: 2).

Accounting for these metaphorical and imaginary spatial flows requires an understanding of their mediation by guidebooks, documentary channels like *National Geographic* and *Discovery*, films and other media. Frustrated by the lack of studies revealing how sensory, embodied practices are informed by processes of signification, Franklin and Crang (2001) and Meethan (2001) both argue that more rigorous understandings are still required concerning the subject/discourse or symbolic/material relations which constitute tourism consumption. In response, the following chapters explore such relationships by attending to 'embodied experiences as part of the semiotic relations within tourism' (Abram et al. 1997: 7). In Chapters 5 and 6 a diverse range of representations and framings – including hotel interiors, Hollywood films or decades of television news coverage – are set against the various ways in which tourists talk and walk about the site. In other words, the book explores the interconnections between the symbolic economies of Angkorean tourism and the material practices involved in actually doing tourism in Cambodia.

Restoration culture

The re-emergence of Angkor as a destination of international and domestic tourism coincided with a process of societal recovery. As we saw earlier, the temples would at once become an intense focal point for both the restoration of a glorious cultural past and the aspirations of an economically vibrant future. In a few short years, heritage and tourism thus emerged as arenas through which various geo-political, nationalist, developmental, and revivalist agendas were simultaneously channeled. This final section sets out a framework for interpreting such processes, and in so doing further situates the themes raised so far within the socio-political context of post-conflict, postcolonial Cambodia.

The arguments presented over the coming chapters join a growing literature which examines the impact of social turmoil and violent conflict on cultural landscapes as sites of collective patrimony. As way of a contribution to this field, the book departs from a number of themes which have already garnered considerable attention. With wars and periods of social unrest almost inevitably resulting in the destruction of material culture – whether it be artwork, sacred texts, buildings or monuments – expressions of lament have become commonplace, with the most critical commentaries typically coming from writers external to, and thus politically disengaged from, the issues being disputed. Not surprisingly, the rise of a world heritage discourse has underpinned a body of writing that has sought to protect 'our' cultural property from being burned, stolen, demolished or bombed (Gamboni 1997, Golden 2004). In March 2001 the Taliban's iconoclasm of the Buddhas at Bamyan generated unanimous condemnation across the world (Ashworth and Van Der Aa 2002). Recently however, more ambivalent voices have also reflected upon the ways in which cultural heritage can perpetuate conflicts, and in so doing sustain anger, hostility, and enmity. Bevan (2006) and Layton and Thomas (2001) point out that decisions to destroy or preserve heritage may reflect a variety of discordant agendas. Citing examples from Bosnia, Kosovo, India, and Israel among others, they demonstrate that, if managed by local groups sensitively, heritage sites can advance reconciliation and reunification. Equally though, the past can be misused in the present to deny previous atrocities or inflame inter-communal tensions.

Within this literature a number of studies have addressed what happens to heritage sites and material culture *after* times of conflict. The principle point of focus here has been the issue of memorialization; a language that reads buildings, statues, and landscapes as 'memorials' embattled with the impossibility of retaining an adequate and respectful memory (Young 1994, Forty and Küchler 2001, Guha-Thakurta 2003, Macdonald 2006). Tunbridge and Ashworth (1996), for example, reflect upon the production of memorials marking the atrocities of World War II, expressing concern that various groups and voices have been written out, and thereby disinherited, from the story of the holocaust.[8]

Understandably, studies examining societies working towards peace and reconciliation have tended to look at those cultural sites either damaged and destroyed by the conflict, or whose symbolic value has been, or continues to be, actively contributing to the contours of the dispute (Brown 1998, Hodder 1998). The case of pre-modern architecture in Cambodia is somewhat different however. As the following chapter notes, the temples were revered across the political landscape throughout the civil war. Grenades, bullets and the looting of prized carvings undoubtedly took their toll, but the temples succeeded in avoiding any programs of systematic destruction.[9] Consequently, their structural forms have not, as such, emerged as memorials to this devastating period in the country's history. In fact, in the decades since the Khmer Rouge ceded power, efforts to commemorate have gravitated towards more vernacular structures and landscapes. The infamous school, turned torture centre, Tuol Sleng, in Phnom Penh, the nearby mass graves of Cheung Ek, and Pol Pot's final place of residence in Anlong Veng, being the most high-profile examples among many (Chandler 2000, Wood 2006).

The situation Angkor finds itself in today thus demands an analysis that explores, but moves beyond, ideas of contested memory and site representation, to include the multitude of issues arising from a rampant growth in tourism. To date the convergence of these two industries in post-conflict situations has been approached via the theoretical vantage points of commodification (Lennon & Foley 2000, Baram & Rowan 2004), semiology (Adams 2003, Bishop & Clancy 2003) or the more technical language of Cultural Resource Management (McManamon & Hatton 2000). The aim here is to pursue similar lines of enquiry, but stretch their intellectual terrain by reading the broader social, economic and political contexts in a way that reveals the tensions and contradictions arising from a violent collision between a desire to embrace rapid modernization and the need to restore and protect an illustrious, but fragile, ancient culture. In other words, by understanding tourism heritage in terms of spatial contestation, performance and networked mobilities, issues of site management and the politics of narration are explored in order to ask larger questions about postcolonial relations, post-conflict nation building, geographies of development, and cultural economies of place.

The pursuit of these various goals brings in to view the ways in which heritage and tourism have triggered Angkor's appropriation by a range of players for particular ends. To help interpret this picture the book draws inspiration from the field of Latin American Cultural Studies, which, through the work of Alvarez, Canclini, Escobar, and Yúdice, amongst others, has sought to understand how and why a multitude of social actors adopt culture as a resource to serve certain purposes or goals within a context of development. Together these authors have brought notions of citizenship, civil society, development, the state and globalization into the fold of cultural studies perspectives on developing countries, and perhaps more importantly, fore-grounded culture within debates over such issues. In justifying this approach, Yúdice argues that the embedding of culture within the economic and socio-political spheres of growth and development has set in motion a 'particular performative force', whereby the cultural has a 'social imperative to perform' (2003: 12). Returning to the theme of performance reminds us what is 'being accomplished socially, politically and discursively' through culture (Domínguez 1992: 21).

Angkor's ability to endure, both physically and symbolically, ensured the restoration and exposition of stone – or to be more specific, ancient stone – would serve as a metaphor for a society undergoing post-war reconstruction and rehabilitation. UNESCO's valuable support for the use of classical antiquities as a cornerstone for a grossly weakened state nationalism has also greatly helped the Royal Government parade the temples on the international stage. However, given recent political events in the country and the concern expressed by Meethan (2001) that such assistance programs often legitimize reductive, state-nationalized understandings of culture, this situation warrants closer attention, as we shall see.

The scale of assistance offered for Angkor in recent years demands that we interrogate national heritage practices in relation to the wider transnational networks and institutional structures within which they operate. Governments, foundations and universities based in various countries around the world have all gained considerable prestige from 'adopting' some of Asia's largest and most elaborate temples for restoration or research. The introduction of such assistance programs in post-conflict situations raises difficult questions and dilemmas regarding sovereignty and neo-colonialism. An analysis of Angkor enables us to fruitfully pursue such issues; and, thus, move beyond accounting for reconstruction and development merely as national or local projects, and instead read heritage as an arena of geo-politics, bi-lateral relations and competing ideologies. Accordingly, the following chapter provides the historical context for such an analysis through a story of monumental conservation, modernity, tourism, and political appropriation that begins in the mid-nineteenth century. Before moving on to such arguments, the final part of this introduction summarizes each of the coming chapters.

Chapter 2 traces Angkor's 'modern' history. An examination of how the site has been appropriated, conceived, and framed within a variety of contexts over the last 150 years – social, political, economic, cultural – provides the foundation for understanding processes of heritage and tourism today. In essence, the chapter not only offers a modern 'social life' of Angkor, but also provides the vital historical contexts for understanding the issues discussed in subsequent chapters.

Moving on to the early 1990s, Chapter 3 examines Angkor's establishment as a World Heritage Site. Tourism and conservation are intensely converging agendas, and within a turbulent, corruption-ridden economic/political environment, the site is legally and geographically isolated. International assistance focuses on the conservation of an 'ancient' temple culture – a situation which re-imposes a former French colonial construction of Cambodian culture, where Angkor is seen as static, dead and frozen in a moment of past glory. The chapter also addresses the expert, student discourse of foreign assistance in terms of power and notions of authority.

Chapter 4 introduces the notion of *touristscape(s)* in order to examine a level of tourism growth perhaps unparalleled anywhere in the world. It is argued that within a World Heritage framework, tourism is conceived in static and geographically bounded terms, where the protective isolation of a monumental landscape, as an emergent *touristscape*, remains precedent. In contrast, an alternative analysis of *touristscapes* focuses on the socio-economic networks and flows which are now intersecting at Angkor. The implications arising from this situation are presented.

Chapter 5 turns to examine the prevailing constructions of Angkor within a socio-cultural landscape of airline adverts, guide books, souvenirs and themed hotels, and how these connect with the ways tourists talk and walk about Angkor. The chapter highlights how distinct, and politically charged, formations of an Angkorean culture, landscape, and history circulate within the contexts of both domestic and international tourism.

Many of the arguments offered in preceding chapters are brought together in Chapter 6 through a detailed analysis of two temple sites: Ta Prohm and Preah Khan. It is argued that the processes discussed earlier converge on these 'partial ruins' in fractious and contradictory ways. It will be seen that a politically imbalanced web of international assistance utilizes the imagery of tourism to re-impose a colonial vision of Angkor as 'ruin', silencing those voices wanting to see the two sites restored as architectural and active religious landscapes.

Finally the Conclusion consolidates the key themes of the book and re-connects the study to other tourism heritage sites around the world. It reflects upon the importance of examining intersecting nationalisms, cultural economies and the various postcolonial, transnational relations which arise through converging agendas of development and cultural rehabilitation in a country like Cambodia.

2 'Lost civilization' to free-market commerce

The modern social life of Angkor

To understand fully Angkor's situation today some initial scene setting is required. Accordingly, the following chapter traces an assemblage of material and non-material processes – including nation building, commerce and branding, tourism, and civic arts – to reveal the ways in which Angkor has been appropriated, commodified, secularized and symbolically exchanged over the last 140 years.

The chapter opens with 'Romantic Tales of Loss and Discovery', examining how the idea of Angkor as a 'lost' civilization solidified with the publication of Henri Mouhot's account of visiting the region in 1860. It is argued that a late nineteenth-century European concern for 'classic' civilizations in a state of ruin – worthy of exploration and restitution – became a dominant cultural, and politically contrived, representation. As French scholarly knowledge on Angkor begun to accumulate, narratives of a Cambodian history were forged. 'Spaces of History, Times of the Nation', reveals how a vision of a glorious 'ancient' Angkor evolved in specific temporal and spatial terms, and through particular scholarly knowledges, to form the basis of a national historiography principally oriented around the material culture of temple architecture. The final section covering the period of French colonial rule, 'Souvenir Angkor', outlines Angkor's mobilization for consumption as a tourist landscape, as a series of exposition replicas in France and as the dominant reference point for a 'modern' Cambodian arts industry during the early twentieth century.

Turning to the years after Cambodia's independence, 'Ominous Modernities' considers Angkor's circulation within the cultural, economic and political spheres of a country grappling with a new, and increasingly turbulent, era in its history. Examples drawn from commercial advertising, modern Cambodian arts, civic monuments and shifts in political discourse demonstrate how Angkor moves across, and becomes embedded within, a variety of symbolic economies.

Romantic tales of loss and discovery

It is commonly stated that the Angkorean period lasted between 802 and 1431 CE. To understand how and why these dates have solidified as two of the most important moments in Cambodian history, it is necessary to leap forward to an event of the mid-nineteenth century: the visit of Henri Mouhot to Angkor in 1860. As we will see over the course of the following chapters Mouhot's encounter would play a definitive role in shaping both the historiography of the country, and the way Angkor is conceived as a heritage and tourism landscape today.

Spurred on by his passion for botany and zoology Henri Mouhot followed in the footsteps of a number of earlier European explorers and missionaries, navigating his way across what is now Thailand, Cambodia, and Laos via the Mekong and other waterways. After securing a commission from the Royal Geographic Society in London, Mouhot arrived in Bangkok in September 1858. From there he took a number of extended excursions, the longest of which took him into Cambodia and up to Angkor. His drawings, the most meticulous of which detailed the animals and landscapes he encountered, bore strong testimony to his interest in botany and the natural sciences. Mouhot was far less occupied with ideas of exploration and claiming 'un-chartered' territory. In fact his diaries explicitly acknowledged and gave credit to those who had been there before him, including Charles-Emile Bouillevaux, a French Catholic missionary who visited Angkor exactly a decade earlier. Mouhot believed that his own efforts were best served by contributing to 'the enrichment of science' (cited in Dagens 1995: 39). Death by malaria in Laos in 1861 would deny him the opportunity to witness the widespread recognition his efforts would eventually receive back in Europe. The serialization of his diaries in *Le Tour du Monde* over 14 weeks in 1863 provided Europe with its first comprehensive account of Angkor's temples.[1] An English translation of his diary would also appear in book form the year after, with a French version published four years later in 1868.

Crucially, the growth of cheap printing technologies enabled these publications to reach far wider audiences than the hand-written accounts of travelers to Angkor from previous centuries. Indeed, we now know that the site not only remained an important destination for Buddhist pilgrims traveling from across Southeast and East Asia from the sixteenth century onwards, but was also visited by a number of Spanish and Portuguese explorers 200 years before Mouhot (Barnett 1990, Cooper 2001). In a recent article examining this 'middle period of Khmer history', Thompson (2004) also cites Japanese and Arabic inscriptions as evidence of a detailed and rich history of Asian travel to Angkor spanning several centuries.

Attempting to convey his own experiences, Mouhot contrasted a 'corrupt and barbarous' nineteenth-century Cambodia inhabited by 'savage tribes' with a magnificent 'Ongcor [that] transported the visitor from Barbarism to civilization, from profound darkness to light' (1864: 282). To resolve a sense of discontinuity between his surroundings and the splendors of Angkor he concluded that the structures were the legacy of a lost civilization which must have disappeared at some point during the intervening centuries:

> There are ruins of such grandeur, remains of structures which must have
> been raised at such intense cost of labor, that, at first view, one is filled with

profound admiration, and cannot but ask what has become of this powerful race, so civilised, so enlightened, the authors of these gigantic works?

(ibid: 278)

He continues:

> If you interrogate the Cambodians as to the founders of Ongcor-Wat, you invariably receive one of four replies: 'it is the work of Pra-Eun, the king of the angels;' 'it is the work of the giants;' 'It was built by the leprous king;' or else, 'it made itself'.

(ibid: 279)

In describing Angkor 'as a sealed book for want of an interpreter' (ibid: 300) Mouhot's accounts proved extremely effective in awakening European 'curiosity and encouraged explorers, archaeologists and photographers to take an interest in the Indochina peninsula' (Cooper 2001: 69). The diaries made their biggest impact in the scientific and scholarly circles of Paris, an environment which, for reasons discussed shortly, was more than open to the theory of a mysterious civilization extinguished from 'history' (Edwards 2007).

Interestingly, many of the details and meticulously crafted descriptions in the English book publication were removed from the French version. This contributed to the emergence of an image of Angkor within French scholarly circles which revolved around ideas of jungle-covered ruins as the remnants of a mysterious and intriguing classical civilization. Mouhot's considerable talent for sketching quite literally added color and depth to his accounts of monumental sandstone structures buried deep in an exotic landscape of wild animals, thick vegetation and 'savage' villagers. Although never crediting himself as Angkor's 'discoverer', it would be an appellation that posthumously stuck back in Europe. Bestowing Mouhot such a title offered France a direct, and pure, connection to erstwhile glory, enabling it to bypass and transcend any counterclaims or alternative postulations on what was at that time a largely vacuous history.

To better understand the significance of such a representation it is helpful to briefly reflect upon the broader socio-political context of late nineteenth-century France. First, the idea of a classical civilization lying buried in the jungle proved an evocative justification for further exploration and research. Indeed, in a country where colonial projects lacked popular support, Angkor would rapidly become a valuable asset for procuring the necessary financial and political backing for such trips. Over the course of the nineteenth century France's interest in the region had expanded from the initial efforts of Catholic missionaries to trade and a program of state-sponsored exploration which was increasingly motivated by a desire for territorial control. On the back of the second opium war of 1856–60, and the broader geo-political race between Europe's imperial powers, Mouhot's account provided an urgency for 'France to add this "jewel" to her crown before Britain snatched it' (Edwards 2005: 14). By offering a potent symbol of 'a virgin territory to be discovered, explored, … an empty space to be comprehended and understood'

(Cooper 2001: 18), Angkor's abandoned ruins added impetus to unfolding French political interests for the region as a whole. Norindr explores the intersections between the cultural representations and political motives of the period to argue that an ahistorical narrative of Angkor served two distinct purposes. First, it enabled the French to position themselves as 'sole and rightful heirs to ... [the region's] ... antiquities'; and second, by reducing Indochina to 'an empty space, a void that could be exploited and colonized' a single administrative, economic and political space could be realized (1996: 5). In other words, the conception of Angkor as a ruin acted as a metaphor for an early colonialist ideology towards the Indochinese peninsula as a whole.

Beyond these immediate aspirations for territorial control in Indochina, the idea of a lost Angkor also resonated with the pan-European fascination at that time for classical civilizations and the inevitable decline of history. The arrival of the Picturesque movement in the 1800s ensured vernacular architecture, gnarled trees and ivy-covered ruins were brought into the fold of a European visual culture. As Woodward identifies, it was an aesthetic whereby 'nature could be improved by the eye of the artist, who adds living trees and rocks, sunlight, water and old ruins to the palette' (2001: 119). In large part, the Picturesque was defined by the attempts of philosophers, visual artists, and poets to represent the subjective and layered nature of memory. In the literary hands of Byron, Ruskin, Diderot and Shelley the ruin became further mythologized as an icon of both lament and optimism. As Romanticism spread across Europe, the movement also took on political motivations, most notably within a post-revolutionary France. For public intellectuals bolstered by the ideals of liberty, equality and fraternity decaying, tree-covered classical structures became a powerful motif for 'human pride, greed and stupidity' (Woodward 2001: 157). In his examination of nineteenth-century France, Green (1990) argues a shift in perception towards nature was driven by the rise of a metropolitan culture. Modernity had prescribed a new aesthetic structure to nature. In reaction to processes of urbanism and industrialization 'another modernity' could be realized through encounters with ruins and other landscapes. The endurance of earlier romanticist ideals ensured notions of the sublime and myth superseded the voracity for an objective, empirical-based rationality which emerged during the renaissance. As a case in point, Woodward describes how Ninfa – an Italian city destroyed and abandoned in the late fourteenth century – was encountered by travelers half a millennium later, 'In the air humid with malaria the vegetation grew with a feverish vigour, as if exhilarating in the absence of human life. The ruins became a jungle, and as a jungle it was discovered by Romantic travelers' (2001: 78).

Not surprisingly, this nineteenth-century vision of landscape dovetailed with contemporary territorial aspirations of empire held within Britain, France, and the Netherlands. As Clarke reminds us, the romantics were in search of a 'vision of wholeness ... a oneness with nature, nature and for a reunification of religion, philosophy and art which had been sundered in the modern western world' (1997: 55). Said has also suggested that for France in particular 'theirs was the orient of memories, suggestive ruins, forgotten ruins' (1995: 169).

The accounts and drawings provided by Mouhot had thus set the tone for a deep fascination for a far-off land of decayed antiquities; an exotic spectacle which, according to Norindr (2006), would become a 'force of passion' for French writers, artists, and filmmakers. Shortly after the establishment of the Protectorate of Cambodia in 1863, Louis Delaporte, at that time a young naval officer, was 'commissioned' to provide the illustrations for a report entitled *Voyage d'exploration en Indo-Chine*. Depictions of Angkor Wat and the Bayon temples included imaginary features like moats or spires, as well as the ever present color of elephants, tigers, thick vegetation and the occasional native (Dagens 1995). Some years later Pierre Loti, one of Europe's most prolific travel writers famed for his tales of voyages across the 'Orient', would also visit Angkor. Published as *Un Pèlerin d'Angkor* (A Pilgrimage to Angkor) 11 years after his 1901 trip, the book would tell the story of grand expedition, adventure and an encounter with wondrous ruins:

> The 'fig tree of the ruins' reigns supreme today as undisputed master over Angkor. Above the palaces, above the temples, which it has patiently broken up, it flaunts everywhere in triumph its pale, smooth branches, spotted like a snake, and its large dome of leaves. At the beginning it was only a small seed, sown by the wind on a frieze or on the summit of a tower. But no sooner did it germinate with its roots, like tenuous filaments insinuated their way between the stones, to go down, down, guided by a sure instinct towards the earth. And when at last they reached the earth, they quickly swelled, waxing on its nourishing juices, until they become enormous, disjoining, displacing everything, splitting the thick walls from top to bottom; and then the building was irretrievably lost.
>
> (Loti 1996: 37)

Similarly:

> Through an inextricable tangle of dripping brambles and creepers, we have to beat a path with sticks in order to reach this temple. The forest entwines it tightly on every side, chokes it, crushes it; and to complete the destruction, immense 'fig trees of the ruins' have taken root there everywhere, up to the very summit of its towers, which act as their pedestal. Here are the doors; roots, like aged heads of hair, drape them with a thousand fringes ... My Cambodian guide insists that we should leave. We have no lanterns, he tells me, on our carts, and we must return before the hour of the tiger. But we shall return to this infinitely mysterious temple.
>
> (ibid: 38–9)

Loti's work formed part of a larger field of French travel writing and fiction on Indochina which emerged around the turn of the century. In their introduction to a collection of essays focusing on such 'cultural representations', Robson and Yee indicate how Indochina became a literary pretext for heroic endeavors and that 'many of the major actors of the colonial conquest staked territorial claims not only through exploration and military prowess but also through textual representation' (2005: 4). The use of abandoned temples as a literary device to portray lost, mysterious and exotic far off lands perhaps reached its zenith in the writing of André Malraux. In his 1930 novel *La Voie Royale* (The Royal Way) Malraux describes the heroic figure – a character loosely based on himself – in search of archaeological treasures and the royal road of the ancient Khmer empire.[2] In Norindr's opinion the novel's depiction of an erotic and feminized Asia needs to be understood more as a 'royal road to the unconscious and the colonialist imaginary' of the Métropole (1996: 105).

In accounting for the above representations offered by Malraux, Delaporte and others, this opening section has examined what would become a crucial moment in Angkorean historiography. The circulation and appropriation of Mouhot's tale of 'discovery' set in motion a framing of Angkor as the architectural, ruinous remnants of a lost, and thus dead, civilization. As Norindr (2006) suggests Angkor became a place *sans histoire*, and as such would emerge as a metonym for a broader French imperialist 'fantasy' of an exotic, enigmatic and seductive *Indochine*. An aura of romance and mystique had been created around Angkor fuelled by a supposed vacuum of history. It was a representation that, by implication, elided localized claims of sovereignty and ancestry. Moreover, in forging a historical rupture between the time of Angkorean creation and the nineteenth century the necessary platform for re-landscaping Cambodia's history into a more politically expedient form was created; a process which, as we will shall now see, would unfold around Angkor during the early decades of the twentieth century.

Spaces of history, times of the nation

> Angkor, symbol of a new Indochina that can be reborn from its ruins, a rebirth made possible by France.
>
> (Norindr 1996: 27)

In 1863 the 27-year-old Ang Vodey, who would be crowned King Norodom I a year later, signed a treaty with France securing the protection of Cambodia from its more powerful Thai and Vietnamese neighbors. The document also marked an expansion of France's territorial control within Indochina which, up until that point, had focused on the southern region of *Cochinchine*, with the port city of Saigon acting as a hub of trade and administration. Three decades later Cambodia became part of the *Fédération Indochinoise* (Indochinese Federation); an administrative territory incorporating Laos and much of modern-day Vietnam. During this intervening period however, officials in Saigon showed little interest in Cambodia's northwest territories. Indeed, just four years after the 1863 treaty, formal sovereignty for these 'remote' regions was handed over to the Siamese.

In contrast, back in the Métropole the sense of Angkor's 'remoteness' further fuelled the intrigue and spirit of adventure first triggered by Mouhot's evocative diaries. As we have seen, his tales of abandoned architectural wonders and mysterious lost civilizations effectively created a narrative of landscape founded upon a *tabula rasa*; an enigma of history that demanded further investigation and research. Accordingly, in 1898 Paul Doumer, the recently appointed Governor of Indochina, established the *Mission Archéologique Permanente* in Saigon. Edwards suggests the establishment of this organization laid the 'foundations for the institutionalization of French control over indigenous pasts and cultures, and their consolidation into national histories and symbols' (1999:184). The formation of the École française d'Extrême Orient (EFEO) three years later cemented this new phase of French intervention. EFEO's first director, Louis Finot outlined three key aims of the organization. First, it would provide France with clear ideas of the people it ruled including their language, traditions, and sense of morality; second, reinforce a sense of French responsibility towards the ancient monuments located within its territories; and third, broaden French scholarship on the orient (ibid: 184–5).

In 1907 a second Franco-Siamese treaty reversed the 1867 agreement, enabling France to reclaim Angkor from a Siam that was increasingly coming under the influence of the British. The new treaty not only ensured France's rival power was unable to gain an administrative hold over the temples, it also paved the way for their incorporation into French cartographic representations of a Cambodian national territory.[3] With dozens of large structures all located within a single region, albeit one spanning several hundred square kilometers, Angkor represented an immense and highly prestigious challenge for EFEO and the newly formed Angkor Conservation Office. Intrigued by the sheer scale and density of construction, scholars would pursue three broad, interrelated lines of enquiry, all of which would evolve over the coming decades.

First, painstaking studies were made of the monuments as architectural forms. With the clearing, numbering, and mapping of each temple a picture of a stylistic and technical evolution steadily appeared. Although the greatest attention was paid to the buildings within the Angkor region, and what would eventually become the Angkor Archaeological Park, studies were also conducted into structures lying further afield in order to trace transitions in style, construction techniques and the materials used. In his brief summary of this process Dagens indicates that, within a broader program of 'scientific' clearing, research and restoration, a consensus was established which allowed some temples to be left untouched enabling visitors 'to rediscover Angkor as it was' (1995: 173).

The process of ripping out tree roots, scrubbing stones and removing vegetation would invariably further undermine the stability of structures that were already toppling and in danger of imminent collapse. To address such concerns EFEO's architects and archaeologists extensively deployed concrete and wooden supports. Seasonal rains and the intense tropical climate not only made such tasks significantly more difficult, but also meant the results were far from durable. The eventual decision to implement anastylosis, a technique of restoration adopted from Europe and extensively applied to Borobudur by the Dutch at the beginning of the century, would allow for a more systematic and rigorous program of dismantling and reconstruction. Anastylosis would enable conservators to discreetly replace missing or shattered stones with new ones if they were deemed vital to the structure's reconstruction. Through the efforts of Henri Marchal and others the technique was carefully perfected, most notably at the small, but highly elaborate, sandstone complex of Banteay Srei.

After seeing the results of anastylosis at a number of other temple sites including Neak Pean and Banteay Samre, the architect Maurice Glaize dismissed concerns held by some scholars that the method was overly intrusive and potentially irreversible. Frustrated by the skepticism towards the value of EFEO's scientific progress, he opined in a 1942 lecture that:

> The archaeologist's efforts are met only with mistrust on the part of the "tourist" who hankers for the picturesque and who, in the midst of the 20th century, travels in style and comfort to visit ruins where he expects to experience the exhilaration of a Mouhot discovering Angkor Wat in 1860. The tourist is driven by an outdated individualism and all that counts for him is a romanticism fuelled by spectacular effects, as symbolised by a section of wall crumbling in the passionate tentacled embrace of voracious trees. The curator is no more than a stage-manager of this vegetal orgy.[4]

A second thread of research, pursued concurrently with this program of restoration, was the study of the countless stone sculptures found in and around the temples. A seemingly endless wealth of free-standing statues, wall-carved figurines and other ornamental features were categorized into phases, or 'styles', within an overall chronology of Khmer art (see for example Giteau 1998, Myrdal & Kessle 1970, Stierlin 1997). Within Angkor's cosmological symbolism wood was the material of a vernacular, living culture, whereas, in representing permanence, stone spoke of another world, one of celestial beauties and divine guardians. In other words, sculptures carved in stone embodied the connections between former rulers, worshipped as ancestral deities, and a pantheon of Buddhist or Hindu gods.

In her chapter 'Taj Angkor; enshrining l'Inde in le Cambodge', Edwards illustrates how this field of research firmly prioritized and reified the cultural and religious influence of India. She describes a process of 'Re-Indianization' whereby early twentieth-century 'Buddhist worship at Angkor presented unwelcome challenges to colonial desires to compartmentalize Cambodia both vertically, through time, and horizontally, through the categorization of religion' (2005: 17). Given that most Cambodians practiced a form of Theravada Buddhism which integrated animist beliefs and the veneration of figures like Vishnu and Shiva, the presence of monks and Buddhist icons detracted from the colonial imagining of a once glorious 'Hindu' past represented by a pristine Angkor. Considered to be an eyesore, the community of monks living in front of Angkor Wat were removed by EFEO in 1909. This was followed by the consolidation of all the temple's Buddhist statues within a single space on the ground floor, an area that was subsequently coined 'the gallery of a thousand Buddhas'. According to Edwards such "'Buddhist" identities spoiled the "Hindu" template presented to tourists

[and] disturbed the colonial presentation of Angkor as both monument *and* frozen moment, a material archive to the "golden" era of Khmer greatness and glory' (Ibid: 17–18, emphasis hers).[5]

The reification of an Indian influence also defined EFEO's third line of enquiry, that of epigraphy. The meticulous translation of Sanskrit inscriptions found on numerous stelae or doorways revealed elaborate stories of kingship and devoted populations, of battles and conquests, and of deities and religious cults.[6] These inscriptions provided a unique key for unlocking the mysteries of why kingdoms were settled and re-settled in different areas, and why powers waxed and waned as territories and armies were won and lost. Supplementary, and more visual, evidence was also gathered from extensive bas-relief carvings found on walls in various temples including Angkor Wat, Bayon and the Baphuon.

Evolving in tandem over the course of the twentieth century, these three areas of research created an ever more detailed picture of Angkor's 'history'. Their points of focus, however, led to a historiography overwhelmingly oriented around an elitist, regal culture. Indeed, writing in the opening pages of his *Introduction to Angkor*, now regarded as one of the seminal texts on the region, George Coedès states, 'The history of the ancient Khmers, or in other words, the Cambodians, is limited to their kings' (1963: 1).

Coedès' assertion indirectly reveals EFEO's lack of interest in understanding, or indeed excavating, more social and vernacular histories. As we shall see shortly, this imbalance towards a classical 'high' culture, and its associated idea of historical decline, would become pivotal to France's political discourse of nation building for Cambodia. But it was also fashioned by the durability of stone in the face of a highly corrosive tropical climate which had destroyed other less resilient forms of material culture long before the French arrived. Given such restraints, colonial scholarship relied upon a limited number of intellectual keys for unlocking Angkor's history. With decades of study built around reading shifting architectural/artistic styles or the interpretation of bas relief carvings and inscriptions, architectural historians and epigraphers provided a chronological blueprint for segmenting and categorizing Cambodia's history into a linear narrative. An emphasis on transitions and ruptures in architecture, sculpture, and periods of kingship cemented the idea of a glorious Angkorean Period; an epoch which would be set against the less illustrious 'pre' and 'post' Angkorean eras.[7]

Within this historiography the reign of Jayavarman VII came to be seen as the apex of Cambodian history. Although the sheer scale and magnificence of Suryavarman II's twelfth-century Angkor Wat ensured it remained a 'peculiarly fascinating archaeological marvel for [the] French' (Cooper 2001: 69), preeminent scholars like George Coedès, Henri Parmentier, and Bernard-Philippe Groslier spent decades interpreting and restoring the key structures of Jayavarman VII's hugely extensive construction program, including his vast city complex of Angkor Thom.[8]

Over the course of a reign spanning nearly 40 years, from 1181 to c1219, Jayavarman VII developed a growing interest in Mahayana Buddhism. Although it was widely acknowledged amongst EFEO scholars that this shift created a religious and political environment incompatible with temple building, the sharp decrease in stone construction after his death was still regarded as a time of decay and waning power. Moreover, as Coedès suggests, Jayavarman VII left 'the country worn out by his megalomania and thenceforth unable to resist the attacks of his young and turbulent neighbor to the west' (1963: 106).[9] Within an analysis that suggested this loss of power was accompanied by a decline in artistry, the eventual looting of Angkor by Thai armies in 1431 was seen as the final annihilation of the skills and resources upon which a glorious era of Angkorean sculpture and architecture depended.

The looting of Angkor was also regarded as the final curtain to a period of Khmer history characterized by immense wealth and power, and the end of an 'empire' that, at its height, had extended across vast territories within Southeast Asia.[10] France's admiration for an idealized Angkor meant its ruins became the material legacy of a once glorious, but now lost, even dead, civilization. With the post-Angkorean period constructed as a time of defeat and dormancy, the French protectorate perceived nineteenth-century Cambodians as culturally, politically, and technically inferior to their ancestors. According to Wright, by suggesting the natives allowed the temples to decay, the French inscribed Angkor with a new artistic, aesthetic terminology to secure their role as the site's rightful custodians. As she states:

> All historic architecture was aestheticised, then classified according to western criteria. Archaeologists and government functionaries lauded the Ecole's formal classification system and its exacting reconstruction effort as the only legitimate way to honour the great art of the past.
>
> (Wright 1991: 199)

In this respect, we can once again see the notion of history as decline transposed onto Cambodia from Europe. It was noted earlier in this chapter that Angkor's temples, lying buried in the jungle, powerfully embodied a classical civilization in 'ruins'. The clearing and restoration of these sites would only serve to reinforce this idea and codify it within a paradigm of scientific research. Given the devaluing of the contemporary era within such a representation, little attention was given to oral histories or the inter-generational transmission of cultural and religious practices. Indeed, within an account of architectural splendor and pristine glory anthropology would hold little kudos or political sway (Luco 2006). In an attempt to overcome this somewhat simplistic idea of 1431 as a moment of abandonment and historical rupture, more recent scholarship has examined shifting geographies of trade, religious continuities or enduring traditions of ceramics (Mabbett & Chandler 1995, Chandler 1996b, Harris 2005). To cite one notable example, the inaugural edition of the *Udaya* journal, published in Cambodia in 2000 by the APSARA authority, was dedicated to the functionality and evolving artistry of ceramics and earthenware. Laying out the aims of the publication, the editors stated, 'Taken together, the contributions in this issue of *Udaya* problematize approaches to the Cambodian ceramic tradition which lean heavily on a simple opposition between continuity and rupture' (APSARA 2000b: 15).

Cooper suggests a narration of Cambodia's history around classical antiq-uities was crucial to France's political project of maintaining its protectorate (2001: 74).[11] In securing the authority and right to restore Angkor, EFEO's expertise also provided the French with a discourse of nation building centered upon ideas of reconstruction and resuscitation. Foregrounding ideas of decline and an impending loss of sovereignty at the hands of more powerful neighbors ensured Cambodia's dependency upon the Métropole. Examining this process as a cultural political dialogue Edwards argues 'French readings of Khmer history tele-scoped the cultural complexity of the previous centuries into a trifocal narrative of Angkorean glory, post Angkorean decay, and colonial redemption' (1999: 163).

One of the tools deployed for constructing such a discourse was cartography. While a number of maps of Angkor were produced in the years after 1907, the region only officially opened as an 'Archaeological Park' in the mid 1920s.[12] Demarcating, maintaining and displaying the temples as a coherent and unified landscape provided a tangible representation of Cambodia's tri-focal history. More specifically, given the threads of research pursued by EFEO, as noted earlier, the notion of a bounded park created a geography of stylistic transitions, whereby carving, ornamentation and construction techniques could be hierarchically cate-gorized. This effectively meant that many of Cambodia's temples lying beyond the park's boundaries were labeled as either pre or post Angkorean, and thus, by impli-cation, of lesser importance. Finally, the mapping of Angkor also reaffirmed the colonial regime as the rightful guardians over the treasured antiquities (Anderson 1991: 181).

The management and presentation of Angkor as a park for tourists, an issue returned to in greater detail shortly, formed part of a broader shift in the French colonial project occurring at that time. Cooper argues that a late nineteenth-century colonial mindset geared towards territorial control and pacification came to be replaced by a more progressive ideology captured in the term *Mise en Valeur*. With the goals and principles of colonialism coming under ever greater scrutiny within Europe *Mise en Valeur* represented an attempt to instill an 'economic … moral and cultural improvement' across the region of Indochina (2001: 29).

For Tully (2002) this shift in French attitudes towards Cambodia, a new phase he describes as a *mission civilisatrice*, gravitated around improvements in health, edu-cation and the restoration of Angkor. However, within his socio-political account of the protectorate, the concept of restoration only extends as far as the actual recon-struction of the temples themselves. In contrast, authors like Cooper, Norindr, Wright, and Edwards have examined this period as a series of unfolding cultural dynamics in order to argue that culture and politics with Indochina need to be seen as 'two complimentary techniques or strategies for asserting power' (Wright 1991: 8). Working within this perspective Edwards (2007) explores Angkor's 'restoration' as a process of secularization, monumentalization, and symbolic mobilization. In addition to tracing the scholarly pursuits of EFEO noted ear-lier, she reviews developments in civic architecture, urban planning, print media and museumology during the early decades of the twentieth century to document the rise of Angkor, and in particular Angkor Wat, as a unifying icon for an emergent *Cambodge*. Departing from the idea that a Cambodian nationalism simply emerged as a colonial ideology imposed upon a passive population, Edwards suggests a vital fusion of 'native and European ... ideas of culture and politics' (1999: 3) occurred, whereby constructions of a noble Khmer citizen, a Khmer cultural heritage, and a Cambodian national history all converged and fused around a totemic Angkor.

By the 1930s, many of Cambodia's educated and intellectual elite lamented their languid nation, a country that had ceded power to both France and its regional neighbors. Newly formed institutes like the *Lycée Sisowath* and the *Institut Bouddhique*, along with the newspaper *Nagara Vatta* (Angkor Vat), attempted to resolve this crisis by fostering an anti-Chinese, anti-Vietnamese movement (Chandler 1996b).[13] Not surprisingly, Angkor was frequently cited as evidence of a Khmer racial and cultural supremacy. This small, but increasingly influential, public sphere also began to adopt an anti-colonial vocabulary as the decade progressed.[14] According to Edwards (2007), the term *jiet* shifted away from its previous associations with birth towards ideas of race and nation. Heavily used in *Nagara Vatta*, the concept would come to play an important role in forming a nationalist ideology increasingly frustrated with and resistant to the idea of a protectorate.[15] Inspired by their understandings of European forms of democracy many of *Nagara Vatta's* writers in the late 1930s began to advocate a similar path for Cambodia via the attainment of independence. Once again, justification for such a quest often drew upon historical references to a glorious Angkor, a testament to Khmer strength which should not be forgotten (Edwards 2007: 15).

Edwards parallels this analysis of Angkor's symbolic and political mobilization within Cambodia with an examination of the role the temples played within a French Metropolitan identity. In turning to consider such issues, the following section considers their consumption as a tourist landscape, as a series of exposition replicas in France, and as the dominant reference point for a 'modern' Cambodian arts industry.

Souvenir Angkor

In this final section examining the French protectorate I wish to look at a trajectory of consumption that formed around Angkor during a period of history so eloquently described by Walter Benjamin (1999) as an 'age of mechanical reproduction'. Particular attention will be given to colonial expositions held in France and the rise of tourism and a modern arts and crafts industry in Cambodia.

As the second half of the nineteenth century progressed ideals of the nation, progress, expansion, power and history provided the impetus for increasingly elaborate 'World Fairs' and a variety of colonial exhibitions across Europe (Allwood 1977, Greenhalgh 2000). After the Great Exhibition of 1851 held in London, France responded with its own Exposition Universelle in 1867. Although the various displays revealed the extent of the country's territorial interests a scarcity of objects from Cambodia meant little attention was given to the country or its temples. It would not be long, however, before scholars, explorers and adminis-trators began gathering artifacts from the temples, floating them down river and loading them onto ships destined for France.

With many of these objects finally coming to rest in the Musée Guimet, which opened in Paris in the late 1880s, replicas of the sculptures would appear in expo-sitions staged in 1878 and 1889. The latter of these two exhibitions would also feature the first reproduction of Angkorean architecture in the form of a central sanctum. The project demonstrated how Europe's fascination for the antiquities of a classical era had become geographically mobile. Initially exported to the territo-ries, and now transported back to the Métropole, it was a representation of the past intended to impress France's colonial prowess on its rival powers and help garner popular support domestically. The gilding of the 1889 pavilion for example, along with the presentation of bas reliefs, inscriptions and temple dancers provided tan-gible evidence of advances in French scholarship in archaeology and ethnographic classification, discourses which also gave both credibility and a distinctive identity to a number of newly opened museums, including the Guimet.

The scholarly advances in constructing a national history for Cambodge out-lined in the previous section would also shape the trajectories of how Angkor was treated as an object of display. The reproduction of an Angkorean grotto in Paris in 1900, a Bayon tower in Marseilles in 1906, and a life-size Angkorean pavilion in 1922 – also in Marseilles – all became the focal points of displays which cate-gorized history and its objects in more geographic and national terms. Within their respective examinations of these expositions Cooper, Edwards, and Norindr all trace Angkor's rise as a metonym and metaphor for an exotic *Indochine*. Accord-ing to Norindr, Angkor, and in particular Angkor Wat, emerged as the 'cradle' of an Indochinese civilization, and thus 'one of the privileged reference points' for a far eastern *fantaisie* (1996: 4). Similarly, Cooper argues that the staging of exhibitions was one of the most effective means for expressing an imagining of *L'Indochine Française* as a 'mythical, dreamed-for-place, an exotic utopia' (2001: 2). Clearly, architecture had become the medium through which a spa-tially, temporally, and culturally distant culture could be presented and publicly consumed. While these two authors emphasize the role expositions played in forg-ing an 'imaginative territorial assemblage *calqué* (traced, copied, translated) from the political boundaries' (Norindr 1995: 38) of a French Indochina, Edwards also indicates how pristine reproductions of Angkor served to reinforce a conviction among scholars, politicians and administrators that their intervention had led to a reincarnation of Cambodian culture.

The ultimate expression of these themes and beliefs came in 1931 with the *Exposition Coloniale Internationalle de Paris*. The most extravagant and elab-orate exposition to date, the show marked the fullest expression of imperial power, with France's colonial territories refined, admired, and displayed as secular spectacle through a process Anderson has described as a 'logoisation' of culture (1991:182). The exhibition planners designed a village to display possessions col-lected from various territories including Algeria, Cochinchina, French Guyana,

Laos and Senegal, amongst others. In addition to these country displays the village entertained its 33 million visitors with evening light shows, elephant and camel rides, electric cars, as well as a zoo and lake. According to Norindr, Angkor was chosen to be the centre piece of the show because it 'embodied the exotic most vividly in the imaginary of the French', and at the same time, captured the ideals of '*la France des cinq continents*' (1995: 47). Costing twelve and a half million francs, the three-quarter size replica of Angkor Wat included detailed reproductions of carvings, sculptures, and bas reliefs along its façades.

In contrast to the faithful reproduction of Angkor's architectural themes on the outside, the interior was remodeled into three floors, which, when seen together, would provide the visitor with an understanding of the close cultural and economic ties between the Métropole and its territory in Indochina. On the ground floor industrial products, natural resources and other trade goods shipped from the colonies were displayed. Above that could be found examples of France's social and cultural programs, such as libraries and museums. Visitors who made it to the final floor were rewarded with an extensive and systematically classified selection of archaeological and ethnographic artifacts. Reflecting upon these displays, Norindr suggests the building was the ultimate realization of an ideology that fused a taste for classical grandeur with the political and moral ideals of the colonial mission.[16] In stating that a replica of Angkor Wat 'signifies a "new" Angkor, symbol of a new Indochina that can be reborn from its ruins, a rebirth made possible by France' (1995: 51) he connects the Paris exposition with the restoration efforts of EFEO seen earlier in this chapter within a single political matrix. This account, by implication, points towards the importance of these expositions in bolstering the legitimacy of France as the natural and direct heir to a great civilization. Indeed, as Robson and Yee have more recently argued, projects like the 1931 exhibition formed part of a broader colonial mindset, whereby 'scientific imperialism, the "mission civilisatrice" and industrialization went hand in hand with France's republican ideology and ambitions as a "great power" on the global stage' (2005: 3).

Exhibited reproductions of Angkor would also accelerate its symbolic appropriation within a world of commerce and branding. In the 1920s Angkor began to be used in adverts for luxury goods trading on ideas of durability, exoticness, and refined taste. To accompany the 1922 Marseille exposition two ocean liners, the *Felix Roussel* and *Angkor*, had their interiors redecorated with seven-headed Naga handrails, carved ceilings and pilasters displaying sculpted apsaras. To accompany the 1931 exhibition Frigéco used the Paris replica of Angkor Wat as a backdrop for its refrigerators to suggest their products were durable and reliable in 'all climates' (Edwards and Winter 2004). Lincoln cars, Cyma watches and Belle Jardinière clothing all used Angkor to signify wealth, elegance, and quality. Such commodification and circulation within a world of branding would strip the temples of all their historical, cultural, and religious meanings. Once unshackled and de-territorialized, they could be imbued with a new, disparate set of values, European ideas of modernity and engineering finesse, or the exotic Orient of silent ruins and resurrected antiquities.

The display of Angkorean architecture and artifacts within France was also paralleled with, and influenced by, the development of the site for touristic consumption. Up until the end of the nineteenth century visits to Angkor were described and written up as trips of exploration, rather than tourism. After docking in Saigon, voyagers would transfer to another boat for the upriver trip to Phnom Penh, the capital of Cambodia from 1886 onwards. The introduction of regular steam boat services by the *Compagnie des messageries fluviales* (River Transport Company) around this time would significantly ease the journey between the two cities.[17] Given that efforts to develop trade and transport links over the coming two decades continued to focus on the region's internal waterways, the great lake Tonle Sap remained the principle point of access for excursions to Angkor. And with the first cars not arriving in Cambodia until the 1900s daily trips out to the temples involved elephant rides or bumpy trips on wooden carts along pathways and the limited network of Angkorean roads.

After their initial scorn for amateur scholars and other temple tourists, EFEO began to acknowledge the need for greater access and accommodation facilities.[18] In 1907 just over 200 tourists were recorded in the Angkor visitors' log. This number would steadily increase over the coming years, in part due to the efforts of the newly established, Paris-based, *Société d'Angkor pour la conservation des monuments anciens d'Indochine*, which promoted the work of EFEO within France. The appearance of cars, buses, and lodges in Phnom Penh during the 1910s coincided with the beginning of an era of grand tours across Indochina. The arrival of the bourgeois European traveler would also lead to a shift in perceptions towards the wild and rugged 'nature' of Angkor's ruins.[19] Up until this point stories of labyrinthine, jungle-covered temples, as offered by Mouhot, Delaporte, Loti and others, had dominated public imaginings of Angkor across Europe, and provided much of the impetus for tourist trips to the region. However, as the region's travel facilities improved, in terms of both scope and comfort, the exhilaration of discovering an Angkorean wilderness lost some of its appeal. To cater to this evolving tourist gaze, Angkor's landscape would be remodeled in a way that harmonized its aesthetics with the well-ordered parklands of Europe.

Over the coming years EFEO and local public administrators implemented programs for maintaining and presenting both the temples and their surrounding environments. In the case of Angkor Wat for example, trees and monks were removed from the complex and the visual impact of the temple was enhanced through the reconstruction of the balustrades lining the long causeway entrance. Other temples such as the Bayon had their foliage stripped and courtyards cleared of rubble and stone blocks. Jean Commaille, EFEO's director until his assassination in 1916, also cleared substantial amounts of forest and vegetation from the interior of Jayavarman VII's Angkor Thom city complex in an effort to make it more accessible to visitors. As noted earlier though, the decision was taken to leave certain temples like Ta Prohm, Preah Khan and Ta Som as partial ruins for those visitors who did want to experience the romance of re-discovering a long-lost, ancient civilization. Although such ideas were being rendered increasingly anachronistic by policies of site management and development, the popular image of Angkor as a series of jungle-covered ruins traced in the opening section of the chapter would endure and continue to seduce. In other words, as a tourist land-scape, Angkor had become an icon of both an enchanting, enigmatic and romantic *Indochine*, as well as the legacy of a great civilization, one that was now being restored and revivified. The chapters that follow explore the political, economic, and cultural mechanisms which ensure these narratives and framings continue to co-exist today.

These framings of Angkor as a tourist landscape would also affect the lives of the dozens of families living within the newly protected area. In order to retain a patina of age more 'modern' intrusions, such as villages or monks, needed to be moved away from the temples and away from the gaze of the tourist. As part of a study on *Contested Heritage: The People of Angkor*, Miura (2004) documents EFEO's rationale for relocating a number of communities living inside Angkor Thom and around Angkor Wat. She indicates how moves to demarcate Angkor as a park came to be underpinned by a conceptualization of the site as an open-air museum, a space of education for the public. Crucially, her analysis reveals that such an approach defined its 'public' as the foreign tourist, rather than the local resident. Interestingly, she cites Henri Marchal's concern over a 1924 proposal to exclude all villagers from the park as an example of the ongoing disagreements between EFEO and local French bureaucrats regarding the geographic (re)location of Angkor's communities:

> ... it would be regrettable from diverse points of view such as the recruitment of workers and the picturesque view. Many painters and artists coming to Angkor were pleased to see groups of indigenous people circulating in the park, with their cattle or carts – the models they associate with the silhouettes of the monuments.
>
> (Cited by Miura 2004: 123)

Notwithstanding such disagreements, Angkor's transformation into tourist space would be virtually complete by the mid-1920s. The exclusion of many families from an area officially designated as the *Park d'Angkor* in 1925 was soon followed by the introduction of visiting charges for tourists, most of whom would follow the recommended *Grand* or *Petit Circuits*. Not surprisingly, EFEO's scholars were becoming increasingly uneasy about the detrimental impact of this flourishing industry. George Groslier, for example, famously lamented 'cars now drive right up to the temple doors, telegraph wires touch its walls, and hotels are built within view of its towers'.[20] The *Hotel des Ruines* Groslier refers to – built near the front entrance of Angkor Wat in 1928 – would be subsequently demolished, and a policy of preventing any further constructions within the park meant the four-storied *Grand Hotel d'Angkor* opened its doors in 1929 a few kilometers down the road in the nearby town of Siem Reap.

The opening of the Grand heralded the beginning of a new age of luxury. In the 1930s, the hotel, along with the *Hotel le Royal* in Phnom Penh, would provide the appropriate accommodation for the wealthiest of round the world cruise ship tourists traveling overland from Saigon and bound for Angkor. They would also accommodate a clientele whose trips had been inspired by the classical dance performances and ornately carved architecture on show in Paris and Marseilles. The simultaneous development of a rail line between Bangkok and Aranyaprathet in Thailand, along with more regional airports, tourist buses and hotels in Cambodia, also enabled travel agents across Europe and North America to promote Angkor as an exotic destination, a place of adventure and incomparable grandeur.[21] On the back of a few short decades of tourism development, Angkor had become a well-ordered and manicured landscape; laid out as a tangible example of a French program of *Mise en Valeur* for the world to come and see.

In addition to shaping Angkor's landscape, international tourism would also deliver an audience for a burgeoning arts and crafts industry in Cambodia. Deeply concerned about the impact of imported goods from Europe, and the resultant cultural modernization, George Groslier had been working towards a national arts program since the early 1910s. Arguing that Cambodia's traditional arts were in 'crisis' Groslier embarked upon a mission of 'rescuing' the country's culture. In her detailed examination of his diaries and daily records Muan (2001) traces his description of an artistic essence, one that was fixed in tradition and the 'climate, flora and fauna' of where the Cambodian people lived (cited in 2001: 20).[22] She proceeds to argue that, for Groslier, the crisis did not involve the end of aesthetic production, but rather a shift towards westernized art forms that 'did not match the ethno-national portrait of "Cambodian art"' that he envisaged.

By the end of the decade a Department of Fine Arts had been established in Phnom Penh under the supervision of EFEO. Once Groslier took over as director, the department focused its attention on creating a cultural industry which linked arts training with the city's Musée Khmer, the country's ancient temple heritage and a steadily growing tourism industry. The School of Cambodian Arts he helped conceive and set up as part of this initiative would train teams of craftsmen to work in the ancient traditions, reproducing the intricate carvings and sculptures found in the temples. For Groslier, the artifacts produced not only ensured a continuity of skills between the ancient past and a fast changing present, but also helped reduce the growing problem of tourists stealing from the temples. More pertinently, and as Muan argues, the school would play an instrumental role in defining the parameters of Cambodian arts throughout the first half of the twentieth century.

In stark contrast to the rise of modernism and its various movements in Europe, art in Cambodia was re-visiting its classical past. The Angkorean civilization had given this young nation a magnificent cultural heritage, a moment of unsurpassable artistic achievement. In Groslier's eyes mimicry and replication were thus natural and honorable aspirations for Cambodians to hold. By situating such efforts within their broader context we can see that the school contributed significantly to a colonial ideology which transposed a concern for the high art of classical antiquity onto the colonial subject. Tourism would reaffirm this aesthetic regime by giving it an economic validity. Temple paintings or replicas of bas reliefs and Angkorean statuary made ideal souvenirs: not only were they authentically Cambodian, but 'tasteful' enough to be proudly displayed in a European home.

In examining these three areas together – colonial expositions, tourism, and a modern arts and crafts industry – this section has traced Angkor's emergence as a site of symbolic and physical consumption during the early decades of the twentieth century. Highlighting the circulation of Angkor at a symbolic level has revealed a variety of framings and discourses. Invoked as a metaphor of an exotic, mysterious Indochine, the grand temples – lying silent and in varying degrees of dilapidation – also emerged as a focal point of intense admiration and awe. If we situate these expositions, the manicuring of a touristscape, and the revitalization of a classical arts tradition alongside EFEO's efforts to restore the temples and narrate a Cambodian history discussed above, a bigger picture of cultural politics surrounding Angkor comes into focus. Accordingly, outlining these various processes illuminates the multifaceted role the site played in the nation building of both Cambodia and France as Métropole. Finally, within this brief overview of the colonial period we have also seen the key historical processes which elevated the temples into the definitive, and omnipresent, point of reference for a modern cultural tourism and heritage industry in Cambodia.

Ominous modernities

> May Heaven protect our King
> And give him happiness and glory;
> May he reign over our hearts and our destinies.
> He who – heir to the builder Monarchs –
> Governs the proud and old Kingdom
> The temples sleep in the forest
> Recalling the grandeur of Moha Nokor.
> The Khmer race is as eternal as the rocks.
> Let us have confidence in the faith of Kampuchea
> The empire which defies the years.[23]

A nation's independence after an era of colonization is invariably accompanied by a sense of hope, optimism and a confidence in the future. Cambodia in 1954 was no exception. Spurred on by the fall of European imperialism elsewhere, many of the country's politicians and key intellectuals sought both independent modernization and a restoration of the honor and pride derived from cultural and political sovereignty. The above opening verses of the country's new national anthem reveal how the arrival of independence after nine decades of French protection would be legitimized through a sense of continuity between the modern era and a resplendent past of architectural glories and territorial power. As the self-proclaimed 'heir to the builder Monarchs', the young king at that time, Norodom Sihanouk, saw independence as Cambodia's opportunity to 'recall the grandeur' of the 'old kingdom' of Angkor. To realize these goals he decided to give up the throne and become the prince to his father, a move that allowed him to enter the world of politics. After his election as Prime Minister in 1955 Sihanouk's *Sangkum Reastr Niyum* attempted to balance neutrality and national integrity with economic prosperity and self-sufficiency for the next 15 years.

For Sihanouk, Cambodian nationalism was an anti-Vietnamese policy. In a cold war environment of increasing regional and internal hostilities, he cultivated a political rhetoric of a nation threatened with a loss of sovereignty. Interestingly, he maintained popular support for a position of weakness by conflating his own vulnerability with the idea of an endangered Cambodia; as the following excerpt from a speech he made in 1963 illustrates:

> My compatriots venerate me with the respect of a god and hold me as a "sacred character" … the truth is that more than five million Khmers identify totally with Sihanouk. To injure, to wound, to humiliate me, is to the strike the Cambodian nation.[24]

Sihanouk secured the necessary credibility for such a stance by aligning himself with an Angkorean past, and in particular the figure of Jayavarman VII – a comparison from which he could command absolutist power through a style of leadership Peou (2000) describes as a paternal authoritarianism. As both Roberts (2001) and Edwards (2007) point out, invoking an Angkorean heritage also bolstered his calls for a post-independence racial and national unity. Accordingly, an Independence Monument was erected in Phnom Penh in 1963, taking its design from the central sanctuaries familiar to ancient Khmer temples (*Prasat*). Five years later Sihanouk commissioned a somewhat more ephemeral paper mâché replica of the Bayon temple for a parade at the city's sports stadium marking the fifteenth anniversary of Independence.[25] In accounting for this 'political theatre', Turnbull (2006) draws our attention to the role played by classical dance, and in particular young costumed apsaras, within a syntax constructed by the palace and the state to promote Angkor as a unifying and populist symbol for the youthful nation.

The symbolic appropriation of Angkor in the years after independence would extend far beyond merely architectural reproductions. Angkor Wat in particular would become a definitive icon of modernity and national progress. *The National Tractor Company, Angkor What Tyres, Royal Khmer Railways* and *L'Aero Club Khmer* were among a number of organizations adopting its towers for their logos. After all, customers purchasing the Angkor brand of trucks, tractors or motorcycles were assured of 'guaranteed quality, perfect servicing and cheap running costs'.[26]

Interestingly, while commerce and industry readily cashed in on Angkor's kudos, the arrival of a 'modern' visual arts movement after Independence resulted in the disappearance of temples from the canvas. Muan (2001) argues a new wave of landscape painting primarily formed around a nostalgia for the tranquility of the pre-modern. Ruins and urban scenes were now out of vogue for Phnom Penh-based artists traveling to the countryside in search of 'traditional' rural landscapes. In a similar vein, students experimenting with ceramics, stone carving, textiles and filmmaking also shrugged off the Angkorean themes widely used in previous decades in an effort to capture this new era in the country's history.

Unlike landscape painters though, these young artists embraced modernity more directly by readily adopting new influences and new technologies (Reyum Publishing 2001).

Although the Royal University of Fine Arts, which opened in Phnom Penh in 1965, would be at the forefront of such energies, the institute also trained young Cambodians in the fields of archaeology and temple conservation. As the 1960s progressed EFEO endeavored to create a body of domestic expertise capable of researching and managing the country's architectural heritage. With their residency in the country jeopardized by the sustained threat of conflict, French scholars continued to train, conserve and research as much as they could.[27] Indeed, under the guidance of Bernard-Philippe Groslier, the son of George Groslier, archaeology was modernized and geographically extended to include sites like Beng Melea and the Great Preah Khan in the east, as well as the settlement of Sambor Prei Kuk to the south. The Angkor park itself continued to be the country's principle tourist attraction for both domestic and international visitors, most of which came from either North America or Western Europe. To raise the profile of Cambodia in the US – as both a tourist destination and a country threatened by an encroaching communism – Sihanouk invited Jacqueline Kennedy to Angkor in 1967. Photographs of the former first lady sipping champagne with the charismatic prince at the *Grand Hotel d'Angkor* became the iconic images of opulence and privilege, an era of ever-widening disparities between a secular, educated and progressive urban elite, and the poorer, more conservative, religious communities of the countryside. The showcase development of Phnom Penh under the guidance of modernist architects like Vann Molyvann for example, belied a countrywide dependency on foreign aid. Frustrated with this scenario, and Sihanouk's ineffectual mode of politics, General Lon Nol succeeded in deposing the Prince as head of state in 1970.

Lon Nol condemned Sihanouk's style of leadership by comparing it with the monarchical decadence of a declining Angkor (Edwards 1999: 387). As Cambodia's liberator from an indulgent nostalgia for a grandiose past, Lon Nol offered the population of the renamed Khmer Republic a more populist, inclusive national history.[28] Once again though, descriptions of a glorious Khmer culture, Khmer ancestry, Khmer blood, and Khmer land were all incorporated into the propaganda of a government Peou (2000) has described as an authoritarian republic. Five years later Pol Pot would take the country in yet another political direction. This time an idealization of Angkor's social and economic foundations defined the parameters of an agrarian utopia. For Pol Pot urbanization and industrialization were the source of many of Cambodia's ills and failures. The only way to reverse rising corruption and wealth inequalities, and pull the country out of a political quagmire was to revert to an agrarian-based economy. The party's vision of wealth creation through the annual export of a rice surplus was founded upon a belief that self-sufficiency could be achieved through the planting of supplementary rubber, cotton, and coconut crops (Vickery 1999). Inspired by the hydraulic theories offered by French scholars over the course of the twentieth century, Pol Pot brutally implemented a form of collectivist agriculture that utilized, and thus attempted to reproduce, Angkor's irrigation technology. As we now know, it was an experiment that would hold horrific consequences for the population.

> The Angkorean dream entertained by the Pol Potists, for which tens of thousands of Cambodians died as they slaved building canals, was in large part historical fantasy.
>
> (Barnett 1990: 121)

Based on misguided beliefs that multiple, season-defying harvests could be achieved through complex irrigation systems, grossly unrealistic aims would lead to progressively worse annual famines. In his examination of CPK speeches, Chandler also indicates how Angkor was cited as an example of the power of mobilized labor and 'national grandeur which could be re-enacted in the 1970s' (1996a: 246). Indeed, it was a grandeur proudly displayed on early DK banknotes – prior to the abolition of money – and to Chinese delegates during a visit in 1977.[29] Although the dearth of references to Angkor within CPK documentation leads Chandler to conclude that an understanding of what the period meant to the party remains sketchy at best, he suggests its status as national and cultural icon meant 'Angkor was simply too *Cambodian* to be discarded'[30] (ibid).

In this respect, we can see that in spite of Pol Pot's desire to create a revolutionary polity, and one that delivered a profound historical rupture, his regime represented a continuity in post-independence political thinking. In briefly examining the very different forms of government instigated by Norodom Sihanouk, Lon Nol, and Pol Pot – which between them spanned three turbulent decades – it has been suggested that Angkor endured as a symbolic resource of cultural, ethnic, and national power. The towers of Angkor Wat, for example, were a constant feature on the flags of every major political party in Cambodia throughout this period. Angkor, as concept and ideal, represented a common thread running through a political landscape that evolved through a combination of realpolitik and competing ideological extremes. Its appropriation enabled leaders to claim guardianship over an invaluable national heritage. In so doing, they would continue a discourse introduced by the French earlier in the century which foregrounded the temples within a vision of national and cultural revival; a paradigm that, as Chandler (1998) has pointed out, at once became both an inspiration and burden for modern politicians. Perhaps most importantly though, association with Angkor authorized absolutist forms of power. As we shall see in the coming chapters, it is a political model which endures to this day and is pivotal to Angkor's current transformation into an engine of capital.

Away from politics, economic liberalization in the early 1990s enabled Angkor to reclaim its symbolic value within Cambodia's popular and commercial culture. Adorning endless commodities from cigarettes to car tires, cement to perfume, Angkor now serves as a marker of quality and Cambodian entrepreneurial pride. Thematic brands – Apsara, Naga, Bayon or Banteay Srei – have become common among digital photography labs, accountants, medical clinics, and seemingly endless hotels all attempting to attract new clients. Across Phnom Penh polystyrene

Figure 2.1 Angkorean montage. (Photos and compilation by Tim Winter.)

reproductions of the temples, reminiscent of the colonial exhibitions held nearly a century earlier, provide illustrious gateways to wedding banquets. And discarding its associations with former revolutionary or communist ideologues, Angkor continues to appear on banknotes, flags, postage stamps, commercial and residential architecture, and even in karaoke videos, as an unambiguous source of civic and social pride (see Figure 2.1).

3 World heritage Angkor

The major social and political transitions occurring in the early 1990s finally provided Cambodians with the realizable goals of peace and economic stability. Such transitions would also mean the Angkor, Siem Reap region could re-enter the global stage, both as a World Heritage Site and as an exciting destination for the international tourism industry. This chapter begins to consider this new era by examining how the region was conceived, valued and managed as a heritage landscape. It opens with an examination of the policies adopted to politically and legally protect the site from its immediate environment, and the implications such a process of isolation would bring. This is followed by a critical analysis of a cultural heritage framework overwhelmingly dominated by temple conservation. Subsumed within a scientist language of world heritage, Angkor was once again conceived as a series of static, even dead, set of 'ancient' monuments. In the section entitled 'Representations of space: neglecting the living' it is argued that within this framework little attention is given to understanding the landscape in anthropological or socio-historical terms, a situation which de-humanizes both history and landscape, and neglects various areas requiring urgent attention such as urban planning and the socio-economic development of the local population. Finally, under the heading 'Cultures of neo-colonialism?' the chapter reflects upon the degree to which a world heritage framework acts as a form of neo-colonialism through its re-imposition of Eurocentric understandings of place, culture, and history.

Safeguarding Angkor: political and legal landscaping in post-conflict Cambodia

In 1989 Prince Sihanouk, at that time President of the UN-recognized Coalition Government of Democratic Kampuchea (CGDK), approached UNESCO in Paris to formally request the designation of Angkor as a World Heritage Site. Restrictions on UN non-humanitarian aid based upon Cambodia's occupation by a Soviet-backed administration in Hanoi had meant field-based activities and assessments of Angkor's condition remained limited until after the 1991 Paris Peace Accords. During that intervening period however, conferences would be held in Paris and Bangkok, paving the way for the site's eventual inscription on the World Heritage List in December 1992. In declaring Angkor as 'a unique artistic achievement, a masterpiece of creative genius ... [which] ... has exerted great influence over a span of time ... [and] ... bears a unique exceptional testimony to a civilization which has disappeared' (UNESCO 1993: 22), the World Heritage Committee took the exceptional step of waiving a number of the usual inscription conditions. The situation in Cambodia also provided the impetus for UNESCO's decision to place Angkor on the List of World Heritage in Danger. The myriad challenges facing UNESCO at that time are examined in this opening section under two basic themes: protecting Angkor from its immediate social and physical environment; and putting in place an institutional infrastructure for its long-term development.

In the face of weak legislative, executive, and judicial branches of a transitional government, it was critical that UNESCO urgently established strong legal and spatial boundaries of protection. To this end, a team of 25 international experts – including cartographers, historians, ecologists, and hydrologists – visited Cambodia in 1993 to draw up a Zoning and Environmental Management Plan, or ZEMP as it became known. Legally reinforced by Royal Decree in May 1994, the ZEMP program spatially demarcated protection and development zones for the Angkor Archaeological Park and nearby town of Siem Reap. The contrasting rural, urban topography of the region required five distinct zones to 'reconcile three major demands – archaeological conservation, urban growth and tourism development – and the productive use of rural resources' (Wager 1995b: 425) (see Figure 3.1).

To cope with the various demands of this variegated landscape, strict legislation was laid out for each zone. More than merely a guide for future policy or strategies, these zones specifically stipulated what forms of construction, land use practices, and land purchases could take place over the coming years:

Monumental Sites: Areas which contain the most significant archaeological sites in the country and therefore deserve the highest level of protection.

Protected Archaeological Reserves: Areas rich in archaeological remains which need to be protected from damaging land use practices and inappropriate development. They will most frequently surround monumental sites, providing protection to adjacent areas of known or likely archaeological importance.

Protected Cultural Landscapes: Areas with distinctive landscape characteristics which should be protected on account of their traditional features, land use practices, varied habitats, historic building, or man-made features from the past or of recent origin that contribute to the cultural value or reflect traditional lifestyles and patterns of land use.

Sites of Archaeological, Anthropological or Historic Interest: include all other important archaeological sites, but of less significance than monumental sites,

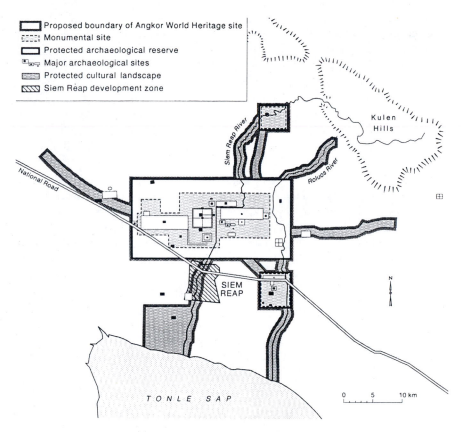

□ Proposed boundary of Angkor World Heritage site
⊡ Monumental site
▢ Protected archaeological reserve
▩ Major archaeological sites
▨ Protected cultural landscape
▧ Siem Reap development zone

Figure 3.1 Map of ZEMP scheme. (Reprinted from Wager, J., 'Developing a strategy for the Angkor World Heritage Site', *Tourism Management*, Vol. 16, No. 7, p. 517. Copyright (1995), with permission from Elsevier.)

that require protection for research, education or tourist interest. These sites are generally small and free standing.

The Socio-economic and Cultural Development Zone of the Siem Reap Region: comprising the whole of the Siem Reap province … this comprehensive zone covers an area of 10,0000 square kilometers including the Phnom Kulen, the shores of the Tonle Sap and the Angkor plain. The region is to be managed as a multiple use area with an emphasis on economic and social development through sustainable use of natural resources and by the development of cultural tourism.

(UNESCO 1996: 194–7)

The abolition of any recognizable cadastral infrastructure since the beginning of the Khmer Rouge era meant land grabbing was a major problem throughout Cambodia

(Ministry of Planning 1996). In an environment of intense corruption, the problem had been compounded in the Angkor, Siem Reap region by a demobilization process involving high-value land being given over to senior military personnel. The ZEMP program therefore provided an essential defense mechanism against the constant threat of land grabbing and unregulated construction. Strict regulation would, however, mean the scheme negated existing provincial and communal frameworks for land administration, some of which had been in existence in some form or another for centuries (UNESCO 1996: 122). The scheme also represented the introduction of an 'alien' legislative infrastructure, which, in its rigidity, would transform the Angkor region into a legal, political, and bureaucratic island, as we shall see.

Given that world heritage listing was driven by a need to safeguard a geographically distributed set of 'ancient' monuments, the above descriptions of each zone appear entirely self-explanatory. It was essential that the archaeological remains and architectural structures of the Angkorean period were protected from the very real dangers of looting and structural damage, and that the overall aesthetic of the landscape was not compromised by modern construction. Somewhat problematically, such necessity would also effectively freeze Angkor as an ancient architectural space, and invoke a strong culture/nature binary whereby numerous villages, rivers, forests, and agricultural areas would all be subsumed within a monolithic paradigm of monumental heritage protection. In this respect, ZEMP reflected 'the territorial imperatives of a particular political system' (Harley 1988: 279), a system, which, over the coming years would largely ignore those features of the landscape not associated with its ancient regal history. Recalling the arguments offered in Chapter 2 reminds us that, far more than just a blueprint for protecting ancient temples, ZEMP mapped out a distinct socio-spatial ideology which would powerfully mould Angkor's future. Indeed, as Bauman notes:

> Before it was the map that reflected and recorded the shapes of the territory. Now, it was the turn of the territory to become a reflection of the map, to be raised to the level of orderly transparency which the maps struggled to reach. It was the space itself which was to be reshaped … in the likeness of the map and according to the decisions of cartographers.
>
> (1998: 35)

Previous events had left Cambodia with desperately inadequate governmental, administrative, and legal structures. Perhaps even more worryingly, the country was also suffering a complete dearth of expertise in crucial areas such as law, monumental conservation, archaeology, community development, tourism, urban planning, or forestry. In recognition of the intense challenges facing Angkor UNESCO created an administrative body, the ICC, which would focus specifically on the newly enlisted World Heritage Site and its environs, including the nearby town of Siem Reap. UNESCO also attempted to establish a national cultural heritage framework by instigating the formation of the Supreme Council on National Culture (SCNC).

The ICC's inaugural meeting held in Tokyo in December 1993 was attended by experts from over 20 countries. With little potential within the SCNC to manage Angkor, the ICC identified conservation and development as their broad agendas for the Angkor, Siem Reap region (UNESCO 1993). Within this overarching remit, it was agreed that the greatest priority should be given to establishing a comprehensive program of cultural resource management. Discussions would therefore focus on issues like capacity building, the renovation of the former Angkor Conservation Office (ACO), the creation of a new documentation center, and how to best protect the countless movable artifacts littered across the Angkor park. Most notably, the Tokyo meeting also provided the forum for identifying which temples required conservation and repair.

Accordingly, during subsequent years the ICC established itself as an elaborate web of international aid, encompassing governmental agencies, privately funded conservation groups, universities, and a number of non-governmental foundations (see Table 3.1). Supported by UNESCO as the ICC's standing secretariat, these organizations would embark upon the prodigious task of stabilizing, researching, and meticulously restoring Angkor's vast corpus of material heritage.

To ensure the site remained insulated from a suspect and unpredictable domestic government, vital political leverage was created by co-chairing the ICC with Cambodia's two largest bi-lateral donors at that time: France and Japan. As we shall see later in this chapter, this situation involved far more than mere architectural conservation. Cambodia's plight as a recipient of aid would lead to Angkor becoming the focal point of an elaborate matrix of geo-political maneuvering. As the 1990s progressed a complex interdependence of national interests would form, with programs ranging from photographic documentation to urban master plans being offered from America, China, France, Germany, Hungary, India, Indonesia, Italy, Japan, Malaysia, Singapore, and the UK.[1]

To complement the ICC and ZEMP programs, the World Heritage Committee called for the establishment of a Cambodian-run management body. To this end the Authority for the Protection and Safeguarding of the Angkor Region, or APSARA,[2] was created by Royal decree in 1994. In the short term APSARA would act as an organizational bridge between the attendant international community and the domestic government. Although the ICC was generally expected to remain in attendance for in excess of a decade, it was hoped that APSARA, as a self-funded, independent and autonomous Cambodian management authority, would fill the void left by the eventual withdraw of international assistance. The organization therefore provided the institutional structure vital for nurturing the Cambodian expertise required for managing the site over the longer term.

In an attempt to ensure its political autonomy, or at least its neutrality, APSARA's board was composed of ministers from across the Royal Government, as well as representatives from the Cambodian Development Council, the Council of Ministers and Siem Reap's provincial Governor (UNESCO 1996: 170–1). The political divides APSARA was faced with bridging are implicitly

Table 3.1 Major international projects coordinated by ICC 1993–1998

Organization	Project sites	Principal focus
JSA (Japanese Government Team for Safeguarding Angkor)	Angkor Wat North Library, Bayon North Library, Prasat Sour Prat	Conservation/Restoration
EFEO (Ecole Française d'Extrême Orient)	Royal Terraces, Baphuon, Angkor Thom	Conservation/Restoration, Archaeology
Sophia University	Banteay Kdei, Angkor Wat Causeway, Tani Site, Srah Srang	Conservation/Restoration, Archaeology, Socio-economic Research
WMF (World Monuments Fund)	Preah Khan	Conservation/Restoration
RAF (Royal Angkor Foundation)	Preah Ko	Conservation/Restoration
GACP (German Angkor Conservation Project)	Angkor Wat	Conservation, Documentation
I Ge S (Ingegneria Geotechnica e Strutturale)	Pre Rup	Conservation/Restoration
CSA (Chinese Team for Safeguarding Angkor)	Chau Sey Tevoda	Conservation/Restoration
ITASA (Indonesian Government Team for Safeguarding Angkor)	Gates of Royal Palace	Conservation/Restoration
UNESCO & ICCROM	–	Human Resource Development

Source: Tim Winter

revealed in UNESCO's account of how the organization was to be politically positioned:

> APSARA does not operate independently from existent governmental structures of a more traditional type, but rather coordinates and focuses national efforts to ensure efficient management and to encourage administrative evolution conducive to the consolidation of fruitful partnerships with the international community.
>
> (UNESCO 1996: 168)

Political independence would, however, come at a price. Suffering from 'an exceeding lack of financial and human resources' (ICC 1998: 21), APSARA's transition from paper to operational reality would be a long and convoluted path. Five years would pass before the authority was sufficiently financed to be fully operational.[3] In spite of its limited resources, the organization was faced with the major challenge of steering the development of a mixed rural, urban area stretching across almost 10,000 square kilometers (UNESCO 1996: 166). The prospect of large-scale tourism was creating a frenzy of interest and activity in the region. In such an environment much of APSARA's efforts went into legislating over construction projects which either infringed upon the Angkor park or contravened the urban planning guidelines for the Siem Reap development zone. Not surprisingly, resistance brought resentment, and relations with the Governor's office and local Ministry of Tourism officials were frequently abrasive. Corruption, grossly inadequate land laws and a politically influential military also compounded APSARA's problems. Nonetheless, as the 1990s progressed the authority managed to successfully block, halt or destroy the vast majority of illegal projects initiated across the region.

APSARA's early years were also characterized by uneasy relations with various government ministries in Phnom Penh. Beyond Angkor, the Ministries of Culture and Fine Arts, Public Works and Transport and Tourism all claimed national jurisdiction over their respective areas. The virtual exclusion of these ministries from Angkor's redevelopment program by the all-encompassing authority of an ICC-backed APSARA – as indicated in the UNESCO statement below – led to widespread resentment among government officials, many of whom felt culturally and politically impotent towards their country's greatest historical asset:

> The new body, known as APSARA, is invested with direct responsibility for research, conservation cultural heritage protection efforts, urban and rural development as well as tourism management throughout the province. These domains, traditionally under the overlapping mandates of several different ministries, are in fact intimately related to one another, and the unique situation of Siem Reap calls with particular force for an integrated approach to their management.
>
> (UNESCO 1996: 118)

Clearly APSARA's remit stemmed from the need to protect Angkor from a post-UNTAC Cambodian political landscape characterized by ever-shifting factions, inter-ministerial conflicts and inherent instability. In this respect we can see that the spatial isolation of Angkor via ZEMP was mirrored in the political isolation of APSARA. The resentment caused by this situation would result in the political realignment of the organization before the end of the decade. As we shall see in the following chapter, Hun Sen's election as sole Prime Minister in 1998 would lead to a radical overhaul of APSARA's structure; a move intended to seize greater control over Angkor's future.

Remaking the nation: logical positivism and cultural heritage

Up until this point it has been argued that the need to protect Angkor isolated the site from its domestic political and legal contexts; a process which resulted in forms of alienation and resentment. Continuing this vein, the following analysis of 'cultural heritage' as a discourse and managerial policy also points to a process of isolation, this time in the form of Angkor's disembedding from its broader historical context.

An examination of the ZEMP scheme has suggested a priority towards safeguarding Angkor's architecture led to a neglect of the region's other topographical features. Crucially, the scheme would be integral to, and a major determinant of, a particular spatial epistemology which was now forming through the listing of Angkor as a World Heritage Site. As the ICC laid out its remit in Tokyo in 1993, it was apparent efforts and resources were to be targeted at the emergency consolidation and safeguarding of the temples. As we have seen, such a strategy appeared entirely natural. The addition of Angkor to the World Heritage list had not stemmed from its ecosystem or vernacular architecture; rather, its unique value to 'mankind' was its spectacular monumental architecture. Damage, neglect, looting, and general deterioration caused by civil war and a decade of Vietnamese occupation had to be urgently addressed and reversed wherever possible.

As the 'cultural arm' of UNTAC, UNESCO was charged with restoring and protecting Cambodia's cultural resources. Reconstructing Angkor's temples was seen as the most potent symbol and demonstration of a country in recovery. The ties between monumental restoration and socio-political reconstruction, first forged during the French colonial period, were now about to reappear. However, the extreme destruction of recent decades, coupled with Angkor's pivotal role as a unifying marker of modern cultural, national, and ethnic identity, would greatly intensify the expectation of cultural heritage as an engine of societal restitution.

For these reasons – and not to mention the global prestige of Angkorean architecture – international efforts overwhelmingly focused on the conservation and preservation of the temples themselves. One of the key documents produced from the Tokyo conference was UNESCO's *Safeguarding and Development of Angkor.*[4] Stretching over 90 pages, the publication outlined the key procedures, institutional frameworks, and challenges facing the Angkor, Siem Reap region. Of the 50 pages dedicated to Future Challenges, 44 were given over to Monumental Conservation

Concerns; two to Archaeological Concerns; two to Regional Development; and a mere one page each to Tourism Development and National Capacity Building. The implications of this imbalance for the development of Siem Reap and tourism will be discussed shortly. The point of interest here, however, is how this publication reflects the particular discourse of cultural heritage which emerged through an overriding need for the preservation of an 'ancient' material culture.

The document unequivocally pointed towards the urgent need for architectural and engineering expertise. As Table 3.1 illustrates, subsequent years would see a network of organizations arriving from around the world, each of which established projects designed to protect and consolidate Angkor's key temple structures. Over the years the ICC consistently expanded with more teams taking on projects. By the beginning of the twenty-first century more than 20 countries had become involved in providing assistance for the Angkor, Siem Reap region. With the vast majority of efforts focusing on temple conservation a highly unusual situation emerged with each country 'adopting' a separate temple. The key exception to this was the assistance program put in place for the immense Angkor Wat structure, which included teams from Germany, America, and Japan. This nationalization of restoration was further reinforced by the presence of country resident ambassadors during annual ICC conferences.

Working under a UNESCO world heritage umbrella, teams were guided by various internationally ratified charters, including the 1954 Hague Convention, 1964 Venice Charter, 1972 World Heritage Charter, and the 1990 ICOMOS Charter for the Protection and Management of Archaeological Heritage. Guidance would also come from the former experiences of EFEO. The immense institutional knowledge EFEO had built up during 70 years of research presented the ICC with a uniquely valuable archival source made up of reports, scholarly publications, fieldwork diaries and thousands of photographs, maps, and drawings. Although it was recognized mistakes had been made, and strategies had evolved over decades of research, EFEO's expertise was crucial to steering the various teams now involved, many of which had little, or no, prior experience of Khmer architecture. EFEO's vast body of knowledge in epigraphy, architectural conservation, art history, and to a lesser degree archaeology, housed in both France and Siem Reap, represented an unquestionably invaluable resource for modern scholars. On the flip side, the pre-eminence of EFEO would also lead to a construction of Angkorean history conceived during a former colonial era being re-invoked and re-authenticated by a late twentieth-century framework of world heritage. More specifically, it would mean an Angkorean historiography which neglected vernacular, social histories in favor of the material heritage of a 'high', regal culture was now re-solidifying, an issue discussed further shortly.

The preservation and management of cultural heritage landscapes around the world has fostered decades of debate and a spectrum of approaches, some more controversial than others. In a field where different sites pose different challenges and require different solutions, consensus has shifted and invariably remained partial at best. It has long been recognized that conceptual definitions of ideas like 'authenticity' vary greatly between Asia, Europe, and North America (Ito 1995,

Jokilehto 1995). Given that teams from these three regions were simultaneously descending on Angkor, the question of consensus needed addressing. Three key factors guided a resolution to this issue, two of which – EFEO and various international charters – have been highlighted above. The third factor concerns the intellectual foundations of the cultural heritage discourse in circulation. The international nature of the ICC demanded a language that could be shared across the table, universally applied, and unequivocally valued by all. Rational science would provide the solution; a unifying medium through which a Khmer temple previously restored by French conservators could be rebuilt once again by a Japanese team supported by experts from Italy, Germany, and the UK. The foundations for this approach can be traced back to the 1972 Protection of the World Cultural and Natural Heritage Convention which, as Hitchcock (2005) points out, was conceived at a time when policies were geared towards the scientific management of tangible heritage.

Over the coming years, annual conferences and symposiums held in Siem Reap would be dedicated to the engineering technicalities of structural foundations, the mineral composition of sandstone carvings, or the load-bearing capacities of arches and precariously tilting columns.[5] Similarly, annual reports and publications rarely departed from discussing cultural heritage as a language of technology and scientific enquiry.[6] Whilst wholly accepting that the dilapidated state of Angkor's ruins undoubtedly demanded such efforts, my critique of this situation sets out to explore the implications of such a rational science-based understanding of the Angkorean landscape.

In the first instance, it is suggested that the heritage discourse surrounding Angkor reflects an approach Smith (2004) has termed 'logical positivism'. As we saw in the Introduction, Smith's critique of such cultural heritage frameworks stems from their application of 'technical procedures and science to conflicts over material culture [which] de-politicize issues through the employment of its expertise' (ibid: 37). In essence, the ICC's orientation towards architectural restoration and CRM 'stresse[d] objectivity and technical rigor' (ibid: 10) to define its authoritative position as the arbitrator of Angkorean history. More specifically, science would provide the ontological foundations for a universally shared definition of 'authenticity'.

Throughout the 1990s the ICC had no projects guided by anthropologists, historians or sociologists to counter the positivistic, and universalizing, language of rational science. In terms of archaeological research, a French project entitled *From Yasodharapura to Angkor Thom* made significant advances in understanding Jayavarman VII's city complex as an 'urban space', and both APSARA and Sophia University successfully unearthed ceramics from excavations undertaken around kiln sites located in the Angkor region.[7] Nonetheless, these sat within an environment characterized by a quest for objectivity and ontological 'truths' which gave little credence to ideas such as historical relativism, plurality or multivocality. The lavish attention paid to the evolution of construction styles and the re-appropriation of buildings by later kings significantly contrasted with a distinct lack of commitment towards tracing histories of ancestral spirit cults, oral traditions or contemporary temple ritual practices.[8] Rendered mute and passive, Angkor's temples were once again framed as the fragile remnants of an ancient past, and the legacy of a glorious, but now dead, civilization.

A cultural heritage framework which principally focused on the materiality of architecture would, by implication, de-humanize Angkorean history, and as such construct a narrative of the past bereft of historical continuity. The dissection of the Angkorean landscape according to a pro-forma allocation, come selection, of temples by team and/or country also inhibited the emergence of an integrated historiography capable of situating Angkor in its broader regional context. Without the narratives of historians, social anthropologists or even more phenomenologically inclined archaeologists, Angkor emerged as an atomized island of research, demarcated as a rural museum of art and architectural glories.[9]

Beyond the Angkor park the Cambodian countryside boasts a seemingly endless abundance of premodern sandstone and brick structures. For obvious logistical reasons, including landmines and infrastructure inadequacies, research and restoration at these sites has remained extremely limited. However, the neglect of these so called 'outlying sites' also stems from a chronological hierarchy, whereby artifacts lying outside Angkor's boundaries are implicitly devalued through their classification as either 'pre-' or 'post-' Angkorean. The combination of this commonly held idea and the problems of gaining access has, in effect, led to the re-affirmation of the tri-focal narrative of Cambodian history constructed by scholars of a colonial era, as we saw in the previous chapter. From around 2000 onwards fieldwork projects by the World Monuments Fund (WMF), EFEO and APSARA conducted at sites like Koh Ker and Beng Melea did begin to address this imbalance. In essence however, the urgent demands for protecting Angkor, the discursive orientation of international expertise, the administrative isolation of the ICC and APSARA, and the considerable logistical challenges of working across the Cambodian countryside have all contributed to a major imbalance of knowledge about Khmer history; a situation which has once again reinstated a 'classical period' of idealized antiquities.

One of the trends unifying nation-states across the world today is the continual search for markers of identity. Distinguished only by their diversity, costumes, cuisines, buildings, bridges, iconic landscapes, art movements, and memorialized individuals have all been rendered conspicuous and incorporated into a logic of heritage and collective patrimony. Invariably, such diversity simultaneously coexists to create a pluralistic and dynamic narrative. In the case of Cambodia, the omnipotence of Angkor in the socio-cultural landscape of history is paralleled by a paucity of other utilizable 'assets'. Justifiable or not, there is a widely held perception that the country has few personalities, engineering triumphs or distinctive cultural industries to complement its achievements in stone. An episode of profound turmoil has given rise to a deep-seated anxiety over what constitutes Khmer and Cambodian identity, and an idealized Angkor undergoing reconstruction has once again become the basis of a state nationalism rooted in a static, if not timeless, vision of a glorious past. As we shall see in the coming chapters momentum for this national imagining has also come from the cultural, economic logics of a rapidly expanding international tourism industry. When considered alongside Cambodia's recent history, the ongoing construction of a monolithic, mono-cultural, unchanging and inflexible identity becomes a cause for considerable concern.

Representations of space: neglecting the living

A common reaction among foreign visitors arriving at Angkor today is a surprise at the number of villages dotted around the site. Indeed, despite being continually inhabited throughout its history Angkor has become framed by the international tourist industry as a desolate, abandoned landscape – a theme explored in greater detail in Chapter 5. By the beginning of the 1990s, it was estimated – notwith-standing the problem of notoriously unreliable statistics in Cambodia at that time – that around 50,000 people were living inside the perimeters of the Angkor Archaeological Park.[10] In light of the arguments offered above it comes as little surprise that these communities did not feature heavily in the inaugural ICC meeting and subsequent conference documentation. In a context of multiple urgent agendas, ideas of community welfare would form part of a broad, but vague, program of social development for the region as a whole.

One area that was given particular attention was the need for 'capacity building'. Throughout the 1990s, EFEO, WMF, JSA and Sophia University successfully recruited a number of residents from the Angkor park to work on their ever-expanding fieldwork projects. Large restoration programs such as the Baphuon or Angkor Wat Causeway, employing in excess of 30 staff at times, provided an increasingly reliable and constant income for local families. Close collaboration with APSARA would also contribute to the development of the domestic resource base required for Angkor's long-term management. Citing such admirable initiatives does, however, point towards the ways in which Angkor's village communities had become encapsulated within a world heritage structure overwhelmingly oriented towards monumental conservation.

In an attempt to preserve the rural character of the Angkor park, legal protection was given to the 'traditional appearance, land use practices, varied habitats, historic building, or man-made features from the past or of recent origin, that contribute to the cultural value or reflect traditional life styles and patterns of land use' (UNESCO 1996: 213). Justification for this strategy came in the form of real estate speculators, consistently submitting proposals for the construction of multi-story concrete hotels or karaoke entertainment centers. The fact that such projects merely remained on paper bears testimony to the success of the regulatory framework put in place by the ICC and APSARA for molding the region's development. Nonetheless, the desire to freeze the site by resisting development would mean discussions of the site as a lived, contemporary space remained firmly at the margins of policy.

Within the heritage matrix of the ICC and ZEMP schemes it was broadly accepted that the communities living in the park, many of which have called Angkor their home for many centuries, required regulation and monitoring for possible infringements of legislation. Preserving the 'traditional character' of the landscape would be achieved by restricting the height of buildings as well as the use of modern construction materials such as metal and concrete. The presence of a rural population also raised concerns about the sustainability of the region's fragile eco-system. Clearly, the variegated nature of Angkor's landscape demanded a multi-focal approach. Yet, given that World Heritage listing had led to a conceptualization of cultural heritage oriented around architectural antiquities, a representation of space emerged which neglected, and in some respects actively resisted, development and modernization for the park's impoverished rural communities.

Aware of the numerous challenges posed by an ever-increasing population, the APSARA authority would attempt to fill this void. Unfortunately, such efforts were greatly hampered by their extremely limited resources increasingly stretched by a rapidly expanding remit. The ongoing tension over the use of trees in the park offers some insight into APSARA's struggle to balance the preservation of a fragile eco-system with community development. The director of APSARA's Department of Culture and Monuments in the late 1990s, Ang Choulean, explained why the struggle to cope with an ever-expanding rural population demanded greater attention at the level of policy:

> [villagers] are forbidden to cut trees. Because of the environment. But at the same time we have nothing to propose to them - in exchange for this ... we still fail in this. We have at least two meetings with the international committee each year. And I think from next year we should, besides discussions on the monuments, we should add to the ordinary discussion how to manage Angkor as a living site. When I say we, Cambodia and the international community, I mean the more than 20, the 30 countries and organizations which compose the ICC ... we all have to try to enrich our discussion and not limit it to the safeguarding of monuments, but to the management of the site as a whole.[11]

As part of this objective Ang Choulean created a small research 'unit' to investigate how the temples were being used as active religious spaces by local communities.[12] Momentum for APSARA's anthropological research also came from a need to counter a growing political will within parts of the Cambodian government to have some of Angkor's Buddhist monasteries either demolished and re-built, or just simply removed. Falling under the jurisdiction of a languid Ministry of Cults and Religious Affairs, the monasteries' resident monks were unable to call upon strong political support from either Phnom Penh or the international community. By the beginning of 2002 significant speculation surrounded the future of various architectural structures within the confines of these monasteries. Local government officials referred to them as 'eyesores', a 'security hazard to the temples' and a 'threat to foreign tourists' (Cambodia Today 2002). According to reports in the Cambodian media, local authorities intended to evict around 170 Buddhist monks and nuns from pagodas which were deemed 'illegally built'. Such references to the law were essentially diplomatic decoys masking a desire to preserve the image of Angkor as an 'ancient' monumental landscape for the international tourist market (Winter 2004); a logic which led certain local officials to question the 'authenticity' of the monasteries, given that a number of buildings were post-1970s re-constructions. Strenuous efforts by APSARA, as well as eventual behind-the-scenes lobbying from UNESCO, ensured the monastery complexes remained intact. Nonetheless, the prolonged threat of their removal revealed how a framework oriented towards monumental stone structures left other features of Angkor's landscape exposed to, and endangered by, a turbulent socio-political environment.

To better understand the implications of this issue it is worth briefly noting the broader social role such monasteries have played in Cambodia in the modern era. As part of his recent study of Cambodian Buddhism, Harris highlights the impact they made in advancing Buddhist education after Cambodia's independence in 1953. Indeed, by the late 1960s, a highly sophisticated and extensive multi-tiered Buddhist education system had been established (2005: 150–1). The country's monastic community or *sangha*, which by that time numbered around 61,000, also played an important role in constructing a post-independence nationalism. In broad terms, Harris's account reveals how pre-revolutionary Cambodian Buddhism operated as a socially and politically engaged religion, essential to the fabric of society. It also illustrates why the destruction inflicted upon the *sangha* during the 1970s had such a devastating impact on the country. Given that the monastic order's subsequent attempts to restore their pre-revolutionary institutional structures have been consistently hampered by internal disputes and a treacherous political environment, we can see that the rejuvenation of Buddhism has been an important, but troubled, part of a broader cultural and religious revivalism.

As possibilities for domestic travel have increased in recent years, the monasteries situated around Angkor's temples have reemerged as highly revered spiritual and educational destinations for tens of thousands of visitors each year (see Figure 3.2). Not surprisingly, these sites also form an integral part of the daily rhythms of the Siem Reap community, many of whom visit to offer financial support for the reconstruction of *Vihears* (congregation halls) and *Wats* on a regular basis. Regrettably, logistical and political hurdles meant APSARA's anthropological efforts to better understand the social role Angkor's monasteries play remained limited. It will be seen in the following chapter that such efforts received little recognition from members of the government wishing to see APSARA capitalize upon an exploding international tourism industry. Nonetheless, by providing a more holistic reading of Angkorean restoration, the research conducted by the small team suggested a need for understanding cultural heritage as community driven, socially enacted, and a composite of landscape features. In so doing, it also revealed why the restoration of Angkor as a local, national landscape demands far more than merely monumental architecture.

As the ICC gathered for its first major conference in 1993, it was widely recognized that the return of peace would also mean the return of the international tourist. There was little doubt that Angkor would emerge as a major attraction within a well-established Southeast Asian tourism industry. For this reason the ICC

Figure 3.2 Cambodian visitors to monastery in Bakong Complex. (Photo by Tim Winter.)

identified two broad goals: conservation and development, a philosophy reflected in ZEMP's identification of Siem Reap as an urban development center. With this legal framework in place, and a clearly identified manifesto, it appeared that the issue of social development would be integral to Angkor's future administration. After all, the combination of widespread poverty and an anticipated rise in tourism provided a strong impetus for putting such a strategy in place.

Cambodia's efforts to develop a tourism industry were significantly constrained by its robust image as an unsafe and politically unstable country. Annual visitor numbers remained in the tens of thousands during the mid 1990s.[13] At this time, the vast resources dedicated to safeguarding Angkor's monuments outweighed the interest shown in preparing the region for the massive social and cultural changes tourism would bring. This imbalance is somewhat surprising given that it was widely accepted that Siem Reap would witness a dramatic increase in both domestic and international tourism in just a few short years. Like the rest of Cambodia, the Angkor, Siem Reap region was suffering from major 'deficiencies in infrastructure and human resources' (Ministry of Planning 1996: 157). Yet little attention was given to such problems in an international managerial framework composed of experts in architecture, archaeology, engineering, and stone conservation. The ICC's general disregard for tourism is revealed in the attention the area receives in the committee's official documentation for the crucial five-year period after that Tokyo conference. Within more than 400 pages of annual reports, spanning 1994 to 1998, only 10 were given over to tourism – the majority of which merely summarized the lack of progress with the planned 'hotel zone'.[14]

With international efforts firmly centered on architectural conservation, responsibility for urban development and tourism would lie with APSARA. To this end the organization was founded with three principal departments: Culture and Monuments, Urban Development, and Tourism Development. APSARA's struggle towards operational stability, along with its severe lack of resources, meant that efforts were directed towards maintaining a protective relationship with the attendant international community. Not surprisingly, this situation resulted in resources being largely concentrated in the Department of Culture and Monuments. In addition to successfully operating as a coordinating hub for numerous international projects, the organization began the task of building a Cambodian pool of expertise. In addition to the small anthropological research unit highlighted earlier, young Cambodian scholars were gradually trained in the areas of temple conservation, archaeology, Geographic Information System (GIS) technology, and temple management. Crucially, the direction of the organization as a whole was forged from the top downwards with architects consistently employed for the position of executive director. Most notable among these appointments was the figure of Vann Molyvann: Cambodia's most prominent and respected architect of the twentieth century.

By implication however, the other two sides of APSARA's organizational triangle – the departments of Urban Development and Tourism – received less support and finance. Even as the 1990s came to a close each of the directors of these departments could only call upon the support of less than five trained staff.[15] As part of their comprehensive report into the Angkor, Siem Reap region, the New Zealand consultants, Boffa Miskell and Fraser Thomas, concluded that for both departments 'resources and budget provisions are inadequate for the tasks required' (Miskell & Thomas 1998: 2–36). The report's authors also argued that diminished resources meant staff were 'often not available for consultations and discussions with local agencies and international investors' (ibid). More than merely an inconvenience, such breakdowns in communication would have significant implications for the development of the region.

One of the greatest challenges facing APSARA since its inception has been the need to create a paradigm shift within domestic political structures toward long-term, sustainable development. Their struggle to achieve this with very limited resources led to frequent conflicts and misunderstandings between the organization and bodies like the Ministry of Tourism or Public Works and Transport. As the century came to a close the town of Siem Reap was undergoing a major transformation with the construction of hotels, guesthouses, restaurants, souvenir shops, and entire new market complexes. This rapidly changing landscape would mean APSARA endured constant pressure from a private, entrepreneurial sector invariably operating on individualistic, self-serving principles:

> When it acts to control unacceptable development, or to constrain development, APSARA's input can be viewed as autocratic or negative. It often earns acrimony for the earlier default on the part of others or for limiting

development which others who, lacking an understanding of the zoning guidelines, see as being important.

(Boffa Miskell Ltd and Fraser Thomas Ltd 1998: 2–39)

Finally, in addition to maintaining difficult relationships with the domestic public and private spheres, APSARA also needed to interact with an international aid community providing assistance in Cambodia in areas such as education, health, community welfare, and infrastructure development. During the 1990s the ILO, FAO, UNDP, UNV and MSF, amongst others had all established offices in Siem Reap for administering their operations in the province and across the northern parts of the country. Interviews with key personnel in these organizations suggested a significant level of frustration existed concerning the administrative coordination of the Angkor, Siem Reap region. A broad awareness of the ZEMP scheme and programs of the ICC and APSARA often led to confusion and feelings of alienation from policy discussions oriented towards temple conservation. In the absence of a clear developmental agenda within the ICC and APSARA, these organizations invariably resigned to their exclusion from the existing world heritage administrative structures, and chose to operate independently.

Cultures of neo-colonialism?

Integral to Angkor's listing as a World Heritage Site was the widespread recognition of the need to restore a nation's cultural past. A profound stumbling block in this agenda was the cataclysmic impact of war and genocide on the country's intellectual resources and scholarly expertise. Although a number of intellectuals had been fortunate enough to flee the country during the early days of the conflict, the vast majority of those that stayed were either murdered or died prematurely. As a consequence, the significant advances made within Phnom Penh's universities in the years after independence were all but wiped out, and their forlorn campuses were now far from recognizable as institutes of higher learning or academic expertise (Ayres 2000). In the early 1990s the country faced the immense challenge of overcoming the vacuum of skills required for governing, researching, interpreting, safeguarding, and nurturing its collective patrimony. The UNTAC process marked the beginning of international efforts to help fill this void. The flip side of such a massive influx of aid would be the emergence of a major imbalance between an ineffectual, and in many cases non-existent, state and indigenous civil society, and an increasingly pervasive body of foreign 'expertise'. The world heritage infrastructure put in place for Angkor epitomized this scenario. The convergence of highly skilled and qualified experts drawn from multiple fields and countries, backed up by internationally ratified charters, lay in stark contrast to the minimal resources available in either Siem Reap or Phnom Penh.

A further factor contributing to Angkor's administrative imbalances was the return of France as the ICC's co-chair, and most powerful player. The fate of modern European history had led to an unlikely alignment between Cambodia's former colonial power and the geographical home of UNESCO. The combination of a long history of expertise in the form of EFEO and UNESCO being headquartered in Paris would enable France to consolidate its position as an unrivalled authority on Angkorean and Khmer history. We can therefore see that a discourse of cultural erasure and historical rupture was accompanied by the reintroduction of a highly sophisticated institutionalized knowledge base from Europe.

It has been suggested here that strong continuities can be seen between a contemporary discourse of world heritage and an Angkorean historiography constructed by scholars during an era of European colonialism, as outlined in the previous chapter. The overwhelming focus on stone during both periods has led to the retention of a powerful and rigid cultural binary, whereby the attention given to a 'high' temple culture has prevailed over a concern for researching 'low' vernacular cultures, whether they be historical or contemporary in nature. Little importance has been placed on understanding the role of Angkor within a Cambodian Buddhist 'cosmology', the relationship between local communities and their environment, or the socio-cultural interplays between tradition and modernity occurring in the park today. In other words, by concentrating on the material artifacts pertaining to a regal history, a contemporary discourse of cultural resource management has re-invoked a narrative more characteristic of nineteenth-century European historiography.

Equally problematic is the preservation of a second binary familiar to that period of scholarship: the distinction between 'greater' and 'lesser' civilizations. A concern for the conservation of stone antiquities has once again prioritized the Indian influences of Hinduism and Mahayana Buddhism. Conversely, much less interest has been shown in tracing how these early influences subsequently evolved, or disappeared, across the region in the centuries after an ideology of 'state' temple construction disintegrated. In large part, this understanding of Angkor's history stems from the lingering impact of earlier scholarship which understood Southeast Asian architecture and art through a lens of Indian influence. Even today, works such as *Histoire ancienne des états hindouisés d'Extrême-Orient* (later published in English as *The Indianized States of Southeast Asia*) by George Coedès are revered as magisterial studies, and as such remain highly influential in shaping the field of enquiry.[16]

It has also been argued in this chapter that, as a cultural heritage landscape, Angkor has been encapsulated within a language of science. The need for an objective and universally shared approach within the ICC's international forum has, by implication, created a set of normative 'truths'. Within a discourse predicated upon scientistic positivism, the value of Angkorean stone as immutable and sublime has been empirically self-evident. Somewhat problematically, this approach has served to mask the historical and ongoing influence of EFEO. In other words, the institutional structures of world heritage have become the medium through which a Eurocentric vision of Angkorean history and culture has re-solidified in the late twentieth century. Critically, the debilitation of Cambodia's intellectual and institutional resources in the fields of cultural resource management, has also meant foreign expertise has rarely been subjected to contestation or countering at the local level.

Angkor's role in mediating post-colonial relations between France and Cambodia also reveals much about the contemporary nature of globalization. Chapter 2 illustrated the ways in which Angkor was reified as one of the most highly prized assets of a French patrimony. Today, world heritage enables France to preserve and rejuvenate both architectural structures in Cambodia, as well as the memory of itself as a benign, indeed benevolent, colonial power. Highly prestigious and globally recognizable, Angkor provides a valuable platform for the international propagation of French expertise, language, and cultural influence. In this regard, Angkor's architectural antiquities have entered the arena of inter-state cultural politics, an area which, as Yunis (2000) has illustrated, has become an essential constituent of contemporary globalization.

Of course the international nature of the ICC bears testimony to the fact that France is far from alone in claiming a stake in Angkorean heritage. The presence of countries like Japan, China, and India reflects the long-standing, pre-nation-state ties Cambodia shares with its regional counterparts. In the case of Japan for example, historical accounts of pilgrims journeying to the site over a number of centuries has led to Angkor's incorporation into a narrative of regional Buddhist influences; whereas for India, Khmer architecture spectacularly attests to the deep historical influence the religions of Hinduism and Buddhism have made on Southeast Asia. Accordingly, during the 1980s the Archaeological Survey of India (ASI) was the only international team to undertake conservation work on Angkor's temples. In describing the restoration of Angkor Wat undertaken by the ASI Bhandari states:

> One advantage the Indian archaeologists have enjoyed in their restoration work of Angkor Wat is their familiarity with the architectural, cultural and religious philosophy of the Angkor monuments. In India itself, stone monuments abound and decades of work in archaeological excavation, restoration and preservation have given them expertise and experience in handling the Angkor monuments with reverence and care.
>
> (Bhandari 1995: 119)

Despite such claims of expertise and familiarity, ASI's use of concrete and strong bleaching chemicals to restore the temple became the subject of much controversy among other international experts in architecture and conservation. As a consequence, their requests to return to the ICC a decade later were met with a certain degree of skepticism. By 2003 however, the ASI eventually secured rights to manage the partial ruin of Ta Prohm – an issue taken up in Chapter 6's examination of the tensions and disputes which surrounded their plans for restoring this complex landscape.

In addition to reestablishing cultural and political connections of the past, the ICC has also provided the forum for the advancement and strengthening of a series of contemporary intergovernmental developmental aid relations. Given Cambodia's difficulties, the submission of multi-million dollar projects for the Angkor region by countries like Japan, China, Malaysia, and Singapore – not all of which came to fruition – have all been delivered as part of bigger programs of bi-lateral assistance. The provision of resources and expertise for reconstructing the country's most prized national heritage has undoubtedly generated both kudos and good will for those countries seeking political influence in the development of both Cambodia and Southeast Asia as a whole. The devastation of the country has therefore been a pivotal factor in the creation of a heritage management framework largely driven by the geo-political maneuvering associated with international aid and dependency.

To conclude that Angkor has merely been 'dissected' across a number of international players and stakeholders would, however, miss the role a framework of world heritage has played in reasserting the site's iconic status as national heritage. Decades after an era of colonialism, a paradigm of cultural heritage which explicitly aims to highlight the importance of safeguarding national treasures has provided Cambodia with a unique opportunity to consolidate a sense of sovereignty over its past. Ongoing collaboration between an attendant international community, APSARA, and the Royal Government has successfully steered Angkor's emergence as a unifying cornerstone of identity for a population whose claim over its architectural past was only secured once the nation-state had been forged in the late nineteenth century.

Simultaneously however, Cambodia's attempts to construct a fragile post-conflict nationalism around Angkor have been accompanied by a series of cultural politics interventions from both within and beyond Asia. Whether Angkor's listing as a World Heritage Site has weakened or strengthened the influence of a former colonial power remains open to question. Not least because this chapter has revealed that the site's transformation into global heritage has also enabled countries such as Japan, India, and China to reassert their own claims of religious, cultural, or civilizational patronage. In conclusion then, we can see that a decade of international assistance and investment, accompanied by domestic efforts to rebuild scholarly and technical expertise, has been characterized by a network of seemingly paradoxical cultural, economic, and political relations.

4   Remapping Angkor

From landscape to touristscape(s)

The early development of the Angkor, Siem Reap region as a world heritage landscape took place against a backdrop of steadily increasing tourist arrivals. By the end of the 1990s however, newspapers, trade journals, and travel magazines frequently drew upon a vocabulary of 'explosion' or 'boom' to describe the extraordinary rise in tourism which was now occurring. The following two chapters explore this fast-growing industry. Chapter 5 interprets tourism as a socio-cultural landscape of representations, narratives, and embodied encounters. In contrast, the pages that follow focus more on economic and political processes to illustrate how Angkorean tourism has been molded by governmental development strategies, policies of site management, and imbalances in infrastructure across the Southeast Asian region.

The chapter begins with 'The Rise of Expedient Angkor', which considers the site's emergence as an economic resource for the Royal Government. It will be seen that national elections held in 1998 represented a major turning point in Angkor's development. With the region now viewed as a financial 'cash cow', the APSARA authority is restructured towards revenue generation, and brought closer to a government characterized by major shortcomings in transparency and governance. To understand the implications of this shift, 'Facilitating an Emergent Touristscape' begins by examining the initial fear, and resultant neglect, of tourism within the world heritage framework. As a rhetoric of 'cultural tourism' emerges in response to the shifting political, economic environment, tourism is addressed as an issue of facility provision and impact management. It is suggested this approach remains dominated by a discourse of monumental conservation and landscape zoning, which together frame Angkor as a static, singular, and geographically bounded *touristscape*. The section highlights how this approach has resulted in vast inequalities in wealth, an absence of community participation, and uneven local development. Despite the subsequent turn towards a language of 'sustainable development' in 2002, it is argued that such a discourse still fails to situate Angkor, and Angkorean tourism, within their national and regional Southeast Asian contexts.

Inspired by Appadurai's (1988) notion of 'scapes', the final section, 'Fractured Touristscapes', examines tourism through the lens of networks and flows operating at various socio-spatial levels. Particular attention is given to the contexts of Cambodia and mainland Southeast Asia – environments deemed to have the greatest impact on Angkor's tourism industry. Inadequacies in the physical and social infrastructure within the country are discussed as major factors inhibiting the development of a nationwide tourism industry. It is suggested that this has been greatly compounded by Southeast Asia's uneven development over the last 50 years, resulting in Cambodia being surrounded by countries bearing considerably more tourism resources and regional power. Invariably visited as an extension to other countries, Angkor has become subsumed within a highly interconnected tourism industry. Examining tourism as a series of regional flows and institutional networks illuminates how the site has become further isolated as a world heritage space and why Cambodia has failed to benefit from tourism on a national level.

The rise of expedient Angkor

At the beginning of the 1990s Cambodia's tourism industry was grossly underdeveloped, both in terms of scope and scale, when compared to neighboring Thailand, Malaysia, and a fast-changing Vietnam. Despite the return of a fragile peace, the country remained on the margins of a *Lonely Planet* Southeast Asia topography. Not surprisingly, establishing visitor arrival statistics during this period was a science fraught with difficulties. According to the Ministry of Tourism, 133,000 tourists entered the country in 1994.[1] However, the fact that only 8000 tourists bought tickets for Angkor that same year indicates how the national arrival statistics were significantly bolstered by the large number of UNTAC-related arrivals at that time.[2]

This broad picture of low tourist arrivals would persist for a number of years: in 1998 less than 41,000 tickets were sold for Angkor. The opening chapter also noted that Cambodia's reconstruction throughout this period was heavily dependent upon foreign aid and assistance. Multilateral banks such as the World Bank and Asian Development Bank (ADB), along with governments from Australia, France, Japan, and the US, were pivotal in mapping the parameters of a socio-economic recovery and program of development. The implementation of a three-year structural adjustment program, lasting between 1993 and 1996, would principally focus on the more 'traditional' industries of agriculture and manufacturing, and the export of natural resources like timber and rubber. Within such a framework the role of culture, and associated tertiary industries like tourism, was only given a passing acknowledgment. Similarly, only a broad recognition of tourism's 'future potential' would appear in the Royal Government's *First Socioeconomic Development Plan* produced in 1996. Despite identifying tourism as one of the country's 'main opportunities for rebuilding its economy', the document's somewhat circumspect rhetoric of reform and economic progress offered few details of how this potential would be realized (Ministry of Planning 1996: 156).

In a developmental environment which principally relied upon various economic markers to define societal progress, a concern for restoring and rehabilitating Cambodia's culture was taken up by international bodies like UNESCO.

Buttressing a thoroughly inadequate and politically weak Ministry of Culture, UNESCO's modest budget and resources were largely consumed by the ongoing problem of temple looting and the illicit trafficking of Khmer artifacts. As we have already seen, this provided the impetus for an agenda of 'damage control' which sought to construct a protective sphere around the country's culture: the greatest priority being given to Angkor and other outlying premodern architectural sites. The lack of protection and local management facilities of these sites meant tourism was perceived more as a danger than as an opportunity.

In this respect, we can see that tourism remained a marginal issue within both these sectors of aid. As a consequence, an institutional and intellectual void concerning the relationship between culture, tourism, and development emerged within, and across, the various bodies involved in Cambodia's rehabilitation. The lack of attention given to bolstering the government's Ministry of Tourism meant it largely functioned as a bureaucratic body concerned with generating revenue and the management of technical issues like visa regulations and airport facilities. As such, its intermittent reports outlining a program of national tourism development remained under-researched and loaded with industry-familiar, but conceptually inadequate, jargon.

The steady pattern of year-on-year growth would be temporarily halted in 1997 by a deadly grenade attack in Phnom Penh and the subsequent forceful removal of Prince Ranariddh from his office as Co-Prime Minister. Somewhat ironically, these events also triggered two further political maneuvers, which, in combination, would restore, and indeed rapidly accelerate, the volume and breadth of tourists visiting Angkor. First, in a move to weaken the FUNCINPEC-backed national carrier *Royal Air Cambodge*, Hun Sen ordered the introduction of direct international flights to Siem Reap.[3] Known as the 'Open Skies Policy', this change in legislation marked the end of an enforced transit, and transfer to a domestic flight, in Phnom Penh.

The second, and far more significant event, would be Hun Sen's successful election as sole Prime Minister in 1998. In reflecting upon the CPP leader's quest for absolutist power, David Chandler perceived the upcoming elections as yet another foreclosing of 'pluralism in Cambodian political life', and the return to a more historically familiar political scenario (1998: 45). After the developmental languor caused in part by the compromise government formed under UNTAC – a situation described by Roberts as 'very much an experiment in democracy' (2001: xiv) – the prospect of greater political stability under a more familiar style of 'strong man' leadership created an environment conducive to real economic progress.[4] Crucially, the contemporaneous increase in the number of international flight arrivals, the opening of more land and sea borders, and a steadily improving international image all meant Angkor's long-recognized potential as one of Southeast Asia's premier tourist destinations was starting to become a tangible reality. By the end of the decade the temple complex stood as one of the newly elected government's most important economic assets.

Although the election provided a new impetus for national development and donor assistance, infrastructure projects continued to be oriented around short-term goals and returns. Public and governmental office remained a fragile position. Unable to afford the luxury of constructing nationwide tourism development schemes involving long-term investments, government officials looked to 'cash-in' on Angkor's immediate potential. Establishing an infrastructure for Siem Reap's fast-growing tourist industry offered rapid and lucrative capital returns, making it a highly attractive governmental policy direction – not least because of the inherent coupling of public office with private commercial interests.

In a country renowned for its lack of democracy and deep-rooted corruption, swings between socialist, totalitarian, and capitalist regimes since independence in 1954 had fundamentally blurred the boundaries between the public and private sectors (Kato et al. 2000, Peou 2000). Frustrated by persistent governance problems and a lack of governmental transparency, bodies like the World Bank and ADB were now demanding major reform as a prerequisite for future assistance.[5] Accordingly, in its account of the *Third Consultative Group Meeting* held in Tokyo in February 1999, the ADB stated, 'Many delegates noted that the actual level of assistance would be influenced by progress made in implementing policy reforms, particularly in the areas of good governance ... domestic revenue mobilization and improved attention to social sector issues' (ADB 1999: 16).

The development of Siem Reap's infrastructure – with its associated employment opportunities, incoming flows of international capital and urban regeneration – could be cited by the government as a tangible indicator of such social progress. In other words, the construction of hotels, airports, markets, and other tourist facilities became integral to a developmental discourse of poverty reduction, 'revenue mobilization', and socio-political reform.[6]

Clearly a discordancy had emerged between this new agenda and the ICC's disposition towards monumental protection and conservation. APSARA, ZEMP, and fresh land management legislation approached the development of both the Angkor and Siem Reap regions with a philosophy of minimum impact and damage. With such a framework in place the Royal Government's provincial Ministry of Tourism office in Siem Reap was essentially reduced to the function of collecting taxes from locally run businesses.[7] Frustrated by the Ministry's inability to command a strategic direction for the region as a whole, and the ICC's apparent lack of interest in development and tourism, Hun Sen moved towards a language of 'master plans', as the following excerpt from a speech given to the Ministry of Tourism during its Annual Conference in May 2001 indicates:

> The Angkor temple is the world's priceless heritage and belongs to all mankind. Therefore, we should have a proper master plan and take protection measures for its development. My observation is that the development of the area is considerably slow. Besides the roads which I pushed very hard last year ... it seems nothing has been improved. There are no road signs for direction, no rest rooms and no facilities to serve visitors. This work has to be done as soon as possible by having a project planned and disseminated to

private investors for their participation, if we want to attract tourists to stay
longer and spend more.

(Hun Sen 2001: 2–3)

Responsibility for the lack of attention given to development and the slow response
to an escalating tourism industry was laid directly at the door of APSARA.
Crucially, such a public airing of discontent with the organization's performance
laid the political ground for its restructuring. In June 2001, APSARA's director
Vann Molyvann was removed from his post and replaced by the authority's former vice president Bun Narith. Like Vann Molyvann, Bun Narith was a trained
architect, but lacked the political guile of his predecessor.[8] The greater degree of
governmental control afforded by Bun Narith's appointment was extended further through the restructuring of APSARA from three key departments to five.
This move replaced the organization's previously dominant power base within the
Department of Culture and Monuments with a structure that steered far greater
resources towards developmental issues. It would be a political maneuver which
took Angkor a major step towards being administered as an economic resource of
tourism.

The creation of a new Economic Development Department signified the transition of APSARA into a management body which now complemented its existing
conservation and research activities with a strong commercial interest. The major
financial rewards emanating from the authority's control over projects such as the
planned 'Hotel Zone' – a project discussed in greater detail shortly – provided the
CPP with a strong incentive to gain control over its accounts. During the annual
ICC conference held in July 2001, senior members of the party explained the need
to 'restructure the organization to deal with the new issues of tourism development'.[9] Within a rhetoric of creating 'the premier tourist site in Asia', the desire
to 'manage the visits of tourists' implicitly reflected the government's intention to
maximize the financial rewards of Angkorean tourism.[10]

Far more than merely an economic decision, the restructuring of APSARA
was also politically motivated. In its short life, the organization had been closely
associated with the now aging King Norodom Sihanouk. Created through Royal
Decree, and directed for the most part by one of the King's closest allies, Vann
Molyvann, APSARA always succeeded in maintaining its political distance from
Hun Sen's CPP party. However, once elected as sole Prime Minister, and with
the ever-diminishing capacities of a frail King, Hun Sen looked to pull the organization further under his party's wing. In so doing, he was acutely aware of
the 'value' of controlling Angkor in his quest to become the country's uncon-
tested leader. As Chandler reminds us, 'Angkor has always been a guiding light,
utilized by many twentieth century leaders as a sign of Cambodian strength'
(1996b: 242).

Indeed, Chandler's observation here also steers us towards an understanding of how the restructuring of APSARA needs to be seen as an attempt to
(re)nationalize Angkor. Taking control of its economic value as national tourist-
space – rather than merely global heritage space – also coincides with a desire

to utilize classical antiquities as a cornerstone for a grossly weakened state nationalism. While Cambodia's premodern architectural sites suffered a certain amount of vandalism, theft, and structural damage during the war, the extensive destruction inflicted upon the country's other forms of material and non-material culture triggered an anxiety to reestablish the vital markers of a collective identity. A tourism industry oriented around a glorious Angkor not only served as a metaphor for a state in recovery, but also mobilized the construction, come representation, of a history beyond deprecation and a self-image defined by power and strength. As the twenty-first century began, tourism was now firmly on the agenda and proving a major force of social change. In recognition of this 'new era', APSARA's new Director, Bun Narith, stated; 'the emergency conservation phase is over and we now need to move onto a development phase'.[11]

Facilitating an emergent touristscape

This declaration of a 'new era' of development and tourism was received with a certain degree of trepidation and surprise by both UNESCO and the ICC as a whole. The inaugural ICC meeting held in Tokyo in 1993 explicitly identified a two-pronged strategy pairing both cultural conservation and socio-economic development. As we saw in the last chapter however, efforts in subsequent years were overwhelmingly directed towards archaeological research and monumental conservation and restoration. The wealth of workshops, symposiums, research papers, technical reports, and other publications pertaining to such issues lay in stark contrast to the occasional, schematic consultancy report on tourism.[12] Within this framework extremely little fieldwork research was conducted into the broad social, cultural, and environment issues arising from a growing tourism industry. Rather than being embraced as a positive force for cultural resource management, tourism was conceptually viewed as an imminent danger, one that needed to be repelled at all costs. This perspective is vividly conveyed in the following excerpt from the joint UNESCO/APSARA publication, *Angkor: Past, Present and Future*:

> Tourism threatens to damage this Khmer cultural legacy far more swiftly and decisively than did any ancient invaders, or even the clandestine raiders of today. Savage, unregulated commercial ventures purposely designed to facilitate the 'consumption' of Angkor, exploiting the Khmer heritage only in order to siphon private profit out of the region if not out of the country, constitute a current and very real threat. Fully committed to the necessity for Cambodia to reap socio-economic benefits from the careful management of this extraordinary national resource, APSARA stands against the inevitable temptation to effectively sell Cambodia's irreplaceable cultural heritage like another plot of land, sacrificing the soul of the nation and one principal guarantee of future national vitality for quick individual wealth.
>
> (UNESCO 1996: 166–7)

This desire to protect Angkor's architectural structures and their environs from the impending threat of a tourism industry operating within a highly challenging socio-political environment, led to the formation of a legal and institutional framework which polarized heritage and tourism. Crucially however, and as these two chapters have demonstrated, the scholarly disposition of the two bodies in question meant the latter was essentially overlooked as a topic worthy of sustained and rigorous investigation. Although the above statement by APSARA clearly suggests recognition of an imminent 'boom' in both domestic and international tourism, this did not translate into the deployment of human or other resources within either of the administrative bodies overseeing the region. This was confirmed by Ang Choulean, the Director of the Department of Culture and Monuments of APSARA in his address to the ICC technical committee in December 1999: 'based on what has been done up to now, we will not be able to cope with tourism in the future'.[13] With the conference taking place just over a year after the 1998 elections such comments would pave the way for the changes in Angkor's management structure noted earlier.

One of the defining themes of this December conference was the recognition that 'the new challenge facing the ICC is tourism'.[14] To this end two key issues, come challenges, were discussed. First, the ongoing growth of tourist arrivals to Angkor, both domestic and international. And second, the rapid acceleration in urban construction across Siem Reap occurring beyond their control. A third development of equal significance, but one that was not articulated within the conference room, was the changing attitudes of the Royal Government towards Angkor and their desire to become more involved in its management.[15]

In recognition of this change and the need to urgently address the tourism issue, UNESCO initiated a series of seminars and conferences intended to facilitate a dialogue between a wide variety of international and national bodies. The first major event of this type took place in Siem Reap in December 2000. Hosted by the World Tourism Organization (WTO), a major international conference on Cultural Tourism brought together academics, consultants, and national representatives from Asia, Europe, the Middle East, and North America. This was followed by the smaller UNESCO/APSARA National Seminar on Cultural Tourism in July 2001.

A common thread running through these two events was a desire to promote a form of 'high quality cultural tourism' that resisted the destructive effects of a more pernicious 'mass tourism'. A language of 'cultural tourism' was widely advocated as the means for harmoniously bringing together the cultural elements of a country like Cambodia with the economic benefits of tourism in a mutually beneficial relationship. In theory, this goal would be achieved by reaping the optimum social and economic benefits of tourism whilst affording protection to the cultural assets it draws upon. Essentially, this approach stemmed from justifiable concerns regarding an environment of anarchic development, corruption, and weak legislation. Operating within such a discursive framework, many delegates spoke of the need to promote a form of 'high quality' tourism which inflicted minimal socio-cultural or environmental damage. Accordingly, in reflecting upon the challenges facing Cambodia, Chau Sun Kerya, the Director of the Department of Tourism Development, APSARA, unambiguously told delegates:

> Tourism in Cambodia must first and foremost be cultural tourism ... the policy of cultural tourism that Cambodia intends to implement must have specific goals in order to prevent it from turning into commercial tourism ... [we must] ... promote high quality cultural tourism, and avoid mass tourism by raising the level of accommodation and the quality of services offered.
>
> (APSARA 2000a: 1–4)

One of the defining features of this approach was the reliance upon certain touristic prototypes. Invoking a language of 'high quality', 'cultural' and even 'special interest' tourists reflected a desire to attract only those visitors that offered superior economic returns with minimal impact. This policy directly responded to UNESCO's previously expressed concern that an industry which focused on 'low quality' mass tourists, whose 'contribution to the local economy is more limited', needed to be resisted as it would rapidly cause 'irreversible destruction of Angkor's cultural and natural heritage' (UNESCO 1996: 157). Within the above statement we can also see an explicit reference made to the provision of 'quality services'. More specifically, it reflects how a policy of cultural tourism centered upon the provision of 'high quality' facilities for high-spending international tourists. Once an ICC and APSARA cultural tourism framework for the Angkor region had finally emerged, policy discussions and documentation essentially gravitated around a number of key facility projects. The proposed 'hotel zone' provides a case in point.

A concern about rampant and anarchic tourism development led the ZEMP team to recommend an area of 'largely unoccupied and non-arable land' lying between the Angkor park and town of Siem Reap be reserved for hotels and a visitor centre (UNESCO 1996: 199). It was argued that regulating tourism development in this way would preserve the 'traditional spatial and social organization' of Siem Reap, reduce the strain on the region's resources and infrastructure, and ensure the tourism industry remained geographically separate from the Angkor Archaeological Park (Ibid). Although legally supported by a sub-decree in 1995, the hotel zone witnessed little progress over the coming years. As I outline elsewhere in a more detailed account of the project, a number of proposals put forward for developing the site, including a major urban regeneration plan by the Malaysian corporation YTL, had been rejected during the course of the decade (Winter 2007). Fresh impetus for the scheme came with the restructuring of APSARA and the rapidly accelerating growth in tourism. Re-branded as the *Angkor Tourist City* in 2001, it was clear the project would play a central role in attempting to transform Angkor into a 'high quality' destination for international tourists. A strategy emphasized in the brochure produced for prospective international hotel investors:

> Angkor Tourist City will be developed in compliance with current planning regulations, but in keeping with Khmer architectural traditions. Green areas

and buildings will be blended together. The area will contain tourist and leisure facilities only. It is reserved exclusively for luxury and first class hotels with a capacity of over 60 rooms.

(APSARA 2001: 4)

Stretching across a thousand hectares, the proposed Angkor Tourist City would also interconnect with a computerized ticketing system and an electric shuttle scheme for transporting tourists around the park. These two additional projects would enable the movement and numbers of tourists within the park to be closely monitored at any given time. The ticketing project involved dividing Angkor into a series of zones whereby the total number of tourists and their duration of visit could be regulated. The electric shuttles would ensure a smooth, and timely, transition between these zones, along with a return journey to the hotel at the end of the day. Powered by rechargeable fuel cells, these multi-seated shuttles would reduce both traffic and pollution levels. To maximize these gains, it was proposed that all other motorized vehicles would be banned from entering the park.

Not surprisingly, this proposal became a source of immense controversy within Siem Reap's transport community, as hundreds of tuk-tuk, motorbike, taxi and bus drivers all saw their livelihoods threatened by such a monopoly. From the extensive press coverage of the issue, it was apparent the government had signed contracts for the manufacture of the electric shuttles at least two years prior to the restructuring of APSARA, and that the project had been held up by the former APSARA director Vann Molyvann.[16]

Clearly, when considered together, these projects served a number of ends. For the ICC they constituted 'a policy encouraging high quality/high price tourism'(UNESCO 1996: 159). If successful, they would make a major contribution to the ongoing protection of the temples and their immediate environments. They also offered maximum economic return for minimum impact. Equally importantly, given the international community's general disposition towards tourism as a future of impending danger and destruction, the projects enabled a high degree of bureaucratic and legislative control to be retained for the region as a whole. Landscape planning, architectural design, and the 'quality' of facilities introduced could all be closely monitored. Efforts made to attract hotel chains like *Accor* or *Four Seasons* illustrated how a design for an integrated 'resort' of multiple hotels was largely conceived with the aesthetically desirable western, transnational hospitality corporations in mind (see APSARA 2001: 4).

There is little doubt that the international community's desire to protect the Angkor, Siem Reap region from tourism – and simultaneously ensure its presentation as a 'quality' destination – is paralleled within the Cambodian government. Equally pertinently though, a facility-driven discourse of cultural tourism promises a huge financial windfall. Gaining control over both ticket sales and transport facilities would provide a consistent cash revenue. It would also secure APSARA's dominance over any transport companies, travel agents, and tour operators arranging visitations to Angkor. As one Siem Reap-based tour operator stated after seeing press advertisements for tender applications: 'we fear being exploited and held to ransom with APSARA now operating as a commercial enterprise'.[17] In addition to these operational revenues, the close management over facilities would not only generate extremely lucrative contractual deals, but also deliver long-term income from the business taxes imposed on the countless tourism businesses located in Siem Reap. In this respect, the financial benefits accrued from taking control of the facilities required for a 'high quality, cultural tourism' industry have provided the government with a compelling incentive to adopt such rhetoric.

We can therefore see that seemingly harmonious interests suggested by a facility-driven discourse does, however, belie significantly different agendas at work – a situation demonstrated in the closing speeches given during the National Seminar on Cultural Tourism held in July 2001.[18] In summarizing the key findings of the two-day conference, UNESCO's special representative for Cambodia, Azzedine Beschaouch, stressed the dangers of overly rapid development. While accepting that change was necessary he emphasized the need to control the situation through improved training, greater communication between government departments, and a recognition of the dangers tourists posed to the temples of Angkor.[19] He illustrated his vision for Angkor's future by referring to a number of international best practice examples given during the conference. Interestingly, these same examples also formed the basis of the closing remarks given by Sok An, APSARA's Chairman of the Board of Trustees and the Senior Minister for Council of Ministers. Most notably, Sok An drew on the example of Notre-Dame, Paris, presented as a model of visitor management, to illustrate his own vision for Angkor:

> Yes, we need higher quality tourism. Notre-Dame gets fourteen million tourists a year, Angkor Wat does not get anywhere near that, and we can reach that level. We are using 1 per cent of our potential and we have 98-9 per cent to go.[20]

In stating his desire to see the introduction of international boxing tournaments and golf courses as the means for attaining these aims, Sok An pointed towards a horizon of an ever-expanding cultural tourism industry, one that differed radically from the minimum impact, controlled development advocated by Beschaouch and UNESCO. The possibility for such radically different agendas to coexist side by side lies in the particularities of how the issue of tourism is discussed. Focusing primarily on the pragmatics of hotel zones and transport systems obfuscates any conceptual contradictions that might lie behind seemingly harmonious policies geared towards producing a 'high quality' destination. Moreover, the absence of any substantive research, analysis, and a reliance upon non-empirically-generated tourist prototypes means a framework of cultural tourism becomes embroiled in the machinations of Cambodia's turbulent political economy. Discussions over the logistics and technicalities of policy implementation serve as the common ground for a local, global interplay of agendas accommodated within the loosely defined discursive framework shared across the table. The willingness of both the government and the ICC to adopt cultural tourism as a policy undoubtedly stems from a shared set of desired outcomes. Somewhat paradoxically, however, it also enables significantly divergent national and international agendas concerning Angkor's development to be sustained. The very ambiguities, tensions and under-theorizations inherent to the framework facilitate its appropriation, even subversion, by a government attempting to 'realize its economic objectives and promote is political aims' (Dahles 2001: xiii).

Indeed, it was highlighted earlier that the government's decision to restructure APSARA was driven by a desire to create a new era of development for Angkor. To respond to this shift in agenda, UNESCO, as the coordinating body of the international members of the ICC, moved towards a language of 'sustainability'. Effectively replacing Cultural Tourism, a paradigm of Sustainable Development represented a recognition by the ICC that this new phase in Angkor's history had to be managed and steered in appropriate directions. It would also provide the opportunity to tackle a broader set of issues, including roads, water management, and environmental pollution. To this end, UNESCO set about bolstering APSARA's knowledge and skills base in the much neglected areas of urban planning and social research. By the time the Second Intergovernmental conference for the Safeguarding and Sustainable Development of Angkor and its Region arrived, this time held in Paris in November 2003, the issue of development had become a key topic of discussion.

Marking the tenth anniversary of the 1993 Tokyo Declaration on Angkor, this international conference facilitated a dialogue between bodies from the world of international heritage management, including ICCROM, ICOMOS, the International Council of Museums (ICOM), and WMF, and those organizations more familiar to the area of development such as ILO, FAO, UNDP, IMF, ADB, and the World Bank. The resultant *Paris Declaration* stated that the goals outlined in the Johannesburg Summit on Sustainable Development (September 2002) should inform a program of 'sustainable ethical tourism in the Siem Reap/Angkor region as a tool in the fight against poverty' (UNESCO 2003: 4). Recognizing the previous lack of attention given to this area, it was recommended that 'development projects in the province of Siem Reap/Angkor be discussed in all their aspects, particularly economic, social and environment, within the framework of the periodic meetings of the ICC' (Ibid).

Accordingly, during the following ICC meeting in Siem Reap in February 2004, a number of progress reports were delivered concerning current, or proposed, development-related projects. Community poverty, river pollution, and the need for a harbor on the nearby Tonle Sap lake were among the concerns highlighted by consultants from the World and Asian Development Banks.[21] However, the most urgent priorities identified during the conference revolved around the impact of a fast-growing local tourism infrastructure on the structural stability of Angkor's temples. A number of research projects had concluded that a change in the local aquifer – brought about by the sharp increase in water consumption from hotels, spas, swimming pools, gardens, and bathrooms – was threatening the long-term stability of the monuments.[22] Contrasting this were presentations by APSARA and the government's Ministry of Public Works and Transport summarizing a number of recently implemented construction projects, including the upgrading of various local and provincial roads.[23] One of the government's flagship projects was the proposed reconstruction of Route No. 67, a road that would connect Angkor with the former Khmer Rouge stronghold of Anlong Veng and nearby temple complex of Preah Vihear in the north. The road was seen as an important project for increasing the flow of tourists to Angkor from the border with Thailand in the north. Placed alongside each other, these projects suggest that the discursive orientations, which shaped the previous 'cultural tourism' policies, have been retained within a language of 'sustainable development'. Although now operating across a number of sectors, the ICC continued to be defined by a conceptual polarization between agendas of monumental conservation and tourism development.

It was argued in the previous chapter that understandings of cultural heritage have been informed by science-based disciplines oriented towards the protection and restoration of monumental antiquities. This chapter has traced the emergence of an accompanying positivistic language of development, arguing that policies attuned to a highly challenging social environment have formulated and articulated the relationship between tourism, culture, and heritage in particular ways. Within this environment tourism and heritage have been perceived and discussed in terms of physical 'resources', whether they be endangered temples or luxury hotels. Fearful of rampant and uncontrolled development Angkor's international heritage community have viewed tourism as a threat, an imminent danger, and a destructive force to be repelled. In contrast, for the Royal Government of Cambodia, tourism promises vast flows of capital and state wealth. Working in combination, these two discourses have framed the site as a bounded *touristscape* where people, capital and modern construction need to be spatially managed. It is a situation however, which has led to a number of important voids in knowledge and discursive exchange.

In the first instance, understandings of the broader social and environmental impacts of what by now had become an extremely fast-growing tourism industry remained under-developed. Despite efforts to bolster APSARA's resources in these areas, the organization would consistently struggle to cope with a set of ever greater challenges posed by the rapidly changing environment. For example, since its inception APSARA has successfully upheld the ZEMP legislation concerning construction within the park.[24] For a number of reasons the organization has been far less successful in overseeing the development of Siem Reap – an urban environment which has witnessed a profound and chaotic transformation in less than a decade. By 2003 the hotel zone had failed to materialize. In its absence a construction boom occurred across an ever-expanding town, most notably along National Route No. 6, a key artery connecting the local airport and town. The lack of an ICC or APSARA monitoring programmed with any regulatory teeth led to the construction of thousands of hotel rooms, together with numerous restaurants, shops, karaoke clubs, and travel agents along this two-kilometer stretch of road; a situation which placed a major strain on the local electricity, sewage, and water infrastructures (see Winter 2007).

One of the key driving forces of Siem Reap's strained expansion has been the ever increasing levels of rural to urban migration (Vann Molyvann 2003).

Since the early 1990s thousands of families have moved to the area lured by the prospect of employment in the tourism, hospitality, or construction sectors. For those with language and service industry skills, tourism has proved a lucrative industry to work in. After tips, commissions and bonuses, the monthly income for head chefs, tour guides, and hotel management staff can often exceed 1000 US dollars. The personal income of entrepreneurial business owners has been many times more. Beyond the limited wealth pockets of tourism though, the salaries of school teachers, manual laborers, nurses, or market traders have barely risen beyond a level of 30 to 40 US dollars per month.

While such inequalities are common to places of tourism development, it is suggested that, in the case of Siem Reap, they have been significantly exaggerated by policies oriented around the provision of 'high-quality' accommodation, transport, and entertainment facilities. For the international community, the discourses of cultural tourism and sustainability have been primarily concerned with limiting tourism's detrimental impact on the Angkor Archaeological Park. In contrast, the government has appropriated tourism to wrap Angkor in a language of national, state-driven development. Arising from this 'new era' has been a program of road construction linking the site with other potential tourist sites around the north of the country. The choice of routes, however, strongly suggests these projects are primarily designed to facilitate day trips from Angkor to other outlying temple sites like Preah Vihear and Koh Ker, rather than fostering region-wide development.[25]

It can therefore be seen that neither frameworks have implemented community-oriented policies designed to improve the equitable distribution of tourism-related capital within, and across, Cambodia's population. The emergence of major wealth inequalities in the town of Siem Reap alone has meant agricultural-based communities, whose families have been unable to raise their income above a mere one or two dollars a day, continue to live in the shadow of multi-storied, brightly painted villas.[26] Moreover, despite the income from thousands of four and five star hotel rooms, and millions of dollars of aid and investment, Siem Reap has continued to languish as the country's fifth poorest province.

This chapter has also identified how a heritage discourse focused on architectural antiquities has defined the parameters of what constitutes the cultural within policies of cultural tourism. Instead of fostering more inclusive representations of Angkor as a lived space comprised of village and monastic communities with a plethora of traditions and cultural artifacts, 'cultural tourism' has reiterated the ICC's strong pre-disposition towards a static culture of the ancient past, and, as such, reaffirmed the colonial framings seen in Chapter 2. More specifically, through the dominance of discourses of architectural conservation and archaeology cultural tourism has emerged as a framework founded on scientific and rationalized understandings of culture. In Lefebvrian terms a realist illusion has formed whereby culture is reduced to an 'objective materialism' because the 'imagined' is 'unseen, unmeasurable and therefore unknowable' (Soja 2000: 64). Within this environment, no attention has been given to supporting the family-run arts and crafts industries of communities living in the park; a neglect which reflects an institutional-based conception of Angkor as a museumified space, principally valued for its 'high' cultural *chef-d'oeuvre*.

The polarization of tourism and heritage has also inhibited the emergence of a policy framework capable of comprehending the social, cultural, and economic dynamics of a fast-expanding world of commerce around Angkor. By implication, little understanding has emerged regarding the pivotal role Angkor's national and regional environments have played in shaping its development, as we shall see shortly. As an extension of this theme, the various ways tourism and heritage mutually constitute each other, forming a particular socio-cultural landscape around Angkor, has also been overlooked. Examining this issue in greater detail, and its consequences for the regeneration of Cambodian society at both the local and national level, the following chapter explores how Angkor has come to circulate across a variety of symbolic geographies and contexts. To situate such an analysis within its structural context, the final part of this chapter first considers patterns of uneven economic and societal development in and around Cambodia.

Fractured touristscapes

As Cambodia reopened its borders a trip to Angkor required considerably more time and effort than the 45 minutes it takes to fly from Bangkok today. The dilapidated state of Cambodia's roads meant travelers arriving in Phnom Penh, the country's sole gateway for international air travel at that time, would either transfer to a domestic flight or travel northwards from the capital by river boat. Given the lack of synchronization between flight arrivals and departures, Phnom Penh invariably served as a one- or two-day stopover in either or both directions. The inconvenience of such delays gave momentum to the 1996 'Open Skies policy', which allowed visitors to fly direct to Siem Reap. The arrival of a convenient connection with one of Southeast Asia's main aerial hubs for both the long-haul and intra-regional markets would have an immediate impact on the total numbers of tourists entering the country. With the majority traveling with the explicit, if not sole, aim of seeing Angkor this policy would, however, drastically reduce the flow of visitors beyond the Siem Reap region.

Throughout the 1990s travel across the country remained a slow, arduous and, in some cases, risky exercise. Collapsed or destroyed bridges, seasonal flooding and subsidence would reduce road speeds to less than 20 or 30 kilometers an hour. Even for National Route No.6 – a key artery connecting the country's two economic centers, Phnom Penh and Siem Reap with the Thai border in the northwest – such modest speeds would be unattainable for much of the year (see Figure A). Likewise, train journeys from Phnom Penh along one of the country's two rail routes – either northwards towards Battambang or south to the coastal town of Sihanoukville – lasted between 12 and 18 hours. Not surprisingly, the difficulties of traveling outwards from Siem Reap and Phnom Penh inhibited the growth of a geographical-dispersed tourism industry.

Paralysis within the industry would also be created by the lack of a critical mass of tourism within the country. In the east, provinces such as Ratnikiri and

Mondulkiri, which together offered considerable potential as destinations of 'eco' or 'ethnic' tourism, received less than a few hundred tourists each year throughout the 1990s. In the south, the coastal towns of Sihanoukville, Kep, and Kampot all faced stiff competition from well-established locations in Thailand, Vietnam, and Malaysia as they struggled to (re)construct beach tourism industries. As we shall see in the following chapter, the tourism industry has also been continually haunted by the image of Cambodia as a country in political turmoil and unsafe to visit. In addition to millions of landmines, the enduring presence of hostile political factions represented a real danger for foreign visitors. Media coverage of the kidnapping and subsequent execution of a group of backpackers traveling in the southern province of Kampot in 1994 delivered an unequivocal image of Cambodia as a dangerous and inhospitable place. A decade later the annual number of tourists arriving at Angkor exceeded the one million mark, and yet the country's more 'remote' locations continued to receive only a few thousand visitors per year.

Across Cambodia, attempts to develop a tourism-related business, facility or attraction have consistently faced a wealth of obstacles and challenges. Business ventures have been mired by an array of problems. Shortfalls in skilled staff, construction materials and everyday supplies such as electricity, potable water and food have been compounded by the very real challenges posed by incessant corruption and whimsical taxation schemes. The state's inability to repair or upgrade the desperately inadequate infrastructures beyond Siem Reap and Phnom Penh has been a recurring source of frustration for a private sector wishing to develop more geographically expansive itineraries. Tour operator efforts to develop Sihanoukville as an inbound point of access for the lucrative cruise-ship market, for example, have been consistently stalled by the town's inadequate deep water port and regional airport facilities. As we shall see shortly, this has meant clients have been transferred by air direct to Siem Reap from ports in neighboring Vietnam or Thailand.

To compound the problem of shattered physical and social infrastructures, Cambodia's tourism industry has also been undermined by a lack of skilled human resources. The growth of those institutions familiar to any tourism industry – such as hotels, travel agents, and national tourist boards – has been muted by a dearth of trained staff at all levels. This lack of trained and expertize staff has proved a major barrier to the (re)development of airports, industry-based information technology networks, marketing materials or business strategies.

At a political level, 1990s Cambodia has been characterized by two major transitions: from a socialist style command economy to a free market democracy; and from civil war to peace. Far from occurring as near-overnight transformations – a belief held by many UNTAC officials – the country's development has continued to be plagued by a centralized and convoluted bureaucracy, not to mention a somewhat languid entrepreneurial culture. Quite simply, Cambodia's political and economic climate, compounded by the above social and physical infrastructure problems, has produced an environment far from conducive to the development of a nation-wide tourism industry. To compound Cambodia's difficulties, the development of tourism has been heavily influenced by a regional context characterized by national borders porous to flows of capital, people, technologies and corporate power. It is to these regional *touristscapes* that I now turn.

> The countries of Southeast Asia encompass a remarkable range of levels and forms of development ... clearly seen in rates of economic growth.
>
> (Dixon and Smith 1997: 8)

In turning to consider Angkor's broader regional context two overarching themes will become apparent here. First, that Southeast Asian tourism operates as a complex network of interconnected national tourism industries. Second, historical patterns of uneven socio-economic development across the region have produced imbalanced relationships of power within that network.

Over the course of the second half of the twentieth century, Southeast Asia emerged as an important destination within an ever-growing global tourism industry. Driven by tourists from Europe, North America, and Australasia, as well as of course Asia, this pattern of growth is expected to continue over the coming decades (Teo et al. 2001). Seizing the turn of the century as an opportune moment to map out the course of the coming decades, the World Tourism Organization confidently predicted that the East Asia/Pacific region would establish itself as the world's second largest destination for international tourism by 2010.[27] In explaining this rapid regional expansion they cited China and 'Southeast Asia – especially Thailand, Malaysia, Cambodia and Vietnam' as the principal long-term growth markets for both long-haul and interregional tourism (WTO 1999). If we are to gain a better understanding of the regional differences within this overview of longer term trends, insights can be gained from looking at Southeast Asia's development to date. Tracing the multitude of historical constituents to Southeast Asia's uneven development – a subject which has occupied many scholars in recent decades – is clearly beyond the scope of this chapter. The more modest aim here is to understand some of the economic and political processes which have shaped the evolution of the region's tourism industry.

As an era of widespread colonial rule came to a close Southeast Asia was a region characterized by 'extremely uneven patterns of development' (Dixon and Smith 1997: 4). Centuries of maritime and river-borne trade in an 'age of commerce', coupled with varying degrees of colonial era core-periphery dependencies had contributed to a geography of imbalanced urbanization and wealth distribution (Dwyer 1990, Reid 1993). The gradual solidification of political and economic sovereignty for the region's newly independent nation-states would be negotiated against a backdrop of postcolonial and cold-war geo-political relations. In accounting for this period, Forbes suggests that 'new geographies assembled and disassembled with each iteration of economy and politics' (1999: 2). Across Southeast Asia, radically different economic programs were pursued. In contrast to the outward looking, open market capitalist approaches followed by Malaysia, Thailand, and Singapore, the economies of Burma, Laos, and Cambodia remained essentially static and insular (Robison et al. 1999: 2).[28] Rigg points towards the ability of the former to cultivate efficient public administrations, sound export-oriented macro-economic policies and their human and physical infrastructures as the engines of a rapid development commonly regarded as a 'miracle' (Rigg 1997: 11[29]).

At a time when modernization paradigms were the vogue of development, the region's cultural diversity was regarded as the antithesis of industrialized modernity. Arguing that 'in terms of culture, virtually all early modernization theorists were convergence theorists' (1993: 51) Wood indicates how tourism was enthusiastically adopted as a vehicle for reforming or erasing localized, traditional cultural practices. The author cites the UN's 1967 International Year of Tourism as an example of this strategy. As prescribed trajectories of development shifted, so did attitudes towards ethnic, historical and cultural diversity; such that culture came to be celebrated by organizations 'promoting alternative forms of development' (Rigg 1997: 42). By implication, tourism also emerged as a natural means of utilizing local diversity for the attainment of economic goals. Now widely regarded as a 'passport to development' (de Kadt 1979), tourism was seized upon by countries like Malaysia, Thailand, Singapore, and the Philippines from the 1970s onwards (Richter 1993).

Of course the ability of these countries to reap the rewards of an increasingly 'multipolar global economy' (Forbes 1999: 2), was predicated on sustained political stability; something other countries in the region were unable to enjoy. A succession of conflicts in Indochina, most notably the 'American war', all but destroyed the economies of Laos, Cambodia, and Vietnam. Devastating human loss, shattered infrastructures, sustained internal conflicts, and grossly inadequate amounts of foreign aid would all serve to paralyze GDP growth; a situation plainly apparent in Table 4.1.

Departing from accounts of shifts in national and international political economies, other authors have observed the post-Second World War decades in terms of regional imbalances in urbanization. Hall & Page (2000) for example argue the rise of key extended metropolitan regions, or EMRs, have been crucial

Table 4.1 Growth trajectories: Southeast Asia in global perspective

	GNP per capita average annual growth		GDP average annual growth		
	1965–80	1980–93	1970–80	1980–90	1990–94
Cambodia	0.6	–	–	–	–
Indonesia	5.2	4.2	7.2	6.1	7.6
Laos	0.6	–	–	–	6.2
Malaysia	4.7	3.5	7.9	5.2	8.4
Myanmar	1.6	–	4.7	0.6	5.7
Thailand	4.4	6.4	7.1	7.6	8.2
Vietnam	0.6	–	–	–	8.0

Source: Modified from Rigg, J. (1997) *Southeast Asia: The Human Landscape of Modernization and Development*, London: Routledge, p. 6. (*Original source*: World Bank & UNDP Annual Reports.)

to the growth of the region as a whole. For port cities like Jakarta, Saigon, Singapore, and Manila the consolidation and expansion of long-standing trade relations enabled them to become 'the major focus for their respective national economies and the principal interface with the international economy' (Dixon & Smith 1997: 5).

For those cities geographically and politically best positioned to benefit from open, free market trade, tourism grew rapidly (Hall & Page 2000). Functioning as gateways to a country, emergent EMRs became hubs of transport routes, accommodation facilities, retail districts and other leisure attractions. Equally importantly, they also attracted the regional and head offices of international hotel chains, airlines, travel agents and so forth. In this respect, tourism played an important role in the ever-increasing influence of EMRs within state programs of socio-economic development.

Crucially, and as both Hall & Page and Dixon & Smith point out, EMRs have been highly influential in not only driving the growth of their national economies, but also the region as a whole. In this respect, frequent references to such EMRs as 'hubs' or 'nodes' form part of their metaphorically flavored accounts of the region as a series of interconnected financial, political, commercial or cultural networks. Hall & Page (2000) also suggest the development of the region needs to be understood in sectoral terms, with attention given to specific patterns of investment and construction within certain highly integrated 'polynodal' industries, tourism being one such example (see O'Conner 1995, Low & Toh 1997). As way of reaffirming the validity of this approach, Page argues 'the evolution of gateways and hubs is increasingly being recognized as a powerful spatial entity [shaping] the regionalization of tourism patterns and activities within Southeast Asia' (2001: 85). In the context of Cambodia, there is little doubt that a recent growth in tourism has been heavily dependent upon a number of nearby EMRs boasting sophisticated and highly developed tourism infrastructures.

Today tourism represents one of the world's truly global industries. And like all other 'global' industries, its extremely elaborate and complex matrix of business enterprises are clustered and networked around particular geographies. With the head offices of multi-national corporations invariably remaining in the country of origin of the business, critical masses have formed in the major urban centers of source markets. Countless examples of vertical and horizontal integration, franchise arrangements, and cross-sector partnerships has meant that strategic planning now occurs through dialogues across offices located in London, New York, Prague, Cape Town or Tokyo. Operating as a set of multi-nodal networks, the tourism industry is also defined by certain regional configurations. Given that Southeast Asia has largely evolved as a destination for tourists from Europe, North America, and increasingly the rest of Asia, tour operators and travel agents from these source countries have either opened offices within the region or cultivated relationships with 'local' partners. For a number of obvious reasons, EMRs like Bangkok, Hong Kong, and Singapore have been at the forefront of the industry's ongoing evolution. Not only boasting extensive infrastructure facilities, these cities have served as key gateways for countries like Thailand,

Malaysia, China or Indonesia, enabling them to emerge as primary destinations and the hubs of any regional branding.[30] By definition a 'primary' country has a number of destinations to visit with the requisite transport and accommodation infrastructure to support multi-stop programs. To add value to these itineraries other 'highlights' are added – like Pagan, Angkor, or Vientiane – from the region's secondary countries.

Over the decades an imbalanced regional topography has therefore emerged with the smaller and less developed countries of Cambodia, Laos, and Burma often only visited as a short 'extension' to an itinerary built around one or two neighboring countries. As such, the nature of tourism within these countries is heavily shaped by decisions made in offices located in the region's EMRs. The geographical distribution of these offices has also played a significant role in shaping the flows of more independent travelers, including the well-established backpacker sector. Although seemingly more organic and chaotic, the routes of the non-package tour market have also been dependent upon particular networks of technologies, information, capital and knowledge: all elements which have been systematically captured and organized within countless volumes of *Lonely Planet* guides.

In summarizing the importance of EMRs to the development of tourism across the region as a whole, Page argues we need to understand the historical 'growth of a pattern of primary and secondary tourism destinations functionally related to the gateway hubs' (2001: 85). Page's suggested mode of analysis finds its ratification in the experiences of travel agents working to develop Cambodia's tourism industry:

> This office is directly responsible to our regional head office in Bangkok. All of our marketing is done from there too, we are marketed in Europe as one destination via our parent airline and hotel companies....so if I want to suggest a new itinerary for here it has to go back to Bangkok, possibly even France, to be considered for inclusion in next year's brochure.
>
> (Helene, Operations Director)

> There are strong contractual ties between our parent company in Bangkok and their wholesalers in Japan. Between them they will arrange the itineraries, sometimes the client will make special requests, they fax that through to us here and we arrange everything. But we can't make changes to the itineraries as we have to stick to these strong contractual ties.
>
> (Mr. Hayashi, Country Director)

Together these responses indicate how decisions over itineraries within Cambodia are made from outside the country. A key component to this process is the contractual agreements tour operators need to establish with the major airlines and hotel chains operating in the region. Throughout the 1990s Bangkok main-tained a position of monopoly over air travel both in and out of Cambodia. Long before then the city's Don Muang airport had established itself as an important hub for connecting flights into, and around, Southeast Asia; on the back of which the country's national carrier, Thai Airways, created its extensive port-folio of long- and short-haul flights. Most importantly though, within the 'Open Skies' policy of 1997 a monopoly over the Siem Reap, Bangkok route had been granted to a subsidiary of Thai, Bangkok Air. Enjoying price controls over the route, the airline also secured the lion's share of an ever-increasing flow of traf-fic into Cambodia. By 2000, 80 percent of all tourists arriving in Siem Reap traveled by air, with 46 percent of these flying direct with the airline from Bangkok. Of the 44 percent traveling up from Phnom Penh, more than two-thirds also entered the country from Bangkok. The remaining 10 percent of air travelers to Siem Reap flew from Ho Chi Minh in Vietnam and other regional airports.[31]

These statistics reflect three key regional dynamics. First, the pre-eminent posi-tion the city of Bangkok enjoyed within mainland Southeast Asian tourism at that time.[32] Second, the emergence of Angkor as an 'extension' within itineraries primarily focusing on nearby Thailand, Malaysia or Vietnam: an issue explored in greater detail in the following chapter. Third, the dominant position Bangkok airport secured over the 'short-break', intra-regional market. In recent years the city has developed an extensive leisure infrastructure of shops, hotels and enter-tainment for visitors from Northeast Asia. A one-night stop in Bangkok ideally complements a short-break 'cultural adventure' to the ruins of Angkor.[33]

Throughout the 1990s Thailand also retained a high level of control over Cambodian air space and regulated many of the tariffs, flight schedules, and landing fees for the airports in Phnom Penh and Siem Reap.[34] The commanding position of the Thai airline industry over Angkor and Cambodia was also apparent in a long-running advertising campaign which promoted the national carrier as the 'only airline in tune with the rhythms of Indochina'. One advert, presented in Figure 4.1, depicted the towers of Angkor Wat floating in the clouds, and thus de-territorialized, surrounded by the now familiar signifiers of Thai culture. The juxtaposition of Angkor against the purple silks, costumes and musical instru-ments of Thailand is an example of how 'state borders have been permeated and territories recombined and reconstituted in new ways' by the tourism industries of Cambodia's more powerful neighbors (Forbes 1999: 2).

For those tour operators looking to offer their clients a variety of transport modes, regional imbalances in airport and airline facilities have their parallel on both land and sea. Southeast Asia's well-established cruise ship industry, for example, is reliant upon a series of deep water ports to create its pan-regional tours. Attempts to incorporate Cambodia within such programs have been inhibited by the inadequate facilities along the country's southern coastline. To offer clients a visit to Angkor, one of Southeast Asia's 'cultural highlights' for this industry, operators have had to continue using ports in neighboring countries as points of disembarkation; a situation explained by David, an agent based in Phnom Penh:

> We have a cruise ship market, but using Sihanoukville is virtually impossible, the port is not deep enough for our boats, the lighting is inadequate and the

Figure 4.1 Advertisement for Thai Air. (With the Permission of Thai Airways International.)

airport strip is just too small for the passenger planes we need to get them up to Siem Reap. We therefore dock the boat in Saigon, stay there for a few days and then fly them directly in and out of Siem Reap.

(David, Operations Manager)

As we can see, much of Cambodia's dependency on its regional neighbors has arisen from the inadequacies in its own transport infrastructure. Decades of inadequate investment has meant the country's key ports of entry have been unable to meet the demands of a late twentieth-century tourism industry. An inability to receive cruise liners or long-haul aircraft are just two examples of why the country has been heavily dependent on the infrastructures of neighboring countries. In an effort to address this problem Phnom Penh's Pochentong airport underwent a major expansion program in 2000. Less apparent though has been the development of a social and business infrastructure within Cambodia capable of wresting control from corporations located in EMRs across the region. Indeed, industry observers have consistently expressed skepticism towards Cambodia's chances of overcoming the political barriers which are currently preventing direct flights from Europe or North America. In the meantime, the government has looked to develop its inbound tourism industry by strengthening the country's position within the intra-regional market. The steady growth of direct flights from Hong Kong, Singapore, and Vientiane from the late 1990s onwards would contribute to the loosening of Bangkok's monopoly. It would also mark the beginnings of a long-term shift towards an industry dominated by tourists 'of Asian origin'; an issue that, in itself, will demand a reexamination of Angkorean tourism at some point in the future. Nonetheless, regardless of how Cambodia's portfolio of long- and short-haul source markets continues to shift, there is little doubt the country will follow a pattern of dependency predicted by Page in 2001:

Within Southeast Asia hubs such as Singapore will certainly be influential in shaping future patterns of regional tourism as countries in the region align themselves with regional hubs and gateways that perform a range of tourism functions at different spatial scales.

(2001: 96–7)

To compliment the earlier account of policy frameworks of cultural tourism and sustainable development, which, as we have seen, have conceived Angkor as a static physically bounded *touristscape*, the final part of this chapter has drawn upon Appadurai's idea of 'scapes' to examine the site's national and regional environments as a geography of *touristscapes*. Adopting such an approach has revealed how Angkor's development has been shaped by a combination of under-developed tourism networks at the national level and a multi-polar, region-wide infrastructure of human, technological, political, and financial flows. The geographic distribution of these *touristscapes*, at once both reflecting and reaffirming the imbalanced nature of the region, has been instrumental to the isolation of Angkor, Siem Reap as an island of tourism development. Instead of a geographically dispersed tourism industry emerging, a host of factors have contrived to create a situation of immense disparities in wealth and development across the country. Reabsorbed within a regional tourism industry, Angkor has become Cambodia's sole node within a networked industry of transnational travel.

5   Angkor in the frame

So far the evolution of Angkor as a site of tourism performance has been discussed in relation to broader political and economic processes, infrastructure resources or policy developments. Up until this point we have yet to hear the voice of the tourist. The following two chapters fill this void by addressing Angkor as a site of consumption. Divided into two parts, international and domestic, this chapter weaves together cultural artifacts – spanning airline adverts to guidebooks, paintings to themed hotels – with the narratives and practices of visitors to reveal how distinct, and politically charged, formations of an Angkorean culture, landscape, and history circulate within the context of tourism today.

The chapter opens with 'The Eighth Wonder of the World' exploring the relationship between a vision of an 'ancient' Angkor and its representation as a World Heritage Site. It is argued that the tourism industry principally presents Angkor as the legacy of a classical civilization, and that such a vision reinforces, and is reinforced by, the site's recent designation as world heritage. Through an examination of 'world heritage tours' it is also suggested that a new cultural topography has been inscribed through Angkor's inclusion in itineraries traversing the 'cultural highlights' of Southeast Asia. The idea of Angkor as a classical civilization has also been accompanied by a second, equally dominant, framing: that of the ruin. In 'The Mother of All Lost Cities' representations and narratives of Angkor as a set of 'romantic' ruins reclaimed from the jungle are discussed. In addition to once again tracing the lineage of such a construction back to the colonial framings outlined earlier, it will be seen that Angkor, as ruin, serves as a metonym of nostalgia for a bygone and romanticized Indochina.

The final section examining non-Cambodian tourists, entitled 'I Survived Cambodia', turns to imaginings and representations of the country as a whole. It will be seen that the overwhelming image of Cambodia presented in guidebooks, travel literature and by tourists themselves is one of danger, landmines, and political turmoil. This is an image that both repels and attracts. For some it is just another 'war-torn, dusty Asian country' that holds little interest; for others it is a luring frontier of discovery, risk, and danger tourism. Either way, tourists struggle to connect a glorious and ancient Angkor with a war-torn and contemporary Cambodia. Continually pulling in the analysis of the previous chapter, these three sections illustrate how Angkor has been transformed into a spatial and cultural enclave within a context of international tourism; a landscape socio-historically disembedded from its Cambodian context.

In turning to examine domestic tourism, 'I Was Told It Was Khmai Heritage, Our Very Old Heritage' explores the prevailing framings and narratives which define an encounter for Cambodians today. In contrast to international tourists, domestic visitors firmly root Angkor in its national context, and regard the site as a powerful focal point for an 'imagined community' articulated in ethnic, cultural, and national terms. Once again, the strong continuities between this contemporary framing and earlier colonial constructions are noted here. The final section 'Angkor Gives Strength to the People' considers the annual festival of Khmer New Year. It will be seen that the festival involves a highly variegated form of spatial consumption, whereby roads, rivers, reservoirs, and pagodas located within the park take on immense symbolic value for a population recovering from decades of national turmoil. An analysis of Khmer New Year vividly illustrates how domestic consumption practices are imbued with a strong sense of a Cambodian nation and Khmer cultural history in recovery.

Part one: international tourism

The Eighth Wonder of the World[1]

> Masa (*24, Japanese, Backpacking round Southeast Asia for 3 months, 1 week in Cambodia*): I came to Cambodia to see Angkor Wat.
> Author: Why, when did you first hear about Angkor Wat?
> Masa: Four days ago. What's the date today? Is it the 19th? I wanted to come because I knew it was world heritage. Although I had an image of Cambodia as a dangerous country, I had no special image of Angkor apart from that it was world heritage.

In Chapter 1 it was noted that in recent years significant attention has been given to the role of heritage tourism as a mediator of a global citizenship forged around declarations of a global inheritance (Urry 1995, Meethan 2001). As Graham et al. state:

> It can be argued that the inexorable growth of foreign tourism, and the importance of culture, heritage and art to that industry, is the most powerful expression of the existence of a common global heritage as the property of all peoples. Every international tourist is asserting the existence of a world heritage and the right of a global accessibility to it.

> (2000: 238)

The authors' assertions can claim their greatest authority in the context of UNESCO world heritage listing. In the case of Angkor, there is little doubt its designation as a World Heritage Site in 1992 helped forge a touristic narrative oriented around ideas of a common/universal sovereignty:

> Yukio (*50s, Japanese, businessman in Thailand and Cambodia for four days*): In Japan Angkor Wat is famous as world heritage, so we wanted to come here. I think it is important to have visitors from the world and have it protected by the world. It is a treasure for Cambodia but most importantly a world treasure. I think it is important to protect Angkor by collecting funds from the world.

> Franca (*60s, Italian, retired Doctor traveling Southeast Asia for two months*): I did not particularly want to go to Cambodia as it is a dangerous country but I did want to see Angkor Wat. Before I came here I only really knew it was a World Heritage Site, but that was why I wanted to come, to see something that belongs to the world. I have many video tapes about World Heritage Sites, and I watched the one on Angkor before I came here.

Even for those visitors unaware of the legislative and institutional frameworks initiated by bodies like UNESCO, International Council of Monuments and Sites (ICOMOS) or the World Monuments Fund (WMF), Angkor commonly yields an aura as one of humankind's most illustrious achievements. Interestingly, with the normalization of such ideas, ambiguities and confusion in genealogy now occur:

> Pam (*27, English, currently living in Singapore, direct flight to Siem Reap, staying 3 days*): I didn't realize Angkor was in Cambodia … I was coming to see Angkor Wat. Angkor Wat is one of the seven wonders of the world isn't it, isn't it?
> Author: Do you think it is?
> Martin (*29, English, partner of Pam*): If I was asked to name the seven wonders the world, I would put Angkor Wat in it. I cannot name the seven wonders of the world but if I was guessing I would put it there.
> Pam: Many countries that have something ancient describe them as the eighth wonder of the world, I don't know whether Angkor is an eighth wonder.
> Martin: I'm sure I have seen in the same sentence Angkor and the seven wonders of the world.

Similarly, in trying to recall the first time he heard of Angkor, Barry states:

> Barry (*33, Australian, visiting Southeast Asia for 1 month*): I can't remember exactly, but I remember hearing about Angkor through my dad, he used to talk about the seven wonders of the world, neat things like that. He used to like telling stories, it was a mystical far off land, some sort of monument lost in history, giant blocks of stone made to resemble mountains, one of life's wonders.

Implicitly accompanying the confusion and awe expressed by Pam, Martin and Barry here are feelings of intrigue and historical mystery. For these visitors, along with many others, the 'seduction of place' is an emotional one, arising from a dearth of factual knowledge. Indeed, it is this very absence which constitutes an aura, and the signifier of an illustrious, but long perished history:

> Mariana (*30, Spanish, living in Singapore, in Cambodia for 3 days*): I imagine Angkor as ruins, Asian ruins, not like European churches, these are very grand, ancient Asian ruins of Buddhism, Hinduism, Taoism. From what you read and hear though you don't really get an idea of how people lived at all, only a little bit really, but not much. That's fascinating, there is so much missing, so much mythology.

> Rad (*37, Australian, living in Singapore, in Cambodia for 3 days*): You hear about these world heritage sites so much now, lots of television programs. We know people that even tick them off as they visit them one by one. Angkor is always on the Discovery Channel in Singapore. They present it as just ancient, mystical, enigmatic, all those things, that's why we wanted to come.

> Yukio (*50, Japanese on 3 day tour to Bangkok and Siem Reap*): In Thailand all the temples are shiny and beautiful, but here they are ancient. Thailand has Sukothai and Ayutthia but they do not feel so ancient as Angkor, they do not have the same feel.

Together the various accounts above resonate with Appadurai's observation that 'there is no simple correlation between place and culture' (cited in Meethan 2001: 120). They also reveal the enduring presence of a colonial vision of Angkor as glorious monumental antiquities and sublime artistry. To explore the implications of such processes further it is helpful to situate these narratives within certain regional industry dynamics identified in the previous chapter. For example, one of the defining features of Southeast Asia's ongoing expansion as a tourist destination has been the emergence of itineraries thematically constructed around visits to major heritage sites across the region. For many tour operators and travel agents pan-regional heritage tours have been adopted as one way of securing market position in a highly competitive industry.

8 Day Mekong World Heritage Tour
Starting from Bangkok, the City of Angels, travel to Sukhothai, 'the Rising of Happiness' and the capital of Thailand's first kingdom, dating back to the mid-13th century. Visit the famous historical ruins, parks, museums and the many surrounding temples. The Kingdom of Sukhothai is viewed as the "Golden Age of Thai Civilization", and the religious art and architecture of the era are considered to be the pinnacle of classical Thai style.

Next to Luang Prabang, to explore the ancient capital of the Lan Xang Kingdom. Visit the masterpiece of Lao architecture Wat Xieng Thong, the former Royal Palace, now the National Museum. Take a traditional boat trip along the Mekong River and visit the famous Pak Ou Cave with several thousands of Buddha images, stopping in a local village to experience the local life.

Fly to Danang and proceed to the charming historic city of Hoi An - 32 kilometers away on the banks of the Thu Bon River. Known to early Western traders as one of the major trading centers of Southeast Asia in the 16th Century and recognized by UNESCO as a World Heritage Site in 1999. Hoi An has a distinctive Chinese atmosphere with low, tile-roof houses and narrow streets. During a leisurely discovery tour on foot, visit some of the historic merchant and community houses, places of worship and famous bridges.

Transfer to Hue' across Hai Van Pass, 132 kilometers to the north. Enjoy a sightseeing tour on your own cyclo, visit the imperial city, take a boat trip on the Perfume River to see the Thien Mu Pagoda, one of the oldest religious architectural structures in Hue and then travel by car to visit the magnificent tombs of the emperors.

Finally, fly to Siem Reap to experience Angkor Wat, one of the Seven Wonders of the World, and also declared as a UNESCO World Heritage Site in 1992. Pass through the South Gate to discover Angkor Thom, the fortified Royal City, with the Bayon, the Royal Enclosure, Phimeanakas, the Elephant Terrace and other exquisite temples. Visit the floating village and enjoy a boat trip on the Tonle Sap.

(Diethelm Travel 2002)

Aimed at the mid-range European and North American markets, the program outlined above provides one such example of this popular sector. As the tour operator's Phnom Penh-based representative explained:

The idea of heritage tours, world heritage tours has become very successful for us. There is a particular market, especially in the US, for trips around Southeast Asia, visiting all the premier sites. Themed holidays like this are one of the best ways of adding value to our product. Most of our clients want to see at least one or two world heritage sites whilst they are in Southeast Asia.

The program seamlessly integrates Chinese trading houses located along Vietnam's coast, Thai and Laotian Buddhist structures, with early Khmer monumental architecture – once again identified as one of the seven wonders of the world – within a single, all-encompassing, narrative. It is a marketing model which finds its audience in clients like Bob and Alison, both of whom chose the above itinerary for their tour of the region:

Bob (*66, American*): We really wanted to come to see the cultural highlights of Southeast Asia. We've just come from Sukothai which was just great, but

I really wanted to see Angkor Wat … but on a trip like this it's all great, just fascinating to see so many historical monuments.

Alison (*47, Austrian*): For my husband and I the ideal holiday is one that takes us to many historical places. The world is changing so fast you know. We feel it is important to see these heritage places, where the ancient past is being preserved. We took this trip because it allows us to see the World Heritage Sites we wanted to see. If we see a beach then great, but our priority is places like Angkor and Hoi An.

Naturally, to offer such 'world heritage' programs tour operators are dependent upon a region-wide infrastructure of local partners and the requisite accommodation, transport and entertainment facilities. In a move to consolidate key aspects of this infrastructure, a joint venture was established between Bangkok Airways, the Tourism Authority of Thailand, and three commercially run tour operators. Launched in the late 1990s, the similarly named 'Mekong World Heritage Tour Project' promised clients four UNESCO World Heritage Sites in a single trip.[2] In summarizing why Bangkok Airways decided to participate in the scheme the president of the airline stated:

The idea of introducing Mekong World Heritage Tour Project is to promote cultural tourism by drawing tourists from all over the world to the historical sites in the Mekong Region. Our flights will create a direct connection from each of these destinations and will facilitate more convenient and faster traveling time to the tourist.[3]

Figure 5.1 illustrates how the project's promotional material delivers a cultural topography of a transnational Asian heritage centered around the banks of the Mekong River. Utilizing an integrated tourism infrastructure capable of sweeping tourists around the region in a number of days, the project is a vivid example of how the tourism industry can de-territorialize locations, whereby certain historical, religious and other contextual references are simultaneously erased and invoked:

Michèle (*45, French, 11 day group tour to Vietnam with 3 day extension in Siem Reap*): At Hué they have put these big red flags up to celebrate communism, it is really horrible. I can't believe that is allowed. It's been classified as a World Heritage Site by UNESCO and they put these flags up, it really is unbelievable, I'm glad there is nothing like that here [Angkor].

World heritage tourism is dependent upon both proximity and distance. A commonly shared heritage suggests propinquity and affinity. Yet for that to be realized, 'wonders of the world' need to be temporally distant. Awe increases proportionately with historical magnitude, particularly where latent ruins signify the inevitability of civilizational decline. As fragile remnants of ancient, and now lost and dead cultures, sites like Angkor are transformed into global property.

Figure 5.1 Advertisement for Mekong World Heritage Tour. (With the Permission of Bangkok Airways Co., Ltd.)

To facilitate this process it has been suggested that a discourse of heritage tourism, and in particular world heritage tourism, re-solidifies the former colonial construction of Angkor as the glorious edifice of ancient times. In its majestic monumentality, and as a place of fantasies, Angkor is raised to the sublime, and as such, stands bereft of all its historical ties. A decade of tourism has placed Angkor on the pedestal of mankind. As the site has secured its position as a node within a regional network of heritage tourism spectacles, the colonial vision of famed antiquities is firmly re-inscribed, yet clipped of its nationalistic sentiments. Exactly a century after the temples began their path towards national iconography they have entered a new topography of supra-national, come global, culture. The analysis of domestic tourism presented later in this chapter reveals, however, that this process of symbolic migration is far from complete, and that for Cambodian tourists Angkor's potency as national landmark has only become further reinforced by the traumatic events of recent decades.

As international tourists embark on their 'cultural adventures', 'discover[ing] the intriguing remnants of Southeast Asia's glorious past and ... architectural masterpieces that have withstood ravages of countless centuries'[4] many of the specificities of each site's immediate locality are dissolved. The various itineraries highlighted here, along with many others, typically allocate between one and three days in Cambodia. Flying directly in and out of Siem Reap, tourists are shuttled around Angkor by air conditioned bus, with excursions rarely venturing beyond the obligatory 'local' restaurant or souvenir shop. More specifically, in ignoring the other features of the landscape, tours of the Angkor site are wholly focused on visiting the key temple complexes. Marked out as the synecdoche of an Angkorean civilization and landscape by guides and guidebooks alike, Angkor Wat, Bayon, Preah Khan, Ta Prohm and Banteay Srei are the only stopping points for buses and taxis traveling to and fro from Siem Reap. Angkor's local population are merely passed by and gazed upon from behind glass in air conditioned comfort. It is a form of consumption which gives the visitor little opportunity to challenge the narrative of guidebooks and airline magazines which consistently state these communities have changed little over the last thousand years or so. Presented and consumed as such, Angkor remains mute, a de-humanized landscape, supposedly untouched by the passage of time. As we shall see shortly, with Angkor presented as part of broader, regional geographies, the consumption 'of space as culture' (Meethan 2001: 114) means visitors make few, if any, associations between the site and its local or national context.

The mother of all lost cities

Accessible Angkor

People have been coming and going through Angkor since the 9th Century AD. The stunning, sprawling architecture was built over a period of several hundred years until it was abandoned as the capital of the Khmer empire in 1430s due to economically draining wars.

Since its 'rediscovery' by the western world, anyway – in the middle of the 19th Century, outside interest in the elaborate and sophisticated stonemasonry has grown, until today it is the architectural wonders of the world protected and supported by the United Nations.

Reaching the Angkor complex is no longer as it was when French explorers came across it in the 1860s covered in dense forest. Bangkok Airways flies to nearby Siem Reap a number of times daily, and the town has a growing range of comfortable accommodation.

(Bangkok Airways 2004)

Over recent decades tourism has emerged as a medium through which nostalgia for a bygone era of European exploration and imperial conquest has been channeled. Indeed, as Sofield suggests, against a backdrop of a demise in European power '"nostalgia" is a western concept out of which major tourism markets have been developed' (2001: 110). In pursuing such a theme here, my intention is to illustrate the processes by which a 'colonial nostalgia [is] materialized and made visible' (Gregory 2001: 114) across Southeast Asia through a particular mode of tourism which draws upon a series of tangible and intangible markers of a history of European influence. Like numerous former European territories – including India and Egypt, as demonstrated by Edensor and Gregory, respectively – tourism in Southeast Asia today 'serves as a theatre in which Orientalist fantasies are articulated' (Edensor 1998: 75). As we shall see, the emergence of Angkor as a major destination has been no exception; themed cafes, antique Citroën cars, luxurious hotels and the diaries of nineteenth-century travelers have all become part of the tourism matrix surrounding the site.

For those tourists seeking 'the grandeur and comfort of a golden age' the London-based 'Legends of Indochina' offers a tour that 'retraces the footsteps' of an early English traveler, Alice Beaumont. Their programs explicitly attempt to reenact Alice's 'Grand-Tour of Indochina' of 1902.[5] As their promotional brochure states:

Legends of Indochina is an elite collections of Southeast Asia's finest travel experiences, offering today's visitors all the magic and excitement that has lured travelers to the East for centuries past. By joining together to offer unique travel programmes the de luxe hotels, trains and cruise ships detailed below offer contemporary voyagers an unparalleled opportunity to enjoy their own Grand Tour of the region. Seamless itineraries matched with outstanding hospitality and service smooth travelers through Indochina's most magnificent scenery and sights.

(Yogerst 2001: 20)

By imbuing late nineteenth-century European travel with motifs of indulgence, luxury and excitement a narrative reminiscent of the 'invented tradition' of the grand tour begins to unfold. The need to simultaneously combine luxury and convenience with a sense of adventure and exploration means routes are oriented around stays in a number of colonial era hotels, all of which are reached by regional flights or 'nostalgic journeys' by river boat or train. Itineraries thus interweave late twentieth-century transport facilities – such as the aerial hubs of Bangkok and Singapore – with a 'restored' infrastructure more akin to nineteenth-century travel. Although this combination of modern and period facilities render comparisons and ideas of 're-enactments' superficial at best, such concerns are relegated to the margins of a text essentially constructed for the purposes of marketing:

> Thanks to some clever renovation in the 1990s, I'm able to sleep in the same room as Aunt Alice stayed a century ago, a fabulous place called the Strand where the past lingers beneath potted palms and gently twirling fans. The Union Jack no longer flutters above this intensely tropical city. The empire that ruled a quarter of the planet just a century ago is now ancient history.

> Yet some things never change, as I discover a few days later on a cruise ship down the Ayeyarwady. Our vessel is modern enough, an elegant ship called the Road to Mandalay that has all the creature comforts that you could ever want – from air conditioned state rooms and gourmet dining to lavish teak panelling and swimming pool. But all along the river time stands still, a tableau of rural life unchanged for centuries.

> (ibid: 4)

In addition to emphasizing the transport and accommodation facilities of the early twentieth century, the brochure's map juxtaposes the national boundaries of a post-independent Southeast Asia with a pre-second world war cartographic representation of India and China to cement an imagined geography of the entire region as *Indochina*. In so doing, the map erases numerous political, geographic and historical particularities in favor of a transnational patina of orientalist fantasies.

Although clearly aimed at the high end American and European markets, 'Legends of Indochina' forms part of a broad landscape of tour operators all drawing upon a discourse of nostalgia to lure tourists to, and around, the region. As a first-time visitor to the region, Louise explained why she chose the 'Trail of Indochina' itinerary outlined below:

> Louise (*39, Australian, 14 day tour of Vietnam, Laos and Cambodia*): Before I came I imagined these countries as mystical, romantic. I had this French colonial image in my mind, so this tour appealed to me. Instead of just being shuttled around on a bus from sight to sight I wanted to see how the French lived here, what they built, the richness of the landscape, that's how I knew this area before I came.

Trail of Indochina

14 Days/13 Nights: Siem Reap - Phnom Penh - Ho Chi Minh City – Danang –
Hoi An - Hanoi - Vientiane - Luang Prabang

Recapture the nostalgia of French Indochina on this comprehensive programme visiting Cambodia, Vietnam and Laos. The tour begins with a visit
to one of the world's best preserved architectural wonder - the grand temple
complex of Angkor in Cambodia, where three days are spent exploring its
extensive ruins and admiring its intricate bas-relief. Continue to vibrant
Ho Chi Minh City where tradition and modernisation fuse to create the
dynamic atmosphere of this former headquarters of the L'Indochine Empire.
Proceeding north along the coastline, visit the quaint fishing village of Hoi
An, former imperial capital of Hue and historic Danang before visiting the
capital city of Hanoi, characterised by elegant colonial architecture and traditional charm. Complete this grand Indochina tour with a visit to sleepy
Laos and enjoy its small-town atmosphere and hospitality while exploring its rich cultural heritage in Vientiane and the former royal kingdom of
Luang Prabang.

(Trail of Indochina 2002)

As with the above 'Legends of Indochina' program, distinctions between historical
eras, indigenous and colonial architectures or national territories are all blurred
within a framework of intraregional and thematically presented tourism. References to destinations such as Laos and Hoi An as either 'sleepy' or 'quaint' and
colonial architecture as 'elegant', point towards the reaffirmation of a 'phantasmatic Indochine' (Norindr 1996). The following description presented in the travel
section of the New York Times in July 2002 illustrates how these same allusions
to sleepiness and decay also frame Angkor:

Some people are suckers for lost cities. I am. I've sought out, among others,
Machu Picchu, Pompeii, Petra, Ephesus, Karnak and Uxmal. But Angkor,
the jungle-covered capital of the ancient Khmer civilization in Cambodia,
has always seemed to me the Mother of All Lost Cities ... the romance of its
'discovery' and exploration by the French in the mid-19th Century was part of
Angkor's glamour ... Sometimes I just sat trying to contemplate cosmology
and civilization, or trying to pretend I was Henri Mouhot, who came upon the
ruins in 1861.

(Rose 2002)

Not surprisingly, within a cultural economy of international tourism these themes
are continually embellished, re-contextualized, and commodified for touristic
consumption. Indeed, in certain instances the travel industry constructs a narrative of Angkor using cultural references which have absolutely no connection

to the site itself. For example, as an internationally familiar icon of danger and archaeological intrigue, Indiana Jones has become an indicator of what a trip to Angkor today might entail:

> Henri Mahout's [sic] 'discovery' of the Angkor temples in 1860 opened up this lost city to the outside world. At its zenith, Angkor Wat spread over 256 sq km ... While you don't need Indiana Jones' whip, pistol and fedora to visit Angkor, the swashbuckling archaeologist's spirit of adventure will come in handy. With more than 1000 archaeological sites scattered across 200 sq km of lush Cambodian jungle, Angkor is a beacon to global explorers.
>
> (Wong 2001: 83)

A defining thread running through the two descriptions above is the idea that Angkor remained buried in the jungle awaiting 're-discovery' by French explorers. In a similar vein, the popular guidebook by Dawn Rooney focuses purely on recounting the 'numerous firsthand accounts written by explorers to Angkor in the last half of the nineteenth century and early western travelers from the beginning of the twentieth century onwards' (2001: 14).[6] Entitled *Angkor Observed* the book utilizes numerous quotes from the diaries of travelers, along with hand-drawn sketches of Angkor to present a narrative of exploration, discovery, and awe. Eschewing lengthy descriptions of temple architecture or sculpture, the author frames the site as a series of labyrinthine ruins, engulfed by thick tropical forest. With its focus upon centuries of dormancy and a nineteenth-century moment of awakening, the book conceives Angkor as a landscape 'heavy with time' (Urry 1995). As we shall see in the following chapter, further layers of temporality are added through accounts of Angkor's two 'partial ruins', Ta Prohm and Preah Khan, which together directly connect the reader, come visitor, with histories of loss and re-discovery. In the mean time, the following interview excerpts begin to illustrate how the guidebook forms part of a widely circulated account of Angkorean history oriented around loss and re-discovery:

> Akiko (*40s, Japanese, in Thailand and Cambodia for 3 days*): I knew Angkor was buried by the jungle, and that it was discovered by explorers. I saw a video of how it was lost to the jungle ... I am expecting we will have to travel through the thick jungle on the bus.

> Jean Luc (*45, French, living in Singapore, Siem Reap for 3 days*): I am expecting a lot of damage, beheaded torsos for example. Lots of vegetation, jungle, things like that, because of the books I was reading, you know the famous 'fromagie' on the temples ... the iconic image of Angkor for me is very much the large Buddha heads imprisoned by the roots, well it has been depicted so many times in the books like that, that is what I am expecting.

> Jennifer (*64, American, on 7 day tour of Thailand and Cambodia*): For me Angkor is all ruins and the world's largest monastery, but I hope we can see

them, are they not all covered up in vines? I hope you can see something and that it's not all covered in vines. I hope we can see the buildings.

Rad (*37, Australian, living in Singapore, in Cambodia for 3 days*): I once saw a documentary about Hue in Vietnam and how the city was lost in the jungle. It was about these roots growing through things, I don't remember a lot else. First time I was in Thailand I went to Ayutthia and sort of thought I was going to Angkor, but I was really disappointed as it wasn't lost in the jungle.

Far from merely shaping the text of guidebooks, this idea of Angkor as a ruin is also transmitted into the contemporary via a range of tourism-related cultural artifacts. Late nineteenth-century engravings are reprinted as postcards; battered suitcases have become the *objet d'art* of hotels; and the costumes of empire are now the uniforms of service staff. At the heart of this historical transmission is romance. The figure of André Malraux – despite being arrested for looting one of Angkor's temples in 1923 – provides the theme for numerous hotel suites by personifying a golden age of luxury travel. The romance and nostalgia for an *Indochine* of the past being channeled through Angkor today has perhaps reached a zenith of simulacra in various new luxury hotels in Siem Reap. One in particular, the Victoria Angkor Hotel, has been extensively decorated with antique inkstands, photographs, binoculars and other artifacts in an attempt to evoke a romanticized vision of the 'Far East'. In describing the concept, the hotel manager explained: 'we wanted people who would walk in to feel as if this was not a hotel, but one of those grand Indochina homes from the 1930s, whose owner had traveled through Asia and collected objects'.[7] Pivotal to the hotel's concept is the idea of temples hidden in the jungle. In addition to a suite named after Angkor's iconic partial ruin, Ta Prohm, the hotel is lined with paintings of jungle-ridden, overgrown architecture.

Constructed from the ground up at the beginning of the twenty-first century the hotel stands next to the Grand Hotel d'Angkor, which originally opened its doors in 1929. After a major renovation by Raffles Hotels and Resorts, the Grand Hotel d'Angkor now offers its guests the opportunity to stay in a suite bearing the name of 'Henri Mouhot, Louis Delaporte, John Thompson or Henri Marchal', all rooms which have 'pictures of twelfth century Cambodia, they're called windows'.[8] Guests are even encouraged to travel back in time in their dreams by reading one of the hotel's 'Fables of the Exotic East'. Presented at bedtime each evening, 'these short and interesting stories are individually selected from the nineteenth and twentieth century travel journals and provide readers with unusual insight into "the golden age of travel" and the destination in which they are staying'.[9]

Together these two luxurious hotels are the most definitive statements of a tourism landscape which has re-inserted Angkor as a metonym of a romanticized and highly aestheticised *Indochine*. The term 're-insertion' here alludes to the strong coherence which we can once again see between such contemporary framings and the colonial discourse outlined in Chapter 2. Indeed, once again, with its post-grandeur history dehumanized and eclipsed, Angkor lies dormant, a silent relic enshrouded by vines and the roots of trees.

I survived Cambodia

> Lee (*27, British, traveling for one year on 'world' ticket, traveled from Bangkok by bus*): well I would like to know much more about Cambodia as a nation. We don't know enough about the Khmer Rouge and the killing fields. Cambodian history is modern history. This is a young country.

> George (*75, American, trip to Thailand and Cambodia for 7 days*): I had the feeling that the Government would be watching you, you had to stay on the paths, that you couldn't linger anywhere. I think that was from American TV. They're probably just left over ideas of communism, that kind of thing. It surprises me there is no kind of military oppression.

In turning to consider the ways in which Cambodia has been framed as a tourist destination for foreign visitors, a number of recurring themes are apparent. In broadest terms, the responses from Lee and George illustrate how Cambodia has primarily come to be seen as a 'modern country', one that has been ravaged by war and political turmoil. For many, Cambodia lies somewhere in the midst of a Southeast Asia, come Indochina; a country covered by dense tropical jungle. With its roots in colonial era diaries and literature, this image of the region came into sharpest focus via the countless documentaries, news programs, and Hollywood films produced on the Vietnam, America war; an era that would render the jungle synonymous with hand-to-hand combat and geo-political standoffs:

> Val (*50s, American, Thailand and Cambodia for 3 weeks*): as we were flying in I expected to see much more jungle out of the plane window. Thick jungle. I guess I imagined it that way from all the Vietnam war films you see. I imagined all of this region to be like that, it's known as a place of guerrilla, jungle warfare.

> Barry (*33, Australian, visiting Southeast Asia for 1 month*): I had the idea that the whole of Southeast Asia was dense jungle, Thailand, Cambodia and Vietnam, and that would be from movies, *Apocalypse Now*, *Predator*, from Vietnam war and other jungle type movies. With things, ruins, out there to really explore you know.

In the case of Cambodia, the darkness of the jungle also acts as an ocular metaphor for a lingering ambiguity and confusion over the country's role in the war, and, for that matter, the subsequent rise of an 'inexplicable' Khmer Rouge regime. When combined with the infamous topography of the Cambodian 'killing fields', accounts of urban evacuations and country-wide guerrilla warfare, it can be seen that a popular memory of this period has solidified around a vision of a wild and hostile landscape:

Natalie (*55, Italian, Traveling Thailand, Laos and Cambodia for 2 months*): When I said in Italy that I go to Cambodia people say 'ah ... be careful the Khmer Rouge are still waiting there in the jungle ... there are bombs everywhere', we were told this by all our friends.

Hideo (*40s, Japanese, 3 day trip to Cambodia via Bangkok*): Yes, Cambodia is a place of mines, thick forest with malaria, dengue fever, the Khmer Rouge, it is not a place to bring tourists.

Val (*50s American, in Thailand and Cambodia for 3 week holiday*): When I saw the film the killing fields, that created a lot of interest in this country and in what humanity can produce. It also raised our complicity in the political process. There is certainly a lot of culpability on the part of the American government for messing up the whole of Indochina. A lot of American people who grew up in the sixties have a sense of regret towards this area, we protested against the government to stop these things but we still feel some responsibility ... I now know we were right to try and get the American troops out of this region, even though we didn't know why. I think the killing fields was our fault in a large part. I don't think Pol Pot did what he did by himself, and you can still feel that past here today.

Crucially, such perceptions have been instrumental in defining particular patterns of consumption, with many visitors restricting their trip to a guided tour of the Angkor park. Indeed, the image of Cambodia as a dangerous and hostile place has contributed to the popularity of 'short-break' trips from hubs like Singapore or the one- or two-day 'extension' packages within tour programs to neighboring Vietnam or Thailand:

Alex (*32, German, living in Singapore, in Cambodia for 3 days*): Cambodia's dangerous, for sure. We heard even around Angkor it's not safe, landmines, old Khmer Rouge cronies. We were recommended by friends, that to be safe, take a guide, see the temples and get the hell out of there. So that's what we're doing.

Neal (*45, American, Trip to Thailand and Angkor, in Cambodia for 2 days*): Phnom Penh? Why would I want to go there, it's just some dirty, corrupt, Asian city ... and with everything you know about Cambodia, no I just came here to see Angkor and then get out.

Ming (*44, Chinese, in Cambodia for 3 days*): we know Cambodia is still dangerous, it has that reputation. I come here with my wife and she was afraid to stay here. We wanted to visit Bangkok and then just see

Angkor as it was close. It's always on the television in China, but after that we leave.

Similarly, in response to the fears expressed by previous clients, one Japanese tour operator remarked, 'We are told by our head office not to promote Cambodia. Cambodia is a dirty word, so we sell trips to Vietnam, Thailand, with excursions to Angkor'.

One of the themes running through a number of the above tourist responses is a fear of unexploded ordinance. Since the early 1990s an omnipresent feature of all guidebooks on Cambodia has been a 'Warning, Landmines!' section. Although the text of these sections is tempered with each new edition as more sites are cleared, readers are commonly advised to 'not stray from well-marked paths under any circumstances' (Robinson & Wheeler 1992: 47). Not surprisingly, the very real danger presented by unexploded ordinance has meant a desire to explore has been abated by a voice of caution:

> Michiko (*60s Japanese, 2 day tour to Siem Reap via Bangkok*): we talked to the villagers. They wanted to show us where their village was. We thought about it but we were too worried about landmines to wander off.

> Jacqueline (*60, French, 14 day group tour of Vietnam and Cambodia*): We did not adventure ourselves into the jungle, we wanted to, it feels slightly dangerous. Aren't there animals, snakes in there? And there was no pathway marked. It's true there are landmines! Our guide advised us not to go off the bigger tracks because there are still some landmines.

For certain visitors however, the hidden danger of millions of unexploded landmines generates far more than merely a passing interest counter-balanced with a sense of caution. Since the early 1990s, demining agencies such as the Halo Trust and CMAC have worked geographically outwards from the Angkor Archaeological Park to ensure a number of outlying temple complexes – including Beng Melea, Koh Ker, and Banteay Chmaar – are safe and accessible for a small number of adventure-seeking tourists. Internet-based travelogues and guidebooks have interwoven with the more ephemeral, but equally potent, circuit of backpacker tales, to create a discourse of un-chartered, danger-ridden, territories. It is not only unexploded ordinance that lies in wait; tales of expeditions to remote and dangerous, jungle-buried temples also await their intrepid authors. Sitting at the heart of this desire to 'flirt with space' (Crouch 2005) is the idea of *kairos*, where it is not only important to be (among) the first to encounter a landscape, but also to be there at a particular moment in history:

> Marc (*29, Belgian, Thailand and Cambodia for one week*): We like to travel to places after there has been some kind of insurrection, we thought Cambodia was stabilizing a bit too fast and if you don't come here quickly it will be a normal country and boring. We want a sense of danger, not actual danger.

We don't want actual danger, just perceived danger, and exploring all these remote temples gives you that feeling.

Secrets (*20s, Dutch, Traveling Asia for 1 year*): Maybe it's silly but I like to explore somewhere. You can't explore anything these days, there is no place in the world that is not mapped, discovered and explored. But in a country like this where development has stalled for many decades because of war there is still exploring to be done, not everything is mapped and signed yet. It still feels chaotic.

Implicit here is a broader reading of the country as a whole. Cambodia represents an opportunity to 'explore' a place that has yet to be incorporated into the heavily populated tourist circuits of neighboring Thailand, Malaysia and, even to some extent, Vietnam. More specifically, Marc and Secrets' responses illustrate how, for some, there is a seduction of place in Cambodia's landscapes, both rural and urban, built around leaving the well-trodden path of international tourism. In order to mark this spatial transition, both guidebooks and tourists alike commonly present Cambodia's border crossings as not merely territorial boundaries, but as frontiers of wilderness and danger involving a rite of passage. To quote Marc again:

Marc: I have wanted to come here for years, a friend of ours came here in 1995 and was telling us how the road is dangerous, and if you take the train it will get hijacked, so in my head I have all these maps. For me the border town of Poipet is a name that is utterly dangerous, my friend came across it by accident and he survived certain death...
Dani (*30, Belgian, partner of Marc*): it is now you're telling me all this! In our guide books it says you cannot go anywhere apart from the temples. I was very scared, and we think it's the same thing for Phnom Penh

Marc's account indicates the allure Cambodia holds as a place of insurrection and danger. Sales of T-shirts emblazoned with images of military ordinance or the words 'I survived Cambodia' illustrates how this framing is communicated to, and thus circulates across, a certain touristic community.

However, by pulling these various responses together, we can see that a perception of Cambodia as a 'war-torn, dangerous' country elicits a variety of emotional and physical responses. Bearing in mind that the average length of stay in the country has remained around the two-and-a-half-days mark, it can be reasonably concluded that the longer staying 'adventure' tourist has been far outweighed by the overnight Angkor visitor. With so many trips oriented around the consumption of an Angkorean monumental culture over a few short days, visitors invariably leave Cambodia with a sense of incongruity and discontinuity between the country's two prevailing histories: one ancient and glorious, the other modern and tragic:

Jonathan (*20s, Dutch, in Asia for 1 year, Cambodia for 1 week*): I've been reading David Chandler, Ben Kiernan, lots of books on the recent history.

I'm more interested in that than Angkor. It definitely makes it more alive knowing that people my age have been to war here, you can relate to that, but the ninth Century, imagining what Jayavarman did, that's hard, or to make any sort of connection between the two.

Barton (*30s, Canadian, lives in Singapore in Cambodia for 3 days*): Even though I'm here now, this place makes no sense. All we seem to know is about war and Pol Pot and these amazing temples. But how do the Cambodian people use this place? I wanted to know how it is important for them as a place for national pride to redevelop? Surely it's an asset for the government, beyond making money I mean, culturally, politically. I asked our guide but he didn't seem to know, and the *Lonely Planet* tells you nothing. It's frustrating.

Mariana (*30, Spanish, living in Singapore in Cambodia for 3 days*): Our guide told us all about the carvings and which king owned which temple. But it all seemed so dead, although he did briefly show us some statues used by local villagers. But I wanted to know more about these villages, how they use the temples. What do they want to happen in the future here? Someone said there are thousands of people living in the park but where, what do they do?

Unanswered questions and expressions of confusion here clearly stem from the major voids in information pertaining to anything beyond these two eras. As a consequence, connections between Angkor and its broader social or national context often remain vague or even non-existent:

Neal (*45, American, Trip to Thailand and Angkor for 2 days*): The only thing I knew about Cambodia were the killing fields and landmines, I had no idea Angkor Wat existed before I came. But once our tour leader told us about it we decided to take the two day extension from Thailand. I'm glad we did.

John (*40s, American, on same trip as Neal*): yeah but to learn something about Cambodia would have been good, but we leave tomorrow. It's too fast, I don't feel we've seen anything.

Emilie (*27, French, traveling Southeast Asia for 3 months*): I had a good book on Khmer mythology I read before I came but it concentrated too much on the bas reliefs and not enough on the global stories of how it was created. I think they don't know so much about the history of how people lived, how they worked, ate, that kind of information, which would be good to know.

Weng (*34, Singaporean, holidaying in Thailand and Cambodia for four days*): yes I came here to see Angkor Wat and all these magnificent temples. But all I know about Cambodia is that it is dangerous, that's all I know.

In fact, for some tourists who have traveled purely to see Angkor, their destination country has little or nothing to do with trip at all:

> Denise (*60s, American, also on 7 day tour of Thailand and Cambodia*): I came here purely to see Angkor, no I didn't know it was in Cambodia, I don't know where I would have placed it, not here though. I don't know why.

> Antonio (*26, Spanish, in Burma, Thailand and Cambodia for 1 month*): Angkor in Cambodia? no not really, I knew if I came here it was in this region somewhere.

> Yukio (*50, Japanese on 3 day tour to Bangkok and Siem Reap*): In Japan there is only one photo about Cambodia, the view of Angkor Wat from the west gate. Yes I can go back to Japan happy to have seen that.

Together these various responses illustrate how Cambodia continues to be seen as a destination haunted by war and genocide. In reflecting upon these narratives here it has been suggested that the country both repels and attracts. For some it is just another 'war-torn, dusty Asian country' that holds little interest; while for others it is a frontier of discovery, risk, and excitement. Common to such divergent dispositions however, is a struggle to connect a glorious and ancient history – framed in terms of kings and religious iconography – with descriptions of modern warfare and genocidal regimes. Over the course of the preceding chapters a number of contributory factors to this situation have been identified.

In the first instance, heritage policies arising from the region's listing as a World Heritage Site in 1992 have principally sought to isolate, protect, and restore an endangered monumental culture. From cultural tourism to sustainable development, tourism policies have also largely focused on the provision of facilities and a concern for the destructive impact of a rapidly growing industry on the temples and their environs. As a consequence, little attention has been given to the development of a more culturally holistic and geographically dispersed tourism industry. Angkor has also witnessed the emergence of a short-stay tourism industry brought about by Cambodia's inability to develop a nationwide industry due to its shattered infrastructures and its location within an interconnected region compromised of countries varying in their levels of wealth and development. Finally, this chapter has examined tourism as a socio-cultural environment in order to illustrate how certain discourses of space, culture and history have solidified, framing Angkor as a landscape of monumental antiquities, a place frozen in time and the dormant legacy of a civilization lost to history.

In essence then, it has been argued that Angkor's re-emergence as a destination of international tourism since the early 1990s has been characterized by a process of disembedding and socio-spatial estrangement. From a tourist consumption perspective, this has meant understandings of the ways in which the site connects with its immediate socio-national context – as a landscape of Cambodian heritage – have remained minimal and amorphous. From a developmental stand-point, the convergence of these factors has inhibited the wider geographical distribution of the wealth generated by tourism. As we have seen, the country holds a strong appeal for a limited number of adventure-seeking tourists. Indeed, in recent years Phnom Penh and to a lesser extent Sihanoukville in the south have become reasonably well established on the backpacker trails of Southeast Asia. However, the number of visitors to these cities, and the wealth brought about by international tourism, remain small in comparison to the hundreds of millions of dollars now channeling in and out of Siem Reap each year. Put simply, in less than a decade Siem Reap has become an island of urban development surrounded by sustained rural poverty, both at the provincial and national level.

Part two: domestic tourism

I was told it was Khmai heritage, our very old heritage

In contrast to the plethora of travel agents, television programs, and guide book authors all promoting Angkor from numerous countries around the world, little attention has been given to the development of the site as a domestic tourist destination within Cambodia itself. With the return of political stability the government's economically prudent Ministry of Tourism (MOT) marketing department firmly prioritized the international visitor. To date, the marketing department has published its promotional material mainly in English and French, with Japanese and other Asian languages increasingly featuring in response to the country's shifting source markets. From its humble beginnings of photocopied pamphlets on Angkor in the mid 1990s, the department has steadily pursued more sophisticated strategies, including multi-media country stands at trade fairs around the world or promotional campaigns like the 'two kingdoms, one destination' with neighboring Thailand. In comparison to these efforts to attract the highly lucrative international sector, the economically marginal domestic market industry has remained an area largely ignored by the Royal Government's Ministry.

One medium through which Angkor has been indirectly promoted is Cambodia's domestic television networks. As part of the resurrection of the country's media industry a number of new documentaries have been produced examining the glorious achievements of pre-modern Khmer architects. Highly celebratory in tone, these programs typically detail the religious symbolism of the monuments and their sculpture, or the life of the monarch associated with the temple. Given the widespread decimation of the country's education system over recent decades, these programs have helped to broaden an understanding among the Cambodian population regarding the achievements of their Khmer forefathers. Indeed, despite widely circulated accounts of a historical and cultural 'erasure' during the Khmer Rouge regime, they reflect a continuation in the collective imaginary towards

Angkor as an enduring legacy of a magnificent and powerful ancestry:

> Sok (*20s, from Siem Reap province, visiting Angkor for four days*): it is good for Khmer people to come here, to see those things that were built in ancient times, this is the history of the glorious Khmer past. It is the honor of our country and it is good that Cambodian people come to see that.

> Chiep (*40s, from village south of Phnom Penh, visiting Angkor for 3 days*): here I can trace back my family, my great, great, great grandfather who built Angkor, it's the heritage of the Khmer people.

> Trei (*50s, from Kampong Cham, near Vietnamese border, visiting Angkor for four days*): when it was described to me as a child, they said it was huge, and so old. I have never seen a picture of Angkor Wat, but I was told it was Khmai heritage, our very old heritage.

Clearly, these three responses share a sense of collective patrimony articulated in cultural and ethnic terms. They also point towards an extremely strong continuity in the prevailing narrative framing of Angkor, from the colonial period right through to the present day. As we have seen in Chapters 1 and 2, the temples have maintained a pivotal position within a Cambodian and Khmer identity matrix, whether it be at the level of state politics, its appropriation for modern civic architecture or in the popular culture of the everyday. As the legacy of a classical, golden era of Khmer power, the Angkorean era has also been unequivocally regarded as the apogee of a national heritage; a theme which continues to pervade everyday understandings today:

> Meng (*30s, Resident of Siem Reap*): Angkor Wat is a symbol and creation of Khmer culture, a symbol of national culture. That is why it is important for me, and why it is important for me to come here.

> Chum (*40s, from Samroun district, 7km from Preah Khan, here for the day*): Angkor is Cambodia's history. It is the pride of our country. It is important for the Cambodian people to see what our ancestors have built in the past.

Not surprisingly, these various responses all indicate how Angkor is revered through a lens of past glory, and as 'ancient' heritage. The final part of the chapter examines the annual festival of Khmer New Year in order to argue that the meanings and values Cambodians attribute to the site are more layered and subtle than suggested by a monolithic reading of architectural antiquities. We have seen that the consumption patterns of international tourists are almost exclusively oriented around the temples. The following analysis of the New Year festival reveals a contrasting mode of tourism, whereby the consumption of roads, rivers, reservoirs, and monasteries becomes symbolically charged for a population recovering from decades of national turmoil.

Angkor gives strength to the people

From the mid-1990s onwards an increasing number of Cambodians have chosen the period known as 'Khmer New Year' to visit Angkor. Scheduled in accordance with the lunar calendar, the festival coincides with the hottest part of the dry season, around March and April. As such, it serves as a welcome 'liminal, time out'. (Turner 1995) from agricultural work in temperatures often exceeding 100 degrees Fahrenheit. Given that Cambodians can enter Angkor without purchasing a ticket, assessing the total number of visitors each year has remained a far from exact science. Estimates offered by APSARA and UNESCO for any given year have ranged from 100,000 to 250,000.[10] Regardless of the fact that these celebrations have not been commercially promoted by the government, the dearth of any major celebrations at Angkor since the 1960s means the volume of visitors in recent years has become unprecedented.

Staying in local hotels and guest houses, visitors typically spend between two and five days in and around the Angkor, Siem Reap area. In the absence of any parades, shows or other formally organized events, the festival is characterized by families, couples, and individuals fluidly moving between a broad range of activities including swimming, picnicking, prayer, and visits to some of Angkor's temples and more modern Buddhist monasteries. Hot afternoons are typically spent swimming in the Siem Reap river or West Baray reservoir, driving around the park in open-top vehicles or relaxing over a picnic. Each day thousands of Cambodians spend the last few hours of daylight by the west gate of Angkor Wat, drinking and eating locally cooked food; a prime location that affords a grand view of the temple's iconic towers (see Figure 5.2). With a strong emphasis placed on socializing and meeting new people, the festival is defined by a continual interweaving of leisure, tourism, and religion. Proceeding from the above accounts of Angkor as the material legacy of a once glorious past, the following interview excerpts also illustrate how the site vitally contributes to contemporary identity constructions: cultural, national and ethnic formations which have been profoundly challenged by the events of recent decades.

Sustained poverty and political turmoil, a conflict fought both in the air and on the ground, and major prohibitions on cross-country travel have all converged to deny Cambodians the opportunity to visit and experience Angkor as a landscape of collective heritage. Within a context of societal recovery, the festivities of today therefore represent a reclaiming of the site as a collective 'memory', and a form of consumption which enables a population to better 'understand [its] national identity' (Yalouri 2001: 17):

> Nop (*30s, village 20 kilometers north of Angkor Thom*): Angkor is the Khmer ancestor heritage and each year we like to see more and more people here at new year. It is a place many people want to come and it is good fortune to come as many people are still unable. After the war many people want to see Angkor, to see their heritage.

Figure 5.2 Afternoon picnicking at Angkor Wat. (Photo by Tim Winter.)

In a similar vein, Meng, a businessman from Siem Reap, also associates Angkor's re-population as an active religious and leisured landscape with a departure from the 'dark years' of the 1970s:

> Meng (*30s, Resident of Siem Reap*): It is good to see a lot of people here, and to see a lot of people employed, if there is no life at the temples then it feels like the time of Pol Pot. So I like to see many people at the temples, both visiting and working. If there is no-one selling things and no life it is like the dark years of Pol Pot. It is relief from the war to see people going to the temples and visiting them regularly. This really started from 1980 onwards, people started putting incense at the temples, so this needs to carry on today, before we were not allowed.

For many, a sense of 'national' recovery has a strong geographical dimension, with the ability to meet people from other provinces playing an important symbolic role:

> Howan (*40, Battambang, staying for 3 days*): yes I like the crowds over the new year period. It's a good atmosphere meeting people from other provinces, I like to see that and I like to talk to people from other provinces because we are the same nation. I like to come and see people from different parts of the country. Since I was young, people came to Angkor Wat, up until 1968,

before Lon Nol, and then it started again in 1979. But it was more local people then because it was under Vietnamese control....since the late 1980s more and more people can come, which is good for Cambodia.

Li (*50s, woman living by Vietnamese border, Kampong Cham*): We met when we came here, some of us met in Phnom Penh. But we are all from different provinces now, but we are family, we are all Khmer. We are staying three days. We have heard about Angkor for a long time, and it is the first time we are all able to come together after many dark years for Cambodia. But it is Khmer heritage, built by our ancestors. We wanted to meet here.

For both Li and Howan one of the main barriers to travel has been the debilitating neglect and damage of the country's transport infrastructure. Whereas for others, an inability to travel has stemmed from dangers posed by a long-running civil war. As the father of one family living in an area under the command of the Khmer Rouge as recently as 1998 explained:

Hong (*30, Resident of Pailin, staying for 4 days*): it's good we can now come here over new year to see the crowds, to worship in the temples. I used to come for one day on my own since 1994, but it was not safe to bring my family as we live near the Thai border. I was a soldier on the Thai border and it was too dangerous for us to all travel in the area.

In these responses we can see the festival period represents a metaphoric rebuilding of the nation through a reclaiming of traditions, territories, and material heritage. These personal touristic experiences of Angkor over New Year enable the events in Cambodia's recent history to be simultaneously remembered and forgotten. In this respect, the festival facilitates the emergence of a social memory which valuably informs the articulation of a collective identity. Indeed, by understanding New Year as a series of socio-cultural practices we are reminded of Turner's (1995) notion of *communitas*. Meeting people and developing friendships is an experience that depends on the dynamics and symbolic potency of Angkor's landscape. Indeed, within Crouch's account of tourism as practice, he suggests friendship 'is embodied because it ... makes particular use of space. People being physically together, sharing activities, the body becomes aware of a shared body space that is also social space' (Crouch 1999: 272). In the context of Angkor, it is the pastimes of driving around in large groups, lying in hammocks by the reservoir or sitting on picnic mats in front of Angkor Wat during the New Year period which constitute this social space. In other words, the festivities represent a unique time/space moment of *communitas* within which a sense of a nation in socio-economic and cultural recovery can be realized:

Hok & Huant (*30s, traveled up from Kampong Thom province*): we come every year to see Angkor Wat, to have fun with the family, to see lots of people. We just drive around. A few families from our village have come.

We've been coming for the past five years and now it's different in that there are a lot more people here and there has been more restoration. We don't know much about the history, so we like to picnic here [Angkor Wat] and the baray [reservoir]. These places have the most people, the other places are too quiet. We like to see it crowded, both with foreign people and Cambodian people. No matter how busy we are, we come here over new year, we feel we have to come to see the people at this time.

Sok (*20s, Siem Reap province*): We like to picnic here at the waterwheel, at the Baray or at Angkor Wat. It's cooler, close to the water, good for picnics and it's a good atmosphere at those places. Over new year we like to feed the monks at the Bayon, go to Phnom Kulen to see the waterfall and people there and worship the spirits of Khmer mythology at Banteay Srei, Neak Pean, Preah Khan … I feel it is very important for my family to see this, to do these things and be here at this time.

Evidently, a trip to Angkor involves far more than merely temple visits. Swimming in the Siem Reap river or in the West Baray, driving around Angkor's roads in open-top vehicles and communal barbeques all represent symbolically charged time spent among the crowd. Time spent at Angkor represents a convergence of histories, whereby glorious and tragic pasts are erased, remembered, and transposed into an optimism regarding the future. As Suoan, a young businessman from Phnom Penh put it:

Suoan (*20s, Phnom Penh, staying for 4 days*): Angkor Wat is for the young generations, it is good to see the crowds coming, it is good for the younger generation to see more and more people coming to the temples. I believe they will restore it one day. Angkor Wat is different from other countries in terms of the architecture. It gives strength to the Khmer people and the nation.

For many Cambodians, a trip to the region would not be complete without at least one visit to a local monastery. These visits typically centre around the rituals associated with Cambodia's distinctive fusion between animistic and Buddhist beliefs. The feeding of monks and financially supporting the reconstruction of their facilities after years of neglect and damage has also become important for securing personal merit. In discussing such issues, the head monks of two monasteries situated inside the Angkor Thom enclosure reflected upon the role their facilities played over the New Year period:

There are many people that come here, they come from town, from villages and they go to many monasteries, not just this one. They want to pray here because the monks are here. They use the old temples in the same way as the pagodas, using incense, praying to the Buddha. Many people like to pray for their relations so they bring food to the monks. They believe food earns them merit as when they give food to the monk he prays for their relative so the food feeds the spirit … At this time of year people give money to help build the Vihear, it brings them good luck and when that happens they believe in that pagoda and keep coming.

Similarly:

> People come from Siem Reap town, the province, Battambang, and from the border with Thailand. They especially like to come during the festivals. They like to come to Angkor during the festival time, they like to give money. They believe all the pagodas inside the Angkor area are more significant than pagodas in their local areas, so they like to give donations.

It was noted in Chapter 3 that these monasteries have been threatened by a desire held within certain quarters of the government to present Angkor as a pristine landscape of glorious antiquities. Indeed, by placing the above domestic narratives alongside the management frameworks outlined earlier, it is suggested that such understandings of the site as a 'living heritage' have been ignored within policies principally oriented toward the science of structural conservation and the provision of facilities for international tourists. Moreover, within a discourse of cultural tourism little or no attention has been given to Angkor's role as a landscape of domestic tourism. Evidently, the various Cambodian voices presented here do not sit in opposition to the dominant paradigms. Rather, they represent 'the subjugated popular knowledge', or *le savoir des gens*, to cite Foucault (1980); understandings and voices which have remained under the veil of hegemonic discourse(s). In offering a more anthropologically oriented account of Angkor, the final part of this chapter has attempted to illustrate why the site does not merely remain part of the nation's ancient past, but actively serves as a living heritage and an important constituent of identities still very much in flux and reconstruction.

6   Collapsing policies and ruined dreams

This chapter brings together a number of arguments presented in earlier chapters via a detailed analysis of two temple complexes: Ta Prohm and Preah Khan. Through their preservation as 'partial ruins' these two sites have become popular icons for the Angkor complex as a whole. Examining them as spaces of tourism and heritage reveals the uneasy convergence of various competing value regimes. The chapter begins with 'Ruins in history: romance and nostalgia', which explores a series of representations, narratives, and practices within the context of international tourism. The dominant themes reproduced in guidebooks, travel literature or documentaries are situated alongside the spatial practices of tourists. It will be seen that a sense of meaningful place, oriented around nostalgic visions of nineteenth-century European adventure and discovery, emerges from the interplay between various discursive representations and the embodied experience of clambering over tree routes and fallen stones.

In marked contrast, 'A History in ruins: lament and destruction' reveals why the idea of the ruin denotes fundamentally different values for domestic tourists. For Cambodians touring Angkor today the current depilated state of these sites serves as a metaphor for their country 'in ruins'. Rebuilding Angkor's temples represents rebuilding Cambodia. Visits to these two sites are imbued with sadness and regret, but also with an optimism for a future of social, cultural, and national 'reconstruction'. The chapter concludes with 'A Change in nature: shifting priorities in landscape management', tracing the different approaches deployed in preserving these two sites as 'partial ruins'. In the case of Preah Khan, it is argued that the World Monuments Fund has principally conceived the site in architectural terms, firmly prioritizing the preservation of the 'ancient' monumental structures. In the case of Ta Prohm, however, UNESCO invokes a more romanticized vision of Angkor, as a ruin, to resist the Archaeological Survey of India undertaking major structural restoration – rather than mere preservation. Within a politically imbalanced international community of assistance certain representations of landscape first constructed during a French colonial period are re-invoked through policies of world heritage interlocking with the cultural logics of international tourism. A number of implications arising from this situation are considered. Before turning to such arguments, a brief overview of these two sites is offered.

Ta Prohm and Preah Khan were built during the reign of Jayavarman VII (1181–c1219), a period widely regarded by scholars today as the apex of Khmer history. After decades of instability, Jayavarman VII seized the vacant throne at Angkor and embarked upon an immense construction program including roads, reservoirs, hospitals, rest houses, and numerous temple complexes. Increasingly inspired by a Mahayana Buddhist concern for egalitarianism, Jayavarman VII conceived both sites as poly-functional spaces. Situated just beyond the boundaries of his Angkor Thom city, they were far from secluded 'temples', as they appear today. According to inscriptions, both were home to thousands of monks with a supporting cast of nearly 100,000 villagers living nearby.[1] French archaeologists working in the early decades of the twentieth century suggested Preah Khan principally functioned as a monastery. More recently however, eminent scholars such as Claude Jacques have suggested the complex needs to be seen more as a university rather than the residence of a disengaged monastic community (Jacques and Freeman 1997: 218). Building on the seminal work of Coedès, Jacques has also indicated that Ta Prohm played an important social role in administering supplies to the 102 hospitals scattered across Jayavarman VII's kingdom (Ibid: 205).[2]

Architecturally, both sites have outer walls of laterite surrounding single-storied 'courts'. Each central area is characterized by numerous passageways and small chamber enclosures. An additional feature of Preah Khan is a two-tiered, round-columned building, the exact purpose of which continues to intrigue scholars and visitors alike. Consecrated in the late twelfth century, both sites housed a veritable pantheon of deities. George Coedès identified around 280 gods at Preah Khan and a slightly smaller total at Ta Prohm; all ensconced in shrines dedicated to an array of Buddhist, Hindu, and ancestral spirits. It has also been argued that the temples formed part of a Buddhist trinity, with Ta Prohm sheltering the maternal image of *Prajnaparamita* and Preah Khan honoring the King's father through an image of the *Boddhisattva Lokeshvara* (Coedès 1963: 97).

By the time EFEO began its restoration program at Angkor at the beginning of the twentieth century, both sites were in advanced states of disrepair. In the late 1920s Henri Marchal set about reducing the density of the surrounding vegetation and forest. However, unlike other temple complexes in the Angkor region, most notably Angkor Wat and Banteay Srei, the level of reconstruction remained limited. In fact, and as we saw in Chapter 2, by the 1930s it was decided to maintain both Preah Khan and Ta Prohm as partial ruins; a strategy that served to pacify those who wanted to preserve the deep-seated 'romanticism' associated with Angkor. Indeed, further to the analysis presented in the previous chapter, the following section reveals how both Ta Prohm and Preah Khan have been instrumental in sustaining, if not bolstering, the idea of Angkor as a jungle-buried civilization awaiting resurrection.

Ruins in history: romance and nostalgia

For all would be Mouhot's and closet Indiana Joneses, Ta Prohm is the perfect lost-temple-in-the-jungle: unlike most of the other monuments at Angkor, it has been only minimally cleared of its undergrowth, fig trees and creepers. It is widely regarded as one of Angkor's most enchanting temples. The French writer Elie Lauré wrote: "With its millions of knotted limbs, the forest embraces the ruins of a violent love".

(Cambodia Handbook 2000)[3]

The decision to leave these two temple complexes as 'partial ruins' in the 1930s has been pivotal to the endurance of the re-discovery narrative seen in the previous chapter. As the above excerpt from a recent popular guidebook indicates, visions of Angkor as romantic, jungle-covered ruins reaches its zenith at these two sites. Serving as metonyms of a lost civilization, both Ta Prohm and Preah Khan have become reliable resources for a seemingly endless stream of travel writers and journalists attempting to capture their own experiences of Angkor in emotive and stirring ways:

> The unreconstructed temple of Ta Prohm makes the visitor feel like Indiana Jones. For deep in the jungle a short distance beyond Angkor Thom, Ta Prohm lies more or less as the French naturalists found it 130 years ago. Trees, some of them more than 300 years old, grow right over the collapsing structure of the temples themselves ... it is spooky, overgrown and crude ... when you walk along the narrow path that takes you to Ta Prohm, your heart jumps into your mouth just as it might have for those 19th century Frenchmen who, stumbling through the jungle, came upon it for the very first time.
>
> (Buckley 1999)

For the guidebook author these sites represent powerful mechanisms for drawing the heavily perspiring, shade-seeking, reader back in time. Dawn Rooney's *Angkor Observed* – a text built around 'numerous quotes from the diaries of travellers', as highlighted in the previous chapter – provides a case in point. In her description of these iconic temples, architectural structures in the 'stranglehold' of nature become metaphors of an organic time, a lost time of creeping decay and silent aging:

> When the jungle invades a temple you see nature and stone cohabitating, in both positive and negative ways ... So we see nature and man feeding on one another. In a strange way they have become friends, supporting, protecting each other and simply growing old together. Today, as the trees and stones are in their golden years of life ... the jungle continues its relentless crush on the stones and provides a timeless changing mélange of nature and man.
>
> (Rooney 2001: 93–4)

Given that such guidebooks, along with tour guides and television documentaries, consistently refer to either, or both, of these sites as the 'highlight' of a visit, it's not surprising to learn that they commonly leave a lasting impression among tourists.

Natalie for example, a school teacher from Italy, explained why Ta Prohm and Preah Khan were her two favorite temples:

> Natalie (*55, Italian, Traveling in Thailand, Laos and Cambodia for 2 months*): Oh because of the jungle, it is just eating the stone, the force of nature, to see that nature is stronger than anything man can create. I have been to India many times and Angkor Wat reminded me so much of India, it is beautiful, but the emotion is at Ta Prohm and Preah Khan. It was so unusual to see them being eaten by the jungle, it is beautiful there, I love the jungle. I felt something direct with the nature it was little to do with the architecture.

Patently, Natalie's 'emotion' here draws upon a deep-seated romanticism associated with ruined landscapes, where the 'dialogue with the forces of nature is visibly alive and dynamic' (Woodward 2001: 73). For many visitors, it is this very conversation between nature and culture which lies at the heart of an aesthetic sensibility:

> Dani (*28, Belgian, in Thailand and Cambodia for one week*): Having trees there are part of it, it's overgrown, and these trees enhance that. You can't pull the trees down, they have as much right to be there as the ruins, you can't chop a tree down that is 250 years old. It should stay as it has become part of the ruin. A ruin's a ruin.

> Masa (*24, Japanese, Backpacking round Southeast Asia for 3 months, 1 week in Cambodia*): I would prefer to see the large trees left there. When I saw that it helped me understand more what a 1000 years is, because of the roots. The trees on the temples make us feel the history. If they were not there we would not be able to feel the history any more.

Masa's concern for preserving the trees as markers of time begins to illustrate the subtle ways in which ruins portray history through an interweaving of their 'cultural' and 'natural' elements. Ruins tell stories of the glory and decline of past civilizations through their overgrown vegetation, and simultaneously remind us of nature's eternal power through their decaying architecture. In the contexts of Preah Khan and Ta Prohm this interweaving also means trees, vines, and thick vegetation all allude to a history of European exploration and a golden era of rediscovering lost civilizations. In other words, these elements of nature constitute a cultural landscape haunted by the ghosts of previous dwellings, previous encounters:

> Pauline (*22, French, 'doing Asia' for around 3 months*): I first learnt of Angkor at school, about colonial history, but we learnt nothing about Khmer history. I just remember being taught about temples in the jungle, and about the adventures of French travelers, including André Malraux of course, in these exotic, far off lands.

Figure 6.1 Doorway of Ta Prohm. (Photo by Tim Winter.)

Antonio (*26, Spanish, in Burma, Thailand and Cambodia for 1 month*): These monuments have a natural life, and therefore if it decays that is okay. They remind me of John Ruskin and of course the writing of Victor Hugo.

Gérard (*30s French, living in Indonesia, in Cambodia for 3 days*): The fact that these temples were hidden for many centuries, and rediscovered in recent times by the French, that's very exciting.

Not surprisingly, today's tourists frequently situate their own encounters with the site within a history of mythologized figures. The following responses indicate how the ghosts of former 'explorers' are explicitly invoked as a way of haunting a visit to Preah Khan today:

Pearce (*38, Canadian, traveling Thailand and Cambodia for three weeks*): it was the sheer romantic nature of it, the organic nature and power of the trees … those manmade structures being devoured by the trees … it was sheer self-indulgence, 'I want to be an explorer, the one who discovered it', to come across something and you really get that here.

Jacqueline (*60, French, 14 day group tour of Vietnam and Cambodia*): I loved the ones with the trees. It was more romantic actually as I felt like we were some explorers who had discovered a temple. It gave you the idea of that.

Michael (*40, British, traveling across Asia for six months*): We saw a program on Angkor just before we went away and the image was predominantly of you as the explorer, the archaeologist going through these completely unexplored temples, these magical mystical temples, of you exploring something that hasn't been discovered before … you have this idea that it was not 'touristy' at all. You arrive at this temple, you're Indiana Jones exploring this place.

Accepting Simon Schama's assertion that landscape 'is built up as much from strata of memory as from layers of rock' (1995: 7), the reappearance of Indiana Jones here as a metaphor for exploration and discovery indicates how fluid and playful the layering of history can be. However, if we are to fully understand how these sites have come to be valued and made meaningful by their foreign visitors it is necessary to extend the above narrative and discursive analysis towards an understanding of embodied spatial practice. To this end, De Certeau's notion of 'kinaesthetic appropriation' is instructive here.

Arguably, De Certeau's greatest contribution to spatial theory is his account of place as 'artful practice' (1984). In an effort to counter the epistemological hegemony of architectural or urban planners, and the ideological abstractions of cartography, De Certeau points our attention to the ways in which place is sociopolitically actualized and negotiated through subjective, embodied inhabitations.

Figure 6.2 Tree roots at Ta Prohm. (Photo by Tim Winter.)

The following responses indicate the value of examining the tourist encounter with Preah Khan and Ta Prohm in such terms:

> Barry (*33, Australian, visiting Southeast Asia for 1 month*): My favorites were Preah Khan and Ta Prohm, you find yourself going in caverns and passageways which you need a flashlight for and clambering over rocks, the idea that there are these carvings just lying on the ground. It looks as though nature has run its course with this temple, it is weathered, decrepit, you do get that feeling you are exploring, I love that. The trees just add to the atmosphere, it's old and they add to that.

> Pauline (*22, French, 'doing Asia' for around 3 months*): It was nice to climb, to feel the heat of the steps and squeeze in tight spaces, you feel as though the temple has a life.

> Val (*50s, American, in Thailand and Cambodia for 3 week holiday*): yes it was magical to touch the walls, just to feel the rock.

> VJ (*50s, American, traveling with Val*): but I understand that the acid in your skin, as millions of people touch it, makes the stone wash away. So I didn't do a lot of that. But when I was climbing, walking around, just wandering, I was able to feel what it was like to have been there.

John (*40s, American, Trip to Thailand and Angkor, in Cambodia for 2 days*):
yes by crawling inside we could see how things were constructed and how
they decayed. Walking in small rooms, climbing steps, that's important to
me. It helps you work out how in the world they managed to create it, and
what happened to it over the centuries.

These responses indicate how the activities of climbing and feeling create a sense of
simultaneous proximity and distance, where other times are imagined and brought
close through the body. Within these portrayals of wandering and contempla-
tive reflection there is an implicit concern for an organic fluid and uninhibited
form of spatial consumption. More specifically, for many tourists an encounter
with these sites is bound up with ideas of 'freedom' and the absence of spatial
discipline:

Val (*50s, American, in Thailand and Cambodia for 3 week holiday*): yes one
of the great things about Preah Khan is that you can walk through, wander
through on your own and be left alone. The freedom in the temples is enormous
and it is wonderful and they need to keep that. For those of us who want to
pretend we are ancient people living in the temple we could do that.

Polly (*34, English, living in Singapore in Cambodia for 3 days*): yes I wanted
to be on my own there, to feel the calm and just sit. I just thought it would
be lovely to just sit down and exist for a couple of hours, to appreciate the
beauty. You can't do that in Singapore.

Emilie (*27, French, traveling Southeast Asia for 3 months*): if I was in a
group or on my own, to be able to just hang around and walk wherever you
want … It just wouldn't be the same visit if I was told where and when to
go, how can I explain it? I had some really strong feelings, which surprised
me. I spent hours and hours just watching the carvings, the beauty of them, it
was just a feeling, I can't explain it. I spent hours looking at the carvings and
the trees, and that would be so different if you are told to move through the
temple.

Emilie's preference for maintaining control over her own speed and direction was
central to her decision to tour the site independently. Clearly, she perceived that
such autonomy would be lost in a group and that her experience would have been
fundamentally different. However, if we turn to consider those who do travel as
part of a group with a guide we see the same tactics in place. Even for those visitors directed along orderly, linear routes this desire for an individualistic, creative,
self-exploratory experience triggers a process of negotiation with the discipline
imposed by the presence of the guide:

George (*75, American, trip to Thailand and Cambodia for 7 days*): yes our
guide walked off for a few minutes and that allowed us to sit, wander, even do

our exploring a little bit, really feel the place. They were the most enjoyable moments for me.

Ming (*44, Chinese, in Cambodia for 3 days*): yes our guide was too fast. I wanted to stop and really look at the carvings and the nature, and I did sometimes. There were so many things to see and learn about and so I ignored our guide sometimes to do that.

Michèle (*40s, French, In Cambodia as extension to trip to Vietnam*): roping areas off, that would be very different, the temple lends itself to go in there, exploring, getting lost … that is the whole idea of leaving it like that, to see how it was. We ventured off to find a quiet spot, just to sit and imagine, away from the group.

Angkorean tourism today is characterized by a profusion of 'copycat' itineraries, whereby scores of travel agents and tour operators continually reproduce similar itineraries for their groups. With Preah Khan and Ta Prohm located near the mid points of the *Grand* and *Petit Circuits*, respectively, they are inundated with hundreds, even thousands, of visitors at particular moments of the day: mid-morning or late afternoon being typical examples. For many visitors the crowding which results is an annoyance inhibiting a desired 'solitary gaze' (Urry 1990). In De Certeau's terms many visitors therefore employ a series of 'artful practices' to avoid coming in to visual or physical contact with these 'aliens' in the landscape:

Lee (*27, English, traveling for one year on 'world' ticket, traveled from Bangkok by bus*): Tourists are a distraction, I can't help tuning in on them which is annoying. When there is just me and the temple there is no other distraction, which is why if I see a big group I deliberately walk the other way. Like today, I went through small corridors when I saw a big group in front of me, but by doing that I fell in love with the place.

Jonathan (*20s, Dutch, Traveling Asia for 1 year*): for me the quiet is very important. If it's noisy with other tourists then it makes my experience less than it could have been, they distract you from concentrating and absorbing the surroundings. For instance in Preah Khan there were big groups of Germans and Japanese there and they were so loud. I realize I am very hypocritical because I want the temple to myself and I am just another tourist. But if I knew there were few people going early in the morning then I would go then. I know it's very egotistical but it makes the experience more rewarding, more satisfying if I have it for myself.

Finally, in this second statement we can detect a sense of regret by Jonathan for not having more information at hand concerning the local patterns of tourism. Indeed, to avoid such irritations independent travelers commonly seek information about prevailing tourist flows in order to compose their own personal itinerary.

One of the more popular strategies is to work against the prevailing flows created by guidebooks such as *Lonely Planet*. The wisdom of subverting these texts is demonstrated in the responses below:

> Stuart (*20s, English, 2 month trip to Thailand and Cambodia*): we deliberately went first thing in the morning to get that special light, to get those sounds of the birds, the whole atmosphere of it. But to experience that, it was important to avoid all the other tourists who would visit later in the day.

> Sandy (*26, Australian, traveling Thailand, Laos and Cambodia for 6 weeks*): if there are no other people there, you really do feel like you are the explorer. We were deliberately there very early, there was nobody else there, and in that case you do get that feeling that you are the first person to go there, you can really lose yourself there.

> David (*40s, British, 'traveling' Cambodia and Thailand for 10 days*): yep we read the *Lonely Planet* and it advised that you get there in the late afternoon. So we knew that most people reading this would follow that. Our idea was to do just the opposite of what was recommended and get there around lunchtime. Yeah it was hot, but quiet.

Across these various responses, freedom of movement, the ability to spend time independently, away from other tourists, and create personalized, reflexive, and fluid forms of spatial consumption are all recurring themes. In this respect, we can see a strong continuity between the prevailing symbolic and discursive constructions of Angkor as a ruin and the ways in which these two sites are consumed through enunciatory acts of embodied spatial praxis. Given the dearth of promotional literature within the domestic tourism industry, these bonds between the symbolic and material, the real and the imagined for Cambodians arises not from guidebooks or brochures, but through a range of other texts and contexts all oriented around the idea of an 'imagined community' in revival. It is to this consumption of Preah Khan and Ta Prohm as a domestic tourist space that I now turn.

A history in ruins: lament and destruction

> Chum (*50s, from Banteay Srei district, here for the day*): yes I don't know much about the history at all. My daughter knows more as she goes to school and she tells me. But we like to come here with all the family. It's cool by the water, a good place to eat and meet friends we know from the village here. They tell us about all the life in their village, that is interesting to hear.

Over the course of this book it has been suggested that the vision of a glorious, powerful Angkor continues to play a pivotal role in unifying identities within, and across, various sectors of Cambodian society. In the previous chapter we also saw that such identity formations are being reinvigorated at the populist level through the annual Khmer New Year festival. It comes as little surprise then to find that these themes reappear within the attitudes of domestic tourists towards the conservation and restoration of the actual temples themselves. For many Cambodians touring Angkor today, widespread dilapidation and architectural collapse serves as a metaphor for a country 'in ruins'. It therefore naturally follows that restoration is also metaphorically imbued with the hopes and aspirations of a national reconstruction:

> Chhin (*50s, lives in village 15 miles north of Angkor, here for the day*): yes I would like to see the temples restored because the country has suffered four generations of war and so a lot of Cambodian people aren't knowledgeable about the Khmer history. I was born in Siem Reap. I used to come to the temples during the Sihanouk period and I used to come to the temples until Pol Pot, when I had to leave. I had to move 200 kilometers away, but I returned here in July 1979, I came back to Angkor. I am happy to see it being restored, especially the Baphuon. Philip Groslier was restoring it up until the war and now they are doing it again, which I am happy to see. People in the country are so poor and for them to see the glories of these temples restored makes them happy, to see Cambodia's glory restored once again, yes it makes people very happy.

> Sok (*20s, Siem Reap province, a farmer, arrived by truck, staying at Angkor for 4 days*): yes I want to see Angkor as a modern tourist site, but they need to keep the traditional structures. They should restore the outer moat of Angkor Wat for Cambodian people to sit on, and restore these ruined temples for Cambodians to see their heritage. Cambodia is now at peace and to see Angkor restored is good for the country.

> Hong (*30, Resident of Pailin*): yes, to see more restoration is good, it would be nice for foreigners and Cambodians to see Angkor Wat and all the other temples restored. Cambodians need to be proud of their heritage and country and for many it is only now that they are able to come here. It is important for them to see Angkor rebuilt, it gives strength to our poor country.

As we can see here – infused with visions of country, culture, and history – the ruins of a once glorious past have become charged with aspirations and hopes which extend far beyond the mere buildings themselves. It is a framing which also triggers feelings of sadness and regret towards Angkor's more ruinous structures, not least Preah Khan and Ta Prohm:

> Chhin (*50s, lives in village 15 miles north of Angkor, here for the day*): to rebuild the structures would help the people learn about their history. It's a real shame to see this temple as a ruin with all the forest around it.

Chiep (*40s, traveled from village south of Phnom Penh, staying for 3 days*): It is a shame to see Preah Khan like this. This is my first visit, but I do not like it as much others I have been to like Angkor Wat. When it is restored I would like to come back, but I feel sad to see this now.

Hok (*30s, traveled up from Kampong Thom province*): we don't like to see these ruins, we prefer the temples that have been restored the most.

Implicit within these three responses, however, is a hope that this process of decay and decline is now being reversed through the presence of international expertise. As Hok's wife, Huant, proceeded to add:

Huant: Yes we like to see these international organizations here, they have the skills to restore the temples. They will make it better and better.

A similar confidence in the international community is shared by Kong, a shop owner from Siem Reap town:

Kong (*20s, Resident of Siem Reap*): I am happy to see the international organizations here to help the Cambodian Government in the restoration of our temples. Yes I would like to see Preah Khan restored, but only if they have the expertise, nothing fake, but yes they should restore it. It is good for the Khmer people, Angkor is our national symbol, our national culture, it should be restored. To see them rebuilding the temples makes them feel like living temples, not just of the past.

In their desire to see Preah Khan restored Huant and Kong are clearly enthusiastic about the interventions of international teams in the area of conservation. Yet, for some Cambodians this very internationalization of restoration represents a potential threat to the loss of Angkor's symbolic potency as a national monument:

Howan (*40, traveled down from Battambang for 3 days*): I believe they will restore it one day. I think the money made from tourism should go on restoration, putting the stones back. It is not for our generation, it should be restored for the next Cambodian generations to come. But I am worried that these international organizations will bring their own style of architecture and change the Khmer architecture, that this team from America will change the style of building. I have no idea what is being done here in Preah Khan and it worries me that each temple is being taken over by different countries. Angkor is Cambodian.

Sok (*20s, farmer, Siem Reap province*): yes there should be restoration here but not if it's not by Khmer people. Restoring Angkor is about restoring Cambodia's glory, so yes it is good that experts help us but it should be Khmers who restore these temples.

Notwithstanding these differing attitudes towards the guardianship over Preah Khan's architectural treasures, the activities of restoration generate a belief and optimism in a more favorable future, one that steadily moves away from decades of turmoil and suffering. An important part of the 'restoration' narrative for these sites has been the reestablishment of various ritual practices of nearby villagers. Both Ta Prohm and Preah Khan host a number of statues, carvings, ponds, and trees revered for their *neak ta* and *bâng bât* spirits. As Miura (2004) and Thompson (2004) have illustrated, these spirits constitute a vital religious and spiritual 'infrastructure' surrounding temples like Preah Khan and Ta Prohm. Offerings and prayers are made not just from local residents, but from Cambodians visiting from across the country:

> Howan (*40, traveled down from Battambang for 3 days*): these shrines are important to the spirit of the temple. I am happy to see they are maintained by the people here, the spirits help protect them. And when I come here I like to pray and light [incense] sticks too.

A number of the above responses indicate a preference for visiting the region's more intact temple complexes like Angkor Wat, Bayon or Banteay Srei; with the former widely revered both for the grandeur of its architecture and the power of its *neak ta*, a symbolic combination of power that goes hand in hand. In spite of this hierarchy of temples, both Ta Prohm and Preah Khan continue to receive significant numbers of domestic visitors. To better understand these landscapes as sites of domestic tourism it is once again helpful to briefly reflect upon certain forms of spatial practice.

During the Khmer New Year period numerous open-top vehicles, many of which carry up to 100 members of a village community, can be found parked outside these sites. The popularity of these vehicles reflects a desire to experience Angkor as part of a large group (see Figure 6.3). Equally, for those tourists visiting Angkor as a day or weekend trip throughout the year, travel is frequently undertaken in parties of ten or more, for the reasons highlighted in the following responses:[4]

> Someth (*40s, from village north of Banteay Srei district*): we come to have fun with the family, to see lots of people. A few families from the village have come. Today is the day we are not working, so we can come here together from the village, it's more fun.

> Savuth (*40s, from Phnom Penh*): We have all come up from Phnom Penh, but our son is still there looking after the shop for two days. We have brought our friends from Kampot here. It is their first time here. It's difficult when you have to work all the time. It is better for us to all come together when we can, when we all have the time away from work, so we waited for that. Of course we all want to come together.

In contrast to the pursuit of the solitary encounter highlighted earlier, we can see here the prevalence of Urry's 'collective gaze'. More than merely sites of

Figure 6.3 Open-top driving during Khmer New Year. (Photo by Tim Winter.)

pilgrimage or historical interest for domestic tourists, Preah Khan and Ta Prohm are spaces to walk around, picnic, talk, and meet others:

> Hong (*30, Resident of Pailin*): it is important for me to meet people here, to see other Cambodians, to sit here, picnic, we are able to talk ... and to see foreigners here is good for our country.

> Meng (*30s, Resident of Siem Reap*): to see many people visiting here is good. My family like to watch other tourists ... it is Khmer heritage and so to see other Cambodians here enjoying themselves, talking and walking around, praying at the shrines if they want to, we like to see that. That is why we come.

> Hok (*30s, traveled up from Kampong Thom province*): It's not for religious reasons, we come to relax, to meet people. Our friends have family in the village near here so we all come together.

Evidently, the presence of other Cambodians and foreign visitors features heavily within the various accounts presented here. Given that the vast majority of Cambodian tourists visit these sites without the services of a formal guide, routes and patterns of movement across the temples are organic and diverse; a situation of marked contrast to the prescribed routes followed by guided groups of international visitors. Interestingly, key locations to sit, talk, and picnic arise from a tourist gaze which looks directly back at other visitors. The most popular impromptu sites of seating at Preah Khan do not reflect a search for solitude or the tranquility of the forest; instead they are points of sociability, of chance encounters, outlooks over mini-vistas of animated movement. It is a gaze, however, which oxygenates the broader symbolic and metaphorical values highlighted earlier. Once again, it is apparent that time spent seeing, hearing and talking to people from around, and beyond, Cambodia are the moments through which Angkor and the nation become one in their recovery and restitution.

A change in nature: shifting priorities in landscape management

As the ICC gathered for its inaugural international conference in Tokyo in 1993 one of the few projects already up and running at Angkor was the WMF Preah Khan program. Established in November 1992 the project set about addressing, indeed reversing, two decades of neglect. Throughout the conflict Preah Khan's walled enclosure had been a place of both hiding and protection (Thibault 1998). Sporadically occupied and mined by Khmer Rouge troops up until the 1990s, the site also bears witness to war through its bullet holes and tank track marks incised in sandstone gateways. To reverse Preah Khan's fortunes the WMF cultivated a four-pronged strategy which tackled both the contemporary challenges and the dilemmas associated with managing a 'partial ruin'. Most urgently, any further damage and the very real problem of over-night looting had to be prevented. Second, the precarious nature of many of the site's architectural structures demanded urgent assessment and appropriate remedial action. Once such emergency measures were in place the secondary goals of training a Cambodian team in the skills of conservation and temple maintenance, and preparing the site for tourists, could commence as long-term programs. To achieve these four goals the organization also had to establish a funding program which principally targeted a world of private and corporate philanthropy.

   In constructing a philosophy towards conservation, the decision to preserve the site as a 'partial ruin' meant projects were oriented towards structural preservation and consolidation, rather than large-scale restoration.[5] Although this approach incorporated the vegetation and forest both within the central courtyards and their surrounding areas, the WMF's proclivity towards monumental conservation steered policies towards a set of architectural priorities. To ensure the long-term safety of the temple the organization decided to implement a landscape management plan:

> Preah Khan is one of the few monumental complexes at Angkor that is still surrounded by an almost intact jungle, and this has led the WMF to draw up a short and long term plan to manage the immediate natural environment of the site and control the growth of vegetation.
>
> (ICC 1995: 22)

In 1996 the team expressed concerns about a number of overhanging trees. The ICC was informed about the possibility of major interventions which would prevent any further damage to the central buildings:

> On 8th June two fromager trees fell down onto the south-west courtyard of the Buddhist complex and caused damage to four individual shrines. The trees were removed and the damage repaired. This caused the WMF to wonder about the advisability of cutting down all trees in the vicinity of the temples.
>
> (ICC 1997: 36–7)

In making the difficult decisions of whether to retain or remove individual trees, the organization has consistently focused on the preservation of a monumental heritage and the technical challenges of meeting that objective. The high density of Preah Khan's architecture and lack of accessibility to central areas has meant any attempt to remove trees carries significant risks, both to personal safety and the temple itself. Particularly concerned about a large tree precariously leaning towards the central 'Hall of Dancers', the WMF brought in experts from America's National Park Service to 'design an effective program [that would] remove the problem'.[6] Initial assessments suggested that chopping down the tree posed significant risk to the temple. The WMF therefore reluctantly decided to leave the tree in situ until an appropriate strategy could be formulated. In examining the organization's policy we can see that the decision to preserve Preah Khan as a 'partial ruin' is driven more by technical and financial constraints, rather than the pursuit of a particular aesthetic sensibility.[7] The policies pursued also indicate how a 'priceless architecture' is unequivocally prioritized over the surrounding environment which is principally regarded as an impending danger.[8]

For an organization dependent upon a continual stream of donor support, the WMF have understandably looked towards tourism as a valuable mechanism for maintaining their public profile and generating the funds necessary for a long-term commitment to Angkor. In response to the steadily increasing levels of international tourists visiting Cambodia towards the end of the 1990s, the WMF paid greater attention to issues of site presentation. As their program director stated, 'Yes we saw that as crucial. We see it as our responsibility to look after the maintenance, but we want to be visitor friendly, it is an important part of our project here'.[9]

Not surprisingly the organization's orientation towards architectural conservation has also underpinned their approach to being 'visitor friendly'. Once again, we learn from their 1999 report of activities that the surrounding forest and vegetation are to be the recipients of a scientific program of observation, 'Preah Khan has become a very attractive site for visitors. It is therefore essential to maintain the site in an orderly fashion, to keep it tidy and free of rubbish and keep the vegetation trained' (ICC 1999: 53).

This overall disposition towards the site is also reflected in the *Official Souvenir Brochure* the WMF produced for visitors. Textual descriptions and a detailed map of the central temple area offer the visitor a number of 'highlights'. Together, these highlights draw attention to the key architectural features, with many narrated in terms of their religious iconography. For example, visitors are encouraged to visit the 'Vishnu and Siva complexes', the 'Central Sanctuary', the 'Garudas' or the 'Cruciform Shrine'. The detailed accounts provided for these areas primarily focus on the religious motifs 'of Indian origin'. The minimal attention given to the presence of animistic shrines or iconography is reflected in their account of a decision to leave an area 'dedicated to ancestor worship ... undisturbed, still deep in the jungle'. In this respect, the brochure communicates the idea that those areas of note and worthy of visitation are of Indian origin.

In so doing, the brochure draws upon, and thus reproduces, a narrative of Khmer history and culture first constructed by French epigraphists and architectural historians in the early decades of the twentieth century. With Preah Khan once again conceived and researched through a lens of architectural conservation, the absence of any anthropologically informed information means no acknowledgment is given to the ways in which Hindu and Buddhist deities intersect – both in historical or contemporary terms – with animist beliefs and practices. Indeed, for the project director, providing an account of such areas lies beyond the boundaries of a conservation philosophy founded on rigorous, scientific research, 'As an organization, we wouldn't want to speculate, we need to be ethical and professional'.[10]

Not surprisingly, this strict scholarly approach oriented around religious and architectural historiographies leaves little space for more evocative or romanticized representations of Preah Khan as a ruin. Within their 'visitor friendly' approach to tourism, the surrounding forest is either ignored or narrated as 'nature'. On the brochure map, for example, all the trees situated within the central enclosure have been erased. The only elements featured are the architectural structures, with no reference given to former colonial era interventions which forged the idea of preserving the complex as a 'partial ruin'. In contrast, within the organization's visitor centre – a single-storied wooden structure located just inside the west gate entrance – extensive details are given regarding the species of trees and animals the visitor is likely to see. Displays providing Latin names and their translations categorize the surrounding environment as 'flora and fauna', and as the binary other of an endangered monumental 'culture'.

In an attempt to manage ever-increasing numbers of tourists, the WMF have investigated options for formal routing visitors through the site. As the program director stated:

> We think the temple should be experienced as it was meant to be experienced, i.e. from the east entrance, as Jayavarman VII intended it to be experienced ... I want visitors to enter the compound from the East and we create a one-way system through the temple.[11]

Patently, such visions necessitate greater surveillance and the disciplining of visitors. The decision to conduct research projects into visitor flows in 2001 also suggested the difficult challenge of allowing ever greater visitor numbers and simultaneously retaining a 'quality experience' would be achieved over the longer term by limiting access and perhaps even length of stay. As I have documented in greater detail elsewhere, the WMF's desire to present Preah Khan 'the way it should be experienced' sits uneasily with the dynamics of the tourist encounter highlighted earlier in this chapter (Winter 2003). The installation of routing schemes, signage, and barriers will naturally reduce the tourists' freedom of movement, ability to wander, linger, and sit. Such a 'museumification' will undoubtedly lead to more collective, disciplined, and visually oriented encounters. In reflecting upon the organization's existing and future directions for site management it is evident that the rational, science-based and architecturally focused CRM policies outlined in Chapters 1 and 3 hold greatest influence here. Yet, if we turn to consider Ta Prohm it can be seen that this dominant discourse is upheld by shifting towards more emotive ideas of 'spirit' and 'poetry'.

Over the course of the 1990s virtually all of Angkor's major temple sites had been 'adopted' by at least one international team. The major exception within this situation was Ta Prohm. As Angkor's quintessential ruin, it was widely acknowledged that the temple should be preserved in a way that enabled the visitor to see what Angkor was like when it was 'discovered by the French explorers of the mid nineteenth century'. Consequently, interventions only extended as far as daily maintenance tasks and any emergency measures required to prevent further structural collapse. In 2003 though, after being largely left alone by the ICC for a decade, the temple suddenly became the focal point of intense discussion and speculation.

In 2002 the Indian Prime Minister Atal Behari Vajpayee visited Cambodia twice, during which time he signed an agreement with the Royal Government regarding the management of Ta Prohm. As an extension to their larger loan package of 10 million US dollars, India agreed to provide funds, materials, and the technical expertise of the Archaeological Survey of India (ASI).[12] While in Cambodia, the Prime Minister also announced details of a Museum of Traditional Asian Textiles to be built in a prime location in Siem Reap. The project's exhibitions, workshops and retail space would provide tourists with an understanding of the countries' mutual textile heritage.

The Ta Prohm project was designed to run for 10 years at a cost of around five million dollars. The 'restoration' of the temple would also mark the return of the ASI after an absence of just over a decade. Their use of concrete and harsh bleaching chemicals when dismantling and rebuilding large sections of Angkor Wat's outer galleries and pavilions during the 1980s was subsequently criticized and discredited by other scholars and conservationists. Working on the stones of Ta Prohm would therefore provide the ASI with a valuable opportunity to restore their reputation in the world of international conservation. In recognition of the need for diplomatic sensitivity, the Indian Government drafted in their Phnom Penh-based ambassador to act as the team's spokesperson during early encounters and meetings with other members of the ICC.

As the project began to unfold it was apparent that the ASI would once again approach Angkor through a lens of cultural affinity. Following on from their earlier efforts at Angkor Wat, the similarities between Khmer and Indian architecture and the shared religious motifs would be highlighted. As one of the team's 'veteran archaeologists' told *The Hindu* newspaper in early 2004:

> It is very similar to the style of Lord Ranganathaswamy temple in Srirangam ... One can see there influences of Dravidian architecture in the form of pyram-midical structure of Vimanam or that of Rashtrakutas in door jambs or that of Oriya in 'sukanasika' (a prominent projection in Vimana). Similarly, the concept of 'panchayatana' [having main sanctum at the centre flanked by four sub-shrines on all the cardinal directions] was adopted and improved by them. An Indian example of this concept is the 8th century Lord Amareshwara temple in Amaravati, Guntur district of Andhra Pradesh. The Khmer Kings followed even our methodology in construction of temples. For example, Ta Prohm temple was built using stone as the only core material. This method of construction is called 'suddha'. Indian examples are Lord Kailasanatha temple in Kancheepuram and the Big Temple in Thanjavur, which were built earlier.[13]

Clearly, such expressions of a shared architecture and religious foundation point towards the use of Ta Prohm as a glue for reaffirming long-standing cultural ties between India and Cambodia. Indeed, as India's Ministry of External Affairs reminds us, Angkor's temples are the 'glorious testimony of the profound cultural and social basis of an India-Cambodia historical relationship'.[14]

During the initial phases of the project's development, significant speculation surrounded the ASI's plans for 'restoration'. Members of the ICC and UNESCO were under the impression that, in approaching the complex as a sacred space of Indian origin, the ASI would seek to restore Ta Prohm as a 'living temple'.[15] By implication, this would mean major structural restoration and the revival of the site from its current status as a ruin. During an ICC meeting held in 2002, the ASI told delegates that 'difficult decisions' would have to be made concerning the trees. The team's history of major reconstruction at Angkor Wat during the 1980s added further weight to concerns among members of the ICC about the fate of the trees. In response, UNESCO's special representative, Mr. Azzedine Beschaouch, took the opportunity to remind the ICC that the trees were 'engraved in the memory all over the world'.[16]

With the ASI unable to clearly document their intentions over the following year, UNESCO looked to dampen speculation about the project by taking the unusual step of convening a symposium specifically dedicated to a single temple. Held in Siem Reap in early 2004, the *Round Table on Ta Prohm* was designed to provide a broad philosophical framework for the future management of the site.[17] The ASI began by outlining the broad threads of their approach which would take in areas like epigraphy, soil mechanics, archaeology, and geotechnical engineering. Delegates were reminded by the Secretary for the Ministry of Culture, Government of India, that Cambodia and India have enjoyed long-standing cultural ties which 'pre-date the Christian era'. Contact with India before and after the fall of Angkor was also cited as the basis for a deep heritage of expertise and knowledge which could be tapped into today. Subsequent presentations by experts drawn from across India focused on the technical questions of structural stability, water management and the potential for three dimensional laser surveys. Highly scientific in their approach, each of the projects represented a strong continuity with the discourse of conservation and heritage management outlined in Chapter 3. While a number of the ASI speakers acknowledged the difficult dilemma of consolidation versus actual restoration, possibilities for major reconstruction via established techniques such as anastylosis were consistently raised. In contrast to previous ICC gatherings, however, these technically fashioned presentations were met with skepticism and concern by the team of 'ad hoc experts' appointed by the ICC.

In order to bolster a call for restraint, invited scholars from EFEO were asked to provide an overview of their previous efforts at maintaining the site as a partial ruin. These presentations principally summarized inscription translations and the wealth of documentation produced in the first half of the twentieth century, ranging from hand-written daily reports by curators spanning almost 40 years to monthly reports and editions of BEFEO. It was also highlighted that the EFEO library in Siem Reap housed thousands of photographs, including many documenting the trees within the temple. Considered together, these various archival records constituted a knowledge base for guiding future policy. Indeed, as we saw in Chapter 3, EFEO provided a potent institutional authority for defining the parameters of good practice and 'authenticity'; an issue I will discuss in greater detail shortly.

It was repeatedly recognized during the course of the workshop that Ta Prohm posed a number of 'difficult challenges'; a situation that warranted cautious, modest steps. Maintaining the appropriate balance between the temple and its surrounding eco-system represented new territory for the ICC. The workshop's ad hoc experts unanimously agreed, however, that in order to uphold the 'integrity' of the complex 'any dismantling should be forbidden' and the 'process of letting the trees die should be as slow as possible'.[18] On a somewhat less technical level, it was also stated that the 'trees were part of the memory of the site [that] we need to keep and preserve'. Recognizing the diplomatically sensitive nature of the conservation question the Indian ambassador reiterated these sentiments by highlighting the symbolic value the trees have come to acquire: 'Ta Prohm has become an icon for Cambodia ... Many people around the world associate this country with these trees. They are icons of the country. We do not want any intervention or chopping'.

The Round Table concluded by ratifying a series of 'Recommendations' for the future. Three broad sections covered the importance of conserving the complex as an eco-historical site; following international conservation standards; and the need for documentation and ongoing consultation with the ICC on technical proposals. Within this framework it was evident that interventions should be kept to a minimum and that conservation 'must give priority to fully protect zones of high values with the closest links between the vegetation and the monuments'. To ensure this process followed rigorous, scientific procedures it was suggested that 'a monitoring system' for trees be established 'on the basis of studies, existing documents and old photographs, to draw a history of the evolution of the state (growth and decay) of the trees during the XX century'.[19]

The formulation of these recommendations ensured that this first Round Table successfully established a rigorous and robust framework within which both APSARA and the ASI could operate. As we have seen, a rigidity was once again created within an unfolding policy by addressing dilemmas and challenges as questions of conservation and engineering. Broad references to charters such as the Nara Declaration also focused attention on international standards and conventions in monumental restoration and site management. In effect, it was an approach designed to politically neutralize Ta Prohm's architecture. By encapsulating the site within a language of scientific rationalism the temple could be de-historicized, enabling it to be administered through ideas of authenticity and universality.

To retain these landscapes as partial ruins science and romance are made to work together in varying degrees of tension and harmony. Their co-existence is sustained by the latter being subsumed within the former. At Preah Khan the 'eco-heritage' is demarcated as 'nature', and as the temple's flora and fauna, whereas at Ta Prohm, the trees are sites of poetry, and of memory. And yet, regardless of the narrative, the forest has become the object of a scientific surveillance. Adopting such a positivist approach to conservation disavows other readings of culture and history. The ruin signifies historical and sacred rupture. The preservation of Preah Khan and Ta Prohm as dormant, abandoned temples denies a continuity between their time of creation and their role as active, living sacred spaces. Given the scholarly inclinations of the ICC the lack of attention paid to social histories or vernacular culture has meant no counter discourse has emerged capable of destabilizing a reading of these two sites as ancient, inanimate landscapes. What remains hidden from view is an understanding of how they are valued and used by village communities living nearby, as well as other Cambodians traveling from around the country. As such, the complex and multi-dimensional ontological matrix arising from an amalgamation of Hindu, Buddhist, and elaborate animistic beliefs is primarily reduced to questions of aesthetics and architecture.

At Preah Khan, a delicate balance between architectural security and the preservation of the site as a partial ruin has been shaped by questions of engineering and risk. As with Ta Prohm, the narration of the site's religious significance bears testament to a wealth of EFEO scholarship. The influence of India is acknowledged, and thus fore-grounded, but within a framework of conservation it is once again viewed as a 'priceless' architectural legacy of an ancient civilization. However, in turning to Ta Prohm, we have seen how this dominant discourse is upheld through a shift in the ways the cultural and natural elements of the site are discussed.

Seemingly under challenge by the ASI, the notion of the partial ruin at Ta Prohm is validated in three ways. First, there is the re-introduction of EFEO as the definitive source of knowledge on the site. Put simply, their archives are utilized to authorize the meaning of place. Second, broad references are made to international standards of cultural heritage management to justify a policy of 'minimal intervention' within a language of 'universal standards'.[20] The final mechanism – which both re-empowers the knowledge of EFEO in the contemporary and the value of Ta Prohm as global heritage – is international tourism. What we see is a convergence between the iconic framings and narratives within international tourism outlined earlier in this chapter and policies of heritage. This fusion serves to prioritize a Eurocentric representation of the landscape. By implication, preserving these sites as partial ruins foregrounds a narrative of mid-nineteenth-century discovery over other histories. As we saw in Chapter 2, the account of Mouhot's encounter with Angkor in 1860 has become an entrenched legend and one that erases histories of ongoing inhabitation and the significance of the area as a destination for travelers and pilgrims from across Asia over a number of centuries. A paradigm of science is thus built upon a foundation of historical mythology. Moreover, at the heart of this nostalgia for a golden era of European travel is the idea that Angkor was found as – and thus remains – a dormant relic of a once glorious, but now dead, ancient civilization. In other words, the romance of decay, quiescence and historical rupture – all themes that dominate Angkorean tourism today – have also (re)solidified under a framework of world heritage.

Recalling the analysis of the ICC offered in Chapter 3 we can also see that this situation is sustained through the organization's hierarchies of expertise. With their efforts of the 1980s frequently discredited, the ASI return to Angkor at the beginning of the twenty-first century in a politically weak position. Under the scrutiny of the ICC, their plans to restore Ta Prohm as a 'living temple' suffer from a lack of credibility and remain open to manipulation. At the domestic level, neither APSARA or the Ministry of Culture are in a position to assume full authority for developing an overall philosophy for managing these sites. As partners to the WMF and the ASI, APSARA have played a valuable, yet subsidiary, role of contributing to the areas of documentation, site maintenance, and training. A number of ICC and UNESCO officials confirmed it would be a number of years before the Cambodian government was able to resume full control or independently make strategic decisions.

Disputes within the government regarding Ta Prohm's future provided the evidence for such opinions. For some, the semiotics of Angkor as a ruin represents both economic and cultural potential. The circulation of iconic images of Ta Prohm and Preah Khan within a landscape of tourism provides a sound base for shaping decisions of site management. Out of the ruins arises economic power and prestige on the global stage, whereas for others, prestige and strength are goals achieved by restoring Angkor's physical and symbolical glory. Ideas of romance or poetry are merely outmoded obstructions to be removed through the restoration of sites like Ta Prohm. As the Undersecretary of State for the Ministry of Culture suggested at an ICC conference in 2002, 'What Poetry? There's no poetry here, only culture'.[21] In this political climate the decision to invite the ASI represented a deliberate move to counter EFEO's enduring authority over Angkor.[22] Beyond such geo-political concerns, we have also seen here that Cambodian visitors to these sites look forward to, and expect, significant levels of restoration. Juxtaposing these accounts against policy formulations reveals how such aspirations, along with the values of local residents, have been largely overlooked in an administrative environment increasingly concerned with the representation of particular landscape aesthetics.

This chapter has examined the ties between tourism and heritage industries, both of which, in the case of Angkor, have Eurocentric genealogies. There is little doubt that the changing nature of tourism at Angkor will deliver new dynamics to this socio-political matrix in the future. With countries from Europe, North America, and Australasia dominating arrival statistics throughout the 1990s and in the early years thereafter, the framings I have outlined in this chapter principally pertain to these countries. The degree to which these are 'global', and thus universally shared, is a question which lies beyond the scope of the book. Rather, it has been suggested here that these 'western' framings have provided the dominant discourse molding Angkor development's since it reemerged as a major tourist destination after decades of internal conflict. Indeed, I would suggest the rise of the Asian tourist at the beginning of the twenty-first century promises to destabilize any assumptions that tourism operates at sites like Angkor as a monolithic, global socio-cultural landscape. We have seen in this chapter that the gaze of international tourism has provided a valuable tool for upholding a Eurocentric representation of Angkorean heritage. The arrival of ASI and Indian tourism projects like the Museum of Traditional Asian Textiles in Siem Reap suggest this situation will be unsustainable in the longer term. As Korea, Taiwan, China, and Thailand continue to establish themselves as the most important source markets for Cambodia's tourism industry, the bonds between tourism and heritage at Angkor will need to be unraveled and retied in accordance with a shifting terrain of heritage and cultural landscape values.

7 Conclusion – in (the) place of modernity appears the illusion of history

> Underpinned by the notion that other cultures need preserving from the onslaught of a totalizing modernity and that their authenticity is under threat, such forms of romanticizing nature and the primitive may in fact simply consign the less developed economies to the status of an eco or cultural theme park for the developed world.
>
> (Meethan 2001: 65)

This book has considered one of the most crucial, turbulent periods in Angkor's 1200-year history. While the region might not have been sacked or abandoned, the twin invasions of a global heritage industry and millions of tourists, both domestic and international, have in themselves had a profound and unprecedented impact on the region. In this respect, Angkor presents us with an extreme example of the challenges facing countless heritage tourism landscapes around the world today. Studying this moment of rapid change therefore offers important insights into 'the social, cultural and political contexts that influence the use and interpretation of material culture', an area which, as Smith (2004: 51) argues, remains an under-researched field of enquiry. The context of Cambodia also provides us with a valuable analytical lens for understanding the opportunities and pitfalls tourism and heritage pose for the developing world and the complex role they play within the national and socio-cultural reconstruction of post-conflict, postcolonial societies. To illustrate this further this concluding chapter brings together, and reflects upon, the analytical threads of the book.

The speed at which Cambodia embraced modernity and globalization during the 1990s grossly exaggerated the paradoxes inherent to these two transformative processes. A real energy to develop, to move forward, modernize, and depart from the revolutionary, socialist politics of the recent past, was partnered by an intense desire to look back, to reclaim, and to retrieve what was lost. Post-war anxieties have also at once been muted and heightened by a broader geography of intense regional inter-connectivity, where Cambodia's borders have become increasingly porous to flows of capital, people, ideas, and goods. The desire to re-establish the 'authentic', the 'traditional' or even the 'pure' has been paralleled by a willingness to open up, and to absorb the foreign. It was widely recognized that a key focal point for these interweaving agendas would be the Angkor-Siem Reap region in the northwest of the country. It was a recognition, however, that looked beyond the actual temples themselves, and towards Angkor's role in the emergence of two key industries: heritage and tourism. The development of a 'cultural heritage' industry promised the restoration of identity, history, cultural sovereignty, and national pride. International tourism promised much needed socio-economic development. There was little doubt Angkor would stand in the foreground of both these industries in the coming years.

Cambodia's grossly inadequate human and technological resources in the early 1990s clearly demanded a need for external assistance and regulatory guidance. As we saw in Chapter 3, for foreign experts to secure the protection of an endangered material culture, a legislative and bureaucratic architecture urgently needed to be imposed and enforced as rigorously as possible. One of UNESCO's long-term priorities has been the reconstruction of a body of Cambodian expertise in the fields of archaeology, temple conservation, heritage law, and site management. In many cases, long before 'experts' could emerge and assume responsibility young students needed to be taught rudimentary skills and knowledge. In the world of late twentieth-century cultural heritage management however, acquiring 'basic skills' has invariably involved mastering complex surveying and restoration techniques, or learning GIS and 3D modeling software. Investing in a new generation of scholars and bureaucrats has required hundreds of thousands of dollars of international aid, a cost worth paying for an authoritative domestic body capable of safeguarding Angkor against a turbulent and unpredictable social environment. Away from the Angkor park itself, the introduction of national legislation and community-based education programs have also been vital tools in the battle against temple looting and the burgeoning cross-border trafficking of Cambodia's cultural artifacts (UNESCO 1997, 1999).

The demands and challenges of a post-conflict, post-genocidal situation have therefore acted as powerful forces in the creation of a processual-based form of cultural heritage management, as outlined by Smith in Chapter 1. Given that reconciliation and national reconstruction were urgent and unequivocally worthy goals, the restoration of Angkor presented itself as a self-evident task that warranted international assistance. The technologies and knowledge systems of CRM, archaeology, and architectural conservation could thus bring positive and concrete benefits. Although such interventions would not play a role in reconciling ethnic divisions, as they have in post-war Balkan countries for example, they could still contribute to the reconstruction of trust and social order at the national level.[1] Not surprisingly, at this particular historical juncture questions of epistemology and reflexivity were secondary concerns and perhaps, for some, wholly inappropriate. Attempts to analytically dismantle power, knowledge structures might, after all, rapidly lead to a gridlock of cultural and political relativism, and perhaps even create further volatility in a highly challenging environment.

Reflecting upon the role of archaeology and cultural heritage policies within a variety of non-western contexts, Meskell nonetheless concludes that if a dialogue is to address the complex socio-political challenges of post-war or postcolonial countries in a productive and ethical manner, it must include a reflexivity towards the flows of power that are 'indelibly entwined' within claims of authenticity and universality. After all conflating 'epistemic relativity (all beliefs are socially produced) ... [with] ... judgmental relativism (all beliefs are equally valid)' is both 'irresponsible and counter-productive' (1998: 9). She suggests that regardless of the circumstances we must remain aware of Eurocentric values and patterns of knowledge by situating archaeology within its historical and geographical contexts of orientalism, postcolonialism, and globalization. Only then can we better understand how globally roaming fields of enquiry and knowledge production, such as archaeology and cultural heritage, retain residues of historical power. Indeed, for Meskell the postcolonial challenge is to display the degree to which they 'remain the stepchildren of imperialism' (ibid: 3).

Highly pertinent to Angkor, the questions and themes raised by Smith and Meskell have been given sustained attention here. An account of Angkor's management under French authorities during the early decades of the twentieth century has provided the foundations for a critique of heritage as a historically constituted socio-political discourse in order to ask important questions about in/ter/dependencies and postcolonial cultural politics. It has been suggested that a master, disciple heritage discourse creates a situation whereby Cambodia's history is once again interpreted, constructed, and documented by non-Cambodian scholars. Approaching heritage as the convergence of authority and knowledge reveals how local voices and values are politically marginalized within a hierarchy of international 'expertise' operating in a domestic context characterized by fundamentally weak social and intellectual infrastructures.

As the undisputed source of knowledge on architectural conservation, epigraphy, and archaeology, EFEO provides France with a powerful mechanism for claiming authority over Angkor. The temples clearly remain a point of focus for a lingering romance towards Indochina, an imagining Robson and Yee (2005: 9–10) argue has strengthened, rather than dissipated, in France in recent years. Accordingly, I have argued that a former French colonial vision of Angkor, which essentially conceived the site as a dead, monumental landscape of the 'ancient' past, is being reproduced by a framework of world heritage today. Chapters 3 and 6 demonstrated how conservation and restoration, as technically and scientifically based languages, have been pivotal to the ongoing idealization of Angkor. Science also pulls a veil over hidden forms of power. Indeed, a detailed examination of Ta Prohm and Preah Khan has indicated how the conservation of partial ruins 'discovered' and reclaimed from the jungle sustains a Eurocentric narrative of romantic ruins and colonial restitution. Simultaneously though, we have also seen how world heritage enables government-funded teams from India, Japan, and China to assert claims of religious, cultural or national patronage over Angkor for their respective countries. Given the additional involvement of embassies and organizations from the US, Italy, Indonesia and others, we can see that Angkor has come to be stretched along a number of geo-political or religio-historical lines of interest.

For the Royal Government, rather than resisting the involvement of further countries, new projects have provided new opportunities to dilute existing power, knowledge structures, and in particular the stranglehold of EFEO. Decades after an era of colonialism the government has thus seized upon an elaborate program of foreign assistance to restrengthen sovereignty over a unifying marker of cultural, ethnic and national strength, and grandeur. To treat the introduction of an external cultural heritage discourse merely as a unipolar imposition of power would therefore miss forms of reappropriation at the local or national level. Indeed, as we saw in Chapters 3 and 4, a framework of world heritage has emerged as a politically and economically expedient resource for a country engaged in post-conflict reconstruction, reconciliation, and nation building. As noted, the freezing of Angkor as a site of classical antiquities reflects the government's desire to reaffirm a monolithic, all-encompassing, national culture. Far more than merely the science of temple conservation, heritage at Angkor has thus become a complex political matrix whereby nationalisms, cultural ties created in previous centuries and future strategic partnerships are simultaneously denied, strengthened and (re)negotiated.

While there is little doubting that the protection and conservation of Angkor's architectural structures and archaeological research have been worthy and important enterprises, this book has argued that, in both scholarship and policy, the Angkor-Siem Reap region has been essentially understood as a physical landscape, a geographically bounded, material space. As a consequence, significantly less attention has been given to understanding the site's broader social, political and economic contexts; the wider societal context of a post-conflict, postcolonial Cambodia.

Since the early 1990s, the ICC has been the largest, most powerful body addressing the restoration of Cambodia's cultural heritage. As we have seen though, cultural heritage has been framed through a language of rational science, underpinned by a logical positivism and belief in universality. Science ensures rigor, and that 'international standards' of excellence are maintained across teams from a number of countries. A focus on vestigial glory has, however, retained the binaries of regal/vernacular, classical/non-classical and modern, traditional first introduced in the late nineteenth century. The limitations of such segmentation and demarcation have become apparent over the course of several chapters. In Chapters 3 and 4, for example, it was argued that Angkor's local residents have remained firmly on the margins of policies concerning both conservation and development.

Moreover, while it was noted that UNESCO intervened to overturn plans to relocate a number of monasteries outside the park, little attention has been given to the revival of Buddhism or the other religious practices of local residents. Publications by Ang Choulean (1988) and Ian Harris (2005) have shown us that Cambodia's Buddhism operates as a socially and politically engaged religion, and that it was a cultural heritage decimated by decades of physical and political violence. Given that Angkor is home to some of Cambodia's most important and symbolically charged monasteries, efforts to rejuvenate the *sangha* in the region would have given momentum to a broader religious and cultural revivalism at the national level. As Luco also notes, with the appropriate support, Angkor could have reemerged as a major pilgrimage site for Asian Buddhists.[2] Such forms of heritage tourism would help re-situate the site's monasteries – some of which date back to the

Angkorean Period and beyond – within their wider Asian Buddhist geographies (Thompson 2004).

An analysis of Khmer New Year has, however, highlighted how Angkor has reemerged as an important festival space. As a form of material culture, Angkor reminds Cambodians of their former glory as a people and as a country. Equally, accounts of the symbolic meaning attributed to the site's roads, rivers, picnic areas, and monasteries, along with the aspirations associated with rebuilding ruins like Ta Prohm and Preah Khan, have highlighted why the site is imbued with an optimism about the country's future. By situating domestic encounters within their postcolonial, post-conflict contexts, it has been argued that ruined temples serve as a metaphor for a population struggling to recover from decades of national turmoil. It has also been suggested that over the first decade of world heritage such domestic constructions of place were essentially ignored by a framework concerned with preserving and presenting architectural antiquities for high-spending 'cultural tourists'. In recognition of the lack of attention given to such issues, APSARA created a new department in 2004 to address Angkor as a landscape of 'living heritage'.[3] Although setting out with modest aims, their new research projects marked the beginning of a turn towards more community-based understandings of heritage; ones that approach the region in more humanist, multi-vocal, multi-temporal terms.

One of the recurring themes of the book has been the cultural and political parallels between the contemporary era and a former period of European colonialism. In both eras, heritage and tourism have been two interweaving arenas through which Cambodia's culture and history have been narrated and framed in terms of resuscitation and revival. At the beginning of the twentieth century French scholars and bureaucrats constructed a narrative of reclaiming Cambodia's cultural masterpiece from the jungle. An emergent nationalism would thus (r)evolve around a story of dormancy, decay, and subsequent restoration. As Chandler (1998: 38) has noted, throughout the 1960s and 1970s Cambodia's political leaders remained 'prisoners to the illusion' of Angkorean glory and its association with Khmer power. In a post-Khmer Rouge era a language of restoration would powerfully appear again, this time fuelled by an urgent need to reverse the devastation caused by genocide and more than two decades of violent conflict. In both eras Angkor's temples have stood in the foreground of this picture. And in both eras, they have been canonized as a focal points for collective hopes and aspirations. Indeed, the matrix of foreign assistance in recent years has ensured Angkor remains a phantasmagoria of Cambodian history. Given the recent logistical difficulties of conducting fieldwork across the country international teams have not surprisingly focused their attention on a small area demarcated for special attention and protection. With its cartographic representations, world heritage Angkor has thus reaffirmed an earlier vision of the region as the apogee of a tri-focal narrative; a landscape beyond which lies the less illustrious 'pre'- and 'post'- Angkorean histories. Understandings of Cambodian history, along with visions of Khmer culture and identity, are therefore once again being firmly welded onto a static vision of a glorious and timeless moment of the past.

Tracing continuities with the representations of a former colonial period has also been profitable for understanding Angkor's secularization, commodification, and presentation as a site of consumption. Chapter 2's discussion of the site's construction as an icon of an exotic and mystical Indochine – through various expositions held in France and its transformation into a 'park' – provided the foundation for interpreting the aesthetic and cultural logics which continue to define how Angkor is framed and narrated as a tourist space today. Accordingly, since the early 1990s a cultural economy has formed which packages, narrates, and sells romance, exotic adventure and global antiquities. For today's commercial sector the idea of rediscovery has proved an economically expedient theme in two distinct, but overlapping, ways. First, and as Chapter 5 demonstrated, Angkor has been promoted as a destination once again 'opening up' and 'recovering', a place to travel to before all the tourists arrive. Paralleling this, hotel interiors, tour brochures, guidebooks and even airline magazines have also revisited a story of nineteenth-century 'discovery' to evoke another golden age of travel, a time of adventure before all the mass tourists did arrive. In this respect, the industry's selective use of place and culture formulations socially constructed during the last 150 years has proved highly effective in seducing foreign tourists to the country in ever-increasing numbers. This reappropriation of Angkor's 'modern' history within the cultural economies of contemporary tourism reaffirms Canclini's assertion that, 'It is not that national culture is extinguished but, rather, that it is converted into a formula for designating the continuity of an unstable historical memory that is now being reconstituted in interaction with transnational cultural referents' (2001: 8).

Indeed, for international tourists, persistent visions of an exotic, romantic Indochina, along with images of war and genocide and the fact that visits to the country are typically incorporated within a variety of regional itineraries, mean that few, if any, connections are made between the site and its national context. As a consequence, Angkor's ruins often emerge as a metaphor for a mysterious Indochina; a region replete with once glorious, but lost, ancient civilizations. As with the prevailing heritage discourse, the tourism industry represents Angkor as a space devoid of human history or vernacular culture. An analysis of the partial ruins Preah Khan and Ta Prohm has revealed how such imaginings and framings connect with particular spatialized practices of consumption. The freedom to wander, touch, sit and clamber across trees roots and fallen stones evokes mystery and adventure, and a history of abandonment followed by a moment of discovery. It can thus be seen that various historical and contemporary processes have led to the ascendancy of particular imaginings of Angkor within a cultural economy of international tourism. Understandings of the site's significance as Cambodian heritage, the violence inflicted during an era of colonialism or the individual histories of other countries across the region are all erased within representations that romanticize, aestheticize, and rely upon certain cultural topographies of Southeast Asia. Clearly, international tourism at Angkor has become a medium through which a 'Phantasmatic Indochine', to use Norindr's term, continues to be produced as 'an unproblematic object of visual pleasure and consumption' (1996: 158).

A look at consumption practices within their broader socio-historical contexts has given some idea of how Angkorean tourism, both national and international, continues to harness the fatal attraction of nostalgia and idealized bygone eras. Chapter 6 further pursued this analytical thread to demonstrate how certain touristic narratives and representations have gained ascendancy within the broader public sphere surrounding Angkor. Through a detailed examination of the partially ruined site, Ta Prohm, it has been argued that UNESCO's desire to preserve an aesthetic intended to re-invoke the romance of Angkor's discovery by European travelers in the late nineteenth century has, in part, sought its legitimacy from the need to uphold particular imagery circulating within today's international tourism industry. A political reading of this situation confirms Roy's warning that nostalgia 'obscures agency and culpability. When formalized as heritage, nostalgia goes a step further; it produces legitimacy through aestheticization' (2004: 65). Through an implicit conceptualization of tourism and heritage as mutually constitutive industries, the book has therefore reflected upon how they combine as agents of cultural imperialism; an issue Hall and Tucker argue has yet to receive the 'recognition or interrogation in tourism studies that it deserves' (2004: 6).

Cambodia's recent history has heavily eroded the country's public sphere and profoundly undermined the ability of civil institutions to meet the challenges and contradictions posed by heritage and tourism. The Ministry of Culture and Fine Arts, for example, lacks both expertise and funding to tackle the complex relationships between identity and culture, tradition and modernity in nuanced, variegated terms. In such a context, architectural antiquities, indisputability Khmer and Cambodian in their provenance, remain a boundless source of pride for a population recovering from decades of turmoil. International tourism has provided an important medium for the performance of revived grandeur. Indeed as Chapter 4 illustrated, a post-war, post-socialist government has turned towards the supranational consumption values associated with tourism in order to meet its own ideological interests. In this respect, we can see that the situation in Cambodia exemplifies Yúdice's assertion that, in such cases where consumption culture 'exceeds the territorial boundaries of the nation-state ... the state is not weakened but, rather, that it has been reconverted to accommodate new forms of organization and capital accumulation' (2003: 167).

Beyond the site itself, the temples also remain the dominant reference point for the production of material and non-material cultures. As I have argued elsewhere, the APSARA dance, now presented as the authentic, classical Cambodian dance, has become the obligatory, and often sole, cultural performance international visitors to the country experience. Angkor's narrowing effect on Cambodia's performing arts industry has also been taken up by Turnbull. Within an account that traces the political and economic factors shaping this industry over the course of the twentieth century, Turnbull argues cultural heritage grants since the early 1990s have principally been directed towards 'the country's architectural and archaeological patrimony rather than its equally fragile intangible legacy' (2006: 139). In 1960, Phnom Penh was home to 30 performance art theaters, and the country boasted around 50 theater companies. Today there are only two commercially run theatres for the entire country. Destroyed by fire in 1994, the ruinous Suramarit theatre in Phnom Penh, once the icon of a vibrant culture of independence, symbolizes the political, economic inertia surrounding the country's performance arts.[4] While Turnbull welcomes recent efforts by UNESCO, various NGOs and the Royal University of Fine Arts to restore shadow puppetry and classical and non-classical dance forms, he concludes:

> While Cambodians appear to cling determinedly to the fundamentals of Khmer identity, endless replicating the *kbach*, gilded apsaras, and hanuman masks for commercial gain, their connection to the nation's intangible culture has been more tenuous ... the paucity of the great dance dramas that form the kernel of the performing repertory of live performances makes it difficult for the general public to form any meaningful attachment with this important body of work.
>
> (2006: 140)

Turnbull's account reveals the priorities of the state's cultural enterprise, and its desire to source cultural markers of indisputable provenance. This quest for a homogeneous ethno-national identity has also been examined by Dahles and ter Horst in their analysis of Cambodia's silk industry. They suggest the revival of silk production and designs 'celebrates ethnic Khmer dominance' (2006: 124) in part through a genealogical link with the courts of Angkor. Accordingly, by connecting 'the weaving of traditional silk garments for royal and religious ceremonies ... [with Angkor] ... these garments cannot be anything but traditionally and authentically Khmer' (Ibid: 130).

Together, the examples of domestic tourism, the silk industry, performing arts, and the national museum begin to illustrate what role, direct and indirect, Angkor plays in the restoration of Cambodia's cultural heritage. They also point towards the impact of tourism on such processes. An episode of profound turmoil has understandably given rise to a deep-seated anxiety over what constitutes Khmer and Cambodian identity. Classical, magisterial Angkor, free of any historical contamination, provides an immutable and indubitable marker of identity within a highly interconnected region. Fuelling this process, Angkorean centric heritage and tourism industries are therefore simultaneously advancing and restraining the parameters of the country's social and cultural revival. Dominated by vestigial glories, these two industries significantly increase the risk of the country trapping itself in a static, mono-cultural, mono-ethnic national identity. When considered alongside recent history, this situation becomes a cause for considerable concern.[5] In Chapter 1 Bevan's (2006) observations that the preservation of heritage sites can contribute to ongoing conflict and political hostilities was noted. As history has shown us, an idealized Angkor, cited as evidence of cultural and ethnic supremacy, has been used for virulent and in some cases extremely violent nationalisms. While the site appears to represent a benign marker of identity today, this book has presented a number of symbolic and material processes emerging from heritage and tourism to suggest more critical perspectives concerning current trajectories of nation building in Cambodia are still required.

Today Cambodia exemplifies Ong's (2006) description of economic globalization whereby places of hyper-growth like Angkor become surrounded by zones of abandonment. Historically unprecedented levels of tourism have transformed the region's temples into an immensely important resource for capital accumulation. The degree to which tourism has contributed to economic and political stability for the country as a whole remains open to question. There is little doubt that millions of dollars of income annually has been instrumental to a steady growth in GDP and that the industry has been the driving force for investments in both social and physical infrastructures. Equally however, the flows and distribution of wealth have been hugely disproportionate. In 1990, 46 percent of Cambodia's population were on the wrong side of the $1 a day index, with only Vietnam and Laos faring worse in Southeast Asia with 51 percent and 53 percent, respectively. And yet while Vietnam succeeded in reducing this figure to 13 percent by 2002, Cambodia continued to suffer from some of the highest levels of extreme poverty in Asia, with 34 percent of the population earning less than a dollar a day that year (ADB 2004: 40). The nature of tourism growth traced over a number of chapters here offers some insights into the factors driving these economic and social inequalities both within and beyond the town of Siem Reap.

As we have seen, the trajectory of Angkor's isolation as a heritage tourism landscape began with a ruler and pen in the 1920s. The mapping of the Angkor Archaeological Park on paper by French scholars would provide the blueprint for a zoning scheme of the 1990s which introduced stringent legislation and policies for a 400 square kilometer rectangle. A desire to prevent 'modern' intrusions and preserve the traditional feel of the park underpinned a decision to steer development towards the nearby urban space of Siem Reap. Although a world heritage framework identified the twin goals of conservation and development, Chapter 3 demonstrated why, over the course of the 1990s, the town was largely ignored through a representation of space that firmly prioritized architectural conservation and archaeology. At a time when conferences and training programs focused on carved, buried or precariously leaning sandstone, millions of tons of concrete were being poured in Siem Reap in response to ever-growing tourist numbers. While there is little doubt that Angkor's fragile temples warranted urgent and sustained attention, the neglect of tourism, and its social, economic consequences, would have deleterious consequences. We have also seen how tourism was overlooked by a foreign aid industry assisting with the country's socio-economic recovery. In the absence of any strategic development plans, the private sector has been unable, or unwilling, to make significant investments in developing other destinations beyond the Angkor-Siem Reap region. Over the course of the 1990s Siem Reap thus emerged as an enclave of development surrounded by sustained rural poverty.

The eventual arrival of a language of 'cultural tourism', with its focus on high-quality facilities, at the beginning of the 2000s, did little to improve the social and geographical distribution of the industry. For the international members of the ICC the careful management of hotels and transport flows for 'cultural tourists' reflected a desire to minimize the geographical impact of the industry, whereas for the governing CPP party, control over Siem Reap's tourism infrastructure represented a source of major revenue. Cambodia's precarious political and economic climate throughout this period fostered short-term perspectives towards development. Rather than investing millions of dollars in nationwide, long-term projects, government officials looked to swiftly maximize Angkor's value as a 'cash-cow' of development. Becoming a stakeholder in Angkorean tourism, whether it be in hotels, land, transport companies or tax revenues, would also mean benefiting from a vast influx of capital. The escalation of land prices in Siem Reap exemplify the problems highlighted in the damning report on corruption in the country produced by USAID in 2004. According to the authors, 'since the 1980s, 20-30 per cent of the country's land, the main source of wealth, has passed into less than one percent of the population' (Calavan et al. 2004: 2).

Even within a discourse of 'sustainable development', inadequate attention has been given to dispersing wealth to regions and communities beyond the Angkor, Siem Reap region. Crucially, and as we saw in Chapter 4, any efforts made in this direction have also been hampered by Cambodia's insufficient infrastructures, an image of political and violent turmoil and Angkor's position within an interconnected regional industry. Decades of uneven development since the Second World War has led to the emergence of a number of powerful nodes across the region, through which the majority of tourists, aircraft, images, communications and investments continue to flow. These *touristscapes*, as I have called them here, at once both reflect and reaffirm the geographical distribution of tourism across the region. For Angkor, this has meant the site has all too often been Cambodia's sole stop on region-wide itineraries favoring more developed neighboring countries.

In Chapter 1 it was noted that tourism, as a networked industry, inevitably stretches its frontiers. With the Ministry of Tourism now actively promoting 'ethnic' tourism in Mondulkiri and Ratnikiri, these eastern provinces, along with Anlong Veng in the north and the country's coastline, will continue to emerge as destinations. The great lake Tonle Sap also holds potential for the development of nature and village tourism. As independent travelers and backpackers make inroads across the country the necessary infrastructures will steadily grow and evolve, and Cambodia's image of danger and risk will naturally dissipate in tandem with these developments. Indeed, recent years have seen a significant increase in the country's popularity as a destination for casino and sex tourism, with Phnom Penh and the border town of Poipet emerging as the main centers of commerce. Further growth in these industries will principally come from intra-regional markets, and in particular from Northeast Asia (Winter 2007). Nonetheless, the ongoing growth, even acceleration, of tourism at Angkor – with some estimates suggesting a number of five million by 2010 – mean that regional imbalances and major wealth inequalities within and across communities will be inevitable in the future. As Calavan et al. (2004) warn us, ever-increasing concentrations in national wealth will continue to create major stumbling blocks in the country's socioeconomic recovery and political reform.

In setting out to interpret the various factors shaping these patterns and imbalances of development, *Post-conflict Heritage, Postcolonial Tourism* has attempted to address Gupta and Ferguson's call for a better understanding of how 'dominant cultural forms may be picked up and used – and significantly transformed – in the midst of the power relations that link localities to a wider world' (1997: 5). Through heritage tourism, culture and cultural landscapes will continue to be valuable resources for developing countries seeking growth and economic prosperity. Transforming while they entrap, restoring while they erode, and cultivating while they restrict, there is little doubt that the contradictions and paradoxes inherent to heritage and tourism will continue as we advance into the twenty-first century. In an attempt to offer some insights into such processes, this book has located Angkor within its broader social context to suggest that scholars of tourism and heritage need to pay closer attention to the residues of historical power within today's globalization, the myriad challenges posed by post-conflict reconstruction, and how, within such contexts, places, cultures, and histories become expedient resources for economic and political gain.

Notes

1 From a time of conflict to conflicting times

1 Robinson and Wheeler 1992: 7.
2 During CPK's regime killings varied greatly between regions and over time. For a detailed account of variations between levels of brutality across the country's administrative zones, see Kiernan (1996).
3 Rowley (1996) estimated that their income for 1992 alone was somewhere between $100 and $300 million, making them the richest player in Cambodian politics at that time.
4 Source: Cambodian Rehabilitation and Development Board (1996) Development Cooperation Report 1995/1996. Phnom Penh: Council for the Development of Cambodia.
5 For further details see University of Sydney, *Greater Angkor Project* homepage: http://acl.arts.usyd.edu.au/projects/externalprojects/urbanangkor.html
6 Agraval (2004).
7 For further details on the consumption and appropriation of the site as a sacred landscape see Yalouri 2001: 174.
8 They state, 'Atrocity characteristically involves desecration, destruction, Vernichtung: physical evidence is very likely to be destroyed or concealed ... and each group of perpetrators, victims and bystanders have their own reasons for denying or forgetting. Against such a background, the problem of management and marketing the heritage of atrocity is the cardinal dilemma of dissonant heritage' (1996: 129).
9 For further details see Stark and Griffin (2004).

2 'Lost civilization' to free-market commerce: the modern social life of Angkor

1 For further details on the publication of Mouhot's accounts see Barnett (1990) or Edwards (2007).
2 For further details see Malraux (1930).
3 Edwards (2007) argues cartography was crucial to the formation of a modern Cambodge. In addition to the creation of new territorial and political entities across the region, European cartography imposed radically new conceptualizations of space and place; ones that challenged and in some cases transcended existing spatialities derived from oral traditions, cosmological representations, ancestral toponyms, and temple architecture. For further details also see Chandler (1996a).
4 'L'anastylose, méthode de reconstruction des monuments anciens. Son application à l'art Khmer' Cahiers de Ecole Française d'Extrême Orient, No 29, Hanoi 1942. Cited in Dagens (1995: 176). Coedès would express similar sentiments two decades later. In his 1963 *Angkor: An Introduction* he stated: 'People with a romantic taste for mysterious ruins have always preferred to believe that, in spite of evidence to the contrary, almost nothing was known about the Khmer monuments ... The lovers of romanticism have even reproached the French archaeologists for denuding the ruins

of the vegetation which obscured them, and for making them both accessible and comprehensible. Unfortunately, we were obliged to choose between clearing the ruins or having them devoured by the forest'. p. 10.

5 An example of this hierarchical division can be found in the account presented in the opening chapter of Henri Parmentier's 1959 'Guide to Angkor'. Dominated by explanations of the Indian pantheon of Hindu deities, little attention is given to other religious forms or aspects of Angkorean history. See Parmentier (1959).

6 See for example Coedès (1968) or Dumarcay & Groslier (1973).

7 George Coedès for example demonstrated how the ascension of Jayavarman II to the throne in 802 marked the end of a transition from a pre-Angkorean style of architecture to a full Angkorean form of design. For a general overview see Chapter 7 of his 1963 *Angkor: an Introduction* which outlines changes in column design, the emergent use of Makaras, and other ornamental features.

8 See for example: Coedès (1963), Parmentier (1939), Groslier & Arthaud (1966).

9 After the death of Jayavarman VII in the early thirteenth century, Theravada Buddhism spread across Southeast Asia bringing with it a new austere philosophy. This shift severely undermined the social foundations upon which Angkor's temples were built, such as forced labor, high bureaucracy, slavery, and economic priorities. For further details see Chandler (1996a).

10 Recent scholarship on the region has increasingly problematized the idea of Angkor as an 'empire'. Given the difficulties of conceptualizing what constitutes a premodern state or polity, the degree to which Angkor acted as a centralized authority with control over outlying territories of populations remains a point of debate and contestation. See for example Wolters (1999).

11 Wright (1991) quotes Martial Merlin, an infamously repressive Governor General, who spoke of the French mission to 'reawaken' a civilization that had been 'for centuries now … mentally retarded, more or less asleep' (Conseil de Gouvernement de l'Indochine, Session Ordinaire de 1923 Hanoi: Imprimerie de d'Extrême-Orient 1923: 13). For further details see Wright (1991: 199).

12 This process began in 1911 with a royal declaration that a protection zone of 200 meters should be installed around Angkor's key monuments.

13 Within its pro-Cambodian tone, Nagara Vatta was influential in giving a voice to Cambodians, including scholars from the two institutes mentioned here. Published in Khmer, the paper not only circulated among the educated and elite classes of Phnom Penh, but also reached a far greater audience than previous French publications. See Edwards (2007) for further details.

14 Mabbett and Chandler (1995) also discuss the emergence of an anti-colonial sentiment within Cambodia, arguing that its formation was considerably less vociferous and slower than in neighboring Vietnam. Elaborating further, Chandler (1996b) points out that the French successfully channeled nationalistic sentiments against a communist, and thus by implication anti-colonial, ideology which was spreading eastwards across Indochina at that time.

15 For further details see Edwards (1999: 19–20, 366–8).

16 For an overview of the relationship between culture and politics arising from this architectural reconstruction see Wright (1991).

17 For a detailed explanation of the development of riverine transport and trade links between Cochinchina, Cambodia, and Bangkok see Edwards (2006).

18 In 1907 Lunet de Lajonquière, a representative for EFEO, officially acknowledged that greater attention needed to be paid to improving the access and accommodation facilities for tourists. For further details see Edwards (2007).

19 In tracing this moment of transition Edwards (2007) outlines the influential account of Louis Delaporte which described the disturbing disjunction felt by certain tourists between a European woodland and Angkor's untamed wilderness.

20 Cited in Edwards (1999: 225).
21 According to Edwards, by 1929 Cambodia had developed 2400 kilometers of surfaced road, and among the country's growing number of vehicles 1840 tourist cars and just over 800 buses were registered for commercial use. For further details see Edwards (2006).
22 Muan also cites Groslier's description of 'a "latent aesthetic" which revealed a "Cambodian temperament", an "ancient soul".' (2001: 20).
23 Cited in Steinberg 1959: 285.
24 Cited in Barnett (1990: 122). Barnett goes on to add that Sihanouk was able to present his own 'survival as equivalent to that of the nation's ... [and] ... that Cambodia was close to extinction' (ibid: 123).
25 For further details regarding the replica of the Bayon see Anderson (1991: 183) and Edwards (2007). An avid filmmaker, Sihanouk also constructed a number of storylines around Angkor. *Ombre sur Angkor* (Shadow over Angkor) featured Sihanouk acting in his own production.
26 Slogans taken from advertisements for The National Tractor Company placed in Cambodian newspapers during the mid 1960s.
27 In the face of an escalating conflict EFEO eventually ceased activities and withdrew from Cambodia in 1972.
28 Inclusive in the respect that Lon Nol's ideology moved away from Sihanouk's elitist understanding of Angkorean history. It was, however, a message that once again excluded Cambodia's Chinese, Vietnamese, Malay, and other ethnic minorities.
29 For further details see Kiernan (1996).
30 Emphasis his.

3 World heritage Angkor

1 See Winter (2007) for a detailed account of the Malaysian-based YTL-proposed 'master plan' for the Siem Reap region.
2 From the French original: *Autorité pour la Protection du Site et l'Aménagement de la Région d'Angkor.*
3 Ongoing political problems, most notably the 1997 Phnom Penh coup, meant foreign support for organizations like APSARA was becoming increasingly unjustifiable. In 1999 UNESCO successfully established a new entrance ticket concession for Angkor with the Sokha Hotels Company, a subdivision of Sokimex Petroleum. This created a direct revenue stream for APSARA, with a small percentage of sales revenue taken by the concessionaire. (See ICC (1999) for further details regarding APSARA's ongoing financial difficulties, and APSARA (2000a) for details of Sokha Hotels Company ticket concession.)
4 UNESCO (1993) Safeguarding and Development of Angkor, Tokyo: UNESCO.
5 The ICC has typically met twice a year. Once in the guise of an ambassadorial level meeting which has maintained diplomatic coherence and highlighted broad strategic directions. The second, more scholarly style conferences, entitled Technical Meetings, have focused on heritage policies and key projects. UNESCO has diligently published reports for each of these meetings. For further details see, *International Co-ordinating Committee for the Safeguarding and Development of the Historic Site of Angkor; Plenary Session.* Phnom Penh: ICC. Published from 1993 onwards. See also *Bayon Symposium Report.* Phnom Penh: ICC Published from 1996 onwards.
6 Similarly, UNESCO has also published annual reports summarizing the ICC's key activities for the year. See for example *International Co-ordinating Committee for the Safeguarding and Development of the Historic Site of Angkor; Report of Activities.* Phnom Penh: ICC. Published from 1993 onwards.
7 For details of both Sophia University and APSARA archaeological research see the special edition of Udaya on ceramics; APSARA (2000b).

8 This neglect of traditions and temple usage by the international heritage community forms part of Miura's (2004) PhD thesis, which focuses on the impact world heritage enlistment has had on one particular village within the park. For further details see Miura (2004).

9 In recognition of this specific problem Monash University organized a three-day conference in July 2005 entitled *Old Myths and New Approaches, Advances in the Interpretation of Ancient Religious Sites in Southeast Asia.*

10 For further details see Agraval, (2004) *World Bank Projects in Siem Reap*, Paper presented at ICC Technical Committee Meeting, Siem Reap, 9–10 February 2004. Phnom Penh: World Bank.

11 Excerpt taken from; *Preserving Angkor: Interview with Ang Choulean, Director of the Department of Culture and Monuments of the Apsara Authority.* Interview October 13, 2000 at Apsara Authority office, Council of Ministers Building, Phnom Penh, Cambodia. Available online at: http://www.talesofasia.com/cambodia-interviews-AC.htm (accessed 1 December 2005).

12 For further details of ancestral worship in and around Angkor region see also Thompson, A. (2004) Calling the Souls: A Cambodian Ritual Text, Phnom Penh: Reyum.

13 This estimate is derived from APSARA records of numbers visiting Angkor. It is acknowledged however that due to the lack of transparency in data collection in the mid 1990s the levels stated are potentially under representative. Comparison with Ministry of Tourism records of 1996, which state the levels of tourist entrants to the country reached around 133,000 for the year of 1994, further cloud the picture as these undoubtedly incorporate UNTAC-related arrivals.

14 See ICC (1995) *Report of Activities 1994.* Phnom Penh: ICC; ICC (1996) *Report of Activities 1995.* Phnom Penh: ICC; ICC (1997) *Report of Activities 1996.* Phnom Penh: ICC; ICC (1998) *Report of Activities 1997.* Phnom Penh: ICC; ICC (1999) *Report of Activities 1998.* Phnom Penh: ICC.

15 For descriptions of each APSARA department see Boffa Miskell Ltd and Fraser Thomas Ltd (1998) *Angkor Forest Rehabilitation and Landscape Enhancement Project.* Phnom Penh: APSARA & Royal Government of Cambodia. Section 2.9.

16 See Coedès (1944).

4 Remapping Angkor; from landscape to touristscape(s)

1 Source: Ministry of Tourism/UNDP/WTO (1996).

2 Source: Ministry of Tourism (2000).

3 For further details see 'Direct Siem Reap flights begin Friday' *Cambodia Daily*, Phnom Penh 19 December 1997, p. 18.

4 For a detailed account of Hun Sen's association with the term 'strong man' see Mehta & Mehta (1999).

5 The level of assistance had now been reestablished after donor confidence in the country dropped with the political coup of 1997. For details of specific funding withdrawals during this period see Asian Development Bank (1999).

6 See for example speech given by Hun Sen at the 3rd Consultative Group meeting, Tokyo, February 1999, in which he stated 'Before the first decade of the next century ends, Cambodia would like to fully reclaim its destiny, be a genuine partner in regional and global affairs and be well on its way to becoming a truly free nation, free from want and poverty above all'. Cited in CDC (1999: 8).

7 A situation that became apparent through interviews conducted with the Vice President of the Ministry of Tourism for Siem Reap province, Mr. Hoa Sotha in July 2001.

8 An understanding confirmed by a former UNESCO consultant who had worked closely with Bun Narith during his previous tenure as APSARA director in the mid 1990s.

9 Excerpt from ICC conference statement of Sum Manit – Secretary of State for Council of Ministers, Siem Reap, 6 July 2001.

10 Both taken from ICC conference statement of Sok An – Senior Minister for the Council of Ministers, Siem Reap, 6 July 2001.

11 Excerpt from opening statement of July 2001 ICC conference, Siem Reap, 6 July 2001.

12 See for example Miskell and Thomas (1998).

13 Statement of Mr. Ang Choulean, Director of Culture and Monuments, APSARA, ICC Technical Committee Meeting, 14 December 2000.

14 Taken from opening statement by Etienne Clement – UNESCO Director for Cambodia, 14 December 2000.

15 A situation confirmed through personal communication with UNESCO official, June 2001.

16 Indeed, Vann Molyvann stated that his reluctance to push forward such projects was a significant factor in his dismissal as APSARA director in July 2001. For further details see 'Angkor's Future in Fine Hands, Ex-Official Says' Cambodia Daily, Vol. 20 No. 92, 20 June 2001, pp. 1, 13.

17 Excerpt from interview with country director of one of Siem Reap's largest international tour operators, August 2001.

18 It is worth noting that, despite being entitled a 'national' seminar on tourism, the Cambodian partner to UNESCO for hosting the conference was APSARA, whose remit only extends as far as the Angkor, Siem Reap region, rather than the Ministry of Tourism.

19 Closing remarks given by M. Beschaouch, Special Advisor to UNESCO, Cambodia, during APSARA/UNESCO National Seminar on Cultural Tourism, Phnom Penh, 6 July 2001.

20 Closing remarks by H.E. Sok An, Senior Minister for the Council of Ministers and APSARA's Chairman of the Board of Trustees, during APSARA/UNESCO National Seminar on Cultural Tourism, Phnom Penh, 6 July 2001.

21 Speeches entitled *World Bank Projects in Siem Reap*, by Agraval, Ns, and *Siem Reap Harbor*, Asian Development Bank, both given during ICC Technical Committee Meeting, Siem Reap 9–10 February 2004.

22 Speeches entitled *Water Management* by Water and Power Consultancy Services (WAPCOS) (India) and Japanese Government Team for safeguarding Angkor (JICA) (Japan) given during ICC Technical Committee Meeting, Siem Reap 9–10 February 2004.

23 Speeches entitled *Roads* by Uk Someth, APSARA Authority and *Road National No 67* by Tram Im Tiv, Ministry of Public Works and Transport, RGC, both given during ICC Technical Committee Meeting, Siem Reap 9–10 February 2004.

24 One high-profile case illustrating the ongoing success of the ZEMP scheme for protecting the Angkor park was the removal of a karaoke club undergoing construction inside the Angkor park in 2000. For further details see 'UNESCO Urges Halt to Angkor Karaoke Club' by McPhillips, J. & Van Roeun, Cambodia Daily, 5 December 2000, p. 12.

25 See for example 'Smoother Driving in Siem Reap Next Year', by Souknilundon Southivongnorath Cambodia Daily, Phnom Penh, 27 June 2001, p. 8.

26 See for example: 'Tourism No Help to Siem Reap's Poorest', by Ball, M., Cambodia Daily, 17 December 2002, p. 1.

27 For further details see WTO (1999).

28 For an earlier account also see Fryer (1970).

29 Bearing in mind the pertinent date of Rigg's publication, such accounts would come to be revised to account for the East Asian financial crisis of 1997.

30 See 'Asean Tourism Ministers to Promote Regional "Branding"' by Shaftel, D., Cambodia Daily, 2–3 February 2002, p. 3.

31 Ministry of Tourism (2000).

32 See for example: 'Bangkok Airways Looks to Promote Cambodian Tourism', by Calvert, B, Cambodia Daily, 31 May 2001, p. 14.

33 Bangkok Airways in-flight magazine advertisement, April 2000.
34 This situation was confirmed by the director of Siem Reap, Angkor International Airport, May 2001. See also 'Tourism Group: Thais Undercut Cambodian Travel Industry' by Kim Kimsong, *Cambodia Daily*, 22 February 2002, p. 14.

5 Angkor in the frame

1 Section titles drawn from tourist quotes presented in text.
2 For further details see official *Mekong World Heritage Tour Project* website. Available online at: http://www.mekongworldheritage.com (accessed 8 August 2002).
3 Statement by Bangkok Airways President and CEO, Dr. Prasert Prasarttong-Osoth. Available online at: http://www.bangkokair.com (accessed 8 August 2002).
4 Excerpt from advertisement in Bangkok Airways in-flight magazine, April 2001.
5 Legends of Indochina Tour, for further details see www.legends-of-indochina.com (accessed 12 December 2002).
6 See also Dagens (1995) and Dieulefils (2001).
7 See 'Rebuilding a Bygone Era' *Cambodia Daily Weekend* 3–4 July 2004, pp. 8–9.
8 Taken from 'Grandeur Returns' pp. 21–2, promotional brochure by Percy Seneviratne, published by Raffles International Hotels and Resorts, Singapore.
9 Excerpt from reverse cover of 'Fables of the Exotic East Volume 1' promotional pack published by Raffles International Hotels and Resorts, Singapore, 2003.
10 This lack of data was acknowledged as a significant problem during the ICC technical conference in December 2000 and again at the UNESCO/APSARA workshop on Cultural Tourism in July 2001.

6 Collapsing policies and ruined dreams

1 According to Jacques and Freeman, inscriptions found at Preah Khan and Ta Prohm indicate the populations of their supporting villages reached 97,000 and 79,000, respectively (1997: 205, 218).
2 For a brief but informative overview of the social context of these sites see Higham (2001).
3 Colet and Eliot (1997).
4 At the time of writing no reliable statistics were available for visitor patterns to either of these sites. However, as an indication, a 2004–5 APSARA study on the nearby Bakheng complex observed that the average group number among Cambodians exceeded 30.
5 For further details concerning conservation activities see Sanday (2001).
6 Excerpt from speech by John Sanday, Program Director of WMF, Angkor, during ICC Technical Committee Meeting, 14 February 2003.
7 Early in 2001 the WMF director John Sanday also outlined plans to remove two large trees in Preah Khan and nearby Ta Som complex which threatened further structural damage.
8 Taken from a statement by John Sanday, Program Director of WMF, Angkor: 'we've had many years of working in the jungle, and have concerns of the nightmare destruction of priceless architecture'. Made during ICC Technical Committee Meeting, 14 February 2003.
9 Taken from personal interview with John Sanday, Siem Reap, 6 February 2001.
10 Ibid.
11 Ibid.
12 For further details see 'India to help restore temple at Angkor Wat', *The Hindu*, 11 February 2002, Available online at: http://www.hinduonnet.com/2002/04/11/stories/2002041102831100.htm and 'India offers $ 10m loan to Cambodia', *The Tribune*, 7 November 2002. Available online at: http://www.tribuneindia.com/2002/20021107/main8.htm (Both accessed 15 March 2006).

13 Excerpt from interview with Mr. Narasimhan, *The Hindu*, Online Edition, 21 March 2004. Available online at: http://www.hindu.com/2004/03/21/stories/2004032101021100.htm (accessed 15 March 2006).

14 Excerpt from 'India-Cambodia Relations', Statement by Ministry of External Affairs, India, March 2005. Available online at: http://meaindia.nic.in/foreignrelation/cambodia.htm See also Joint Statement, India and Cambodia, Phnom Penh, 11 April 2002. Available online at: http://meaindia.nic.in/declarestatement/2002/04/11js1.htm (Both accessed 15 March 2006).

15 A situation confirmed through a number of personal interviews with members of the ICC and UNESCO.

16 Cited in 'Conservation at Twenty Paces: The Politics of Angkor Restoration', by R. Turnbull, *Sarika*, Vol. 3 No. 4, Bangkok: 2004, p. 36.

17 'Round Table on Ta Prohm', Hosted by Archaeological Survey of India and Embassy of India, in collaboration with the APSARA Authority, UNESCO and JSA, Siem Reap, 5 February 2004.

18 Excerpts from statements by panel of 'ad hoc experts' appointed for Round Table on Ta Prohm.

19 All cited from 'Recommendations of the Round Table on Ta Prohm Temple, Siem Reap', 5 February 2004.

20 During the Round Table on Ta Prohm, Mr. Etienne Clément, Representative of UNESCO in Cambodia, stated: 'Our strategy is to safeguard the temple in full harmony with international and universal standards'. Siem Reap, 5 February 2004.

21 Cited in 'Conservation at Twenty Paces: The Politics of Angkor Restoration', by R. Turnbull, *Sarika*, Vol. 3 No. 4, Bangkok: 2004, p. 36.

22 In 2002-3 H.E. Sok An, Senior Minister, Minister in Charge of the Office of the Council of Ministers drew upon a number of Sanskrit terms within a number of heritage- and tourism-related speeches in recognition of the long-standing cultural ties between India and Cambodia.

7 Conclusion – in (the) place of modernity appears the illusion of history

1 For an overview of 'Order and Anarchy' in Yugoslavia, and the breakdown of mutual trust between Serbs and Croats see Layton, R. and Thomas, J. (2001) 'Introduction: the destruction and conservation of cultural property', in Layton, R., Stone, P.G. and Thomas, J. (eds) *Destructions and Conservation of Cultural Property*, London: Routledge.

2 Personal Communication during Phnom Bakheng Workshop, 4–6 December 2005, Siem Reap. For further details see Luco, F. (2006) 'The People of Angkor: Between Tradition and Development', in Chermayeff, J. (ed.) *Phnom Penh Workshop on Public Interpretation*, Phnom Penh: APSARA, World Monuments Fund.

3 These efforts have been supported through a collaborative project entitled 'Living with Heritage', established by the University of Sydney in 2005. For further details see: http://www.acl.arts.usyd.edu.au/angkor/lwh/index.php

4 According to Turnbull 'Of the three million dollars on average that the government spends annually on performance culture - a mere 0.25 per cent of Cambodia's national budget - much of it is allocated to a bloated network of around 3,000 administrators. (2006: 139).

5 Partly in response to such concerns, UNESCO assisted with the production of an 'Inventory of Intangible Cultural Heritage of Cambodia'. Published in 2004, this inventory provides an important foundation for the cultivation of cultural policies which seek to create more pluralistic and vernacular connections between the past and the present. For further details see, UNESCO/Ministry of Culture and Fine Arts (2004) *Inventory of Intangible Cultural Heritage of Cambodia*, Phnom Penh: UNESCO/Ministry of Culture and Fine Arts.

Bibliography

Abram, S., Waldren, J. and Macleod, D. (1997) 'Introduction' in S. Abram, J. Waldren and D. Macleod (eds) *Tourists and Tourism: Identifying with People and Places*, Oxford: Berg, pp. 1–12.

Acker, R. (1998) 'New geographical tests of the hydraulic thesis at Angkor', *South East Asia Research*, Vol. 6, No. 1, pp. 5–47.

Adams, K. (2003) 'Global cities, terror, and tourism: the ambivalent allure of the urban jungle' in R. Bishop, J. Phillips and W. Yeo (eds) *Postcolonial Urbanism: Southeast Asian Cities and Global Processes*, London: Routledge, pp. 37–62.

Agraval, N. (2004) *World Bank Projects in Siem Reap,* Paper presented at ICC Technical Committee Meeting, Siem Reap, 9–10 February 2004, Phnom Penh: World Bank.

Allwood, J. (1977) *The Great Exhibitions*, London: Studio Vista.

Alvarez, S., Dagnino, E. and Escobar, A. (1998) 'Introduction: the cultural and the political in Latin American social movements' in S. Alvarez, E. Dagnino and A. Escobar (eds) *Cultures of Politics Politics of Cultures*, Boulder, Colorado: Westview Press, pp. 1–29.

Anderson, B. (1991) *Imagined Communities: Reflections on the Origin and Spread of Nationalism*, London: Cornell University Press.

Ang, C. (1988) 'The place of animism within popular Buddhism in Cambodia: the example of the monastery', *Asian Folklore Studies,* Vol. 47, pp. 35–41.

Anonymous (2002) *Statement, India and Cambodia, Phnom Penh, April 11, 2002.* Available online at: http://meaindia.nic.in/declarestatement/2002/04/11js1.htm (accessed 15 March 2006).

Appadurai, A. (1988) 'Introduction: commodities and the politics of value' in A. Appadurai (ed.) *The Social Life of Things*, Cambridge: Cambridge University Press, pp. 3–63.

— (1990) 'Disjuncture and difference in the global cultural economy', *Theory, Culture and Society,* Vol. 7, pp. 295–310.

APSARA (2000a) *Rapport d'Activities de L'Autorite APSARA pour la periode Juin-Decembre 2000*, ICC Conference Papers 14–15 December 2000, Phnom Penh: UNESCO.

— (2000b) *Udaya No.1 April 2000*, Phnom Penh: Department of Culture and Monuments, APSARA.

— (2001) *Angkor Tourist City Investment Brochure*, Phnom Penh: APSARA Authority - UNESCO - Agence Française de Développement.

Ashworth, G. (1994) 'From history to heritage - from heritage to identity: in search of concepts and models' in G.J. Ashworth and P.J. Larkham (eds) *Building a New Heritage: Tourism, Culture and Identity in the New Europe*, London: Routledge, pp. 13–30.

Ashworth, G. and Van Der Aa, B. (2002) 'Bamyan: whose heritage was it and what should we do about it', *Current Issues in Tourism,* Vol. 5, No. 5, pp. 447–57.

Asian Development Bank (1999) *Country Assistance Plan: Cambodia (2000-2002),* Phnom Penh: Asian Development Bank.

— (2004) *Key Indicators 2004: Poverty in Asia: Measurement, Estimates and Prospects,* Manila: Asian Development Bank.

Ayres, D. (2000) *Anatomy of a Crisis: Education, Development, and the State in Cambodia, 1953-1998,* Honolulu: University of Hawaii Press.

Ball, M. (2002) 'Tourism No Help to Siem Reap's Poorest, 17 December', *Cambodia Daily,* p. 1.

Bangkok Airways (2004) 'Accessible Angkor', *Fah Thai,* In-flight magazine, September–October 2004, p. 12.

Baram, U. and Rowan, Y. (2004) 'Archaeology after nationalism: globalization and the consumption of the past' in Y. Rowan and U. Baram, (eds) *Marketing Heritage: Archaeology and the Consumption of the Past,* Walnut Creek, California: Altamira Press, pp. 3–23.

Barnett, A. (1990) 'Cambodia will never disappear', *New Left Review,* Vol. 180, pp. 101–25.

Bauman, Z. (1998) *Globalization the Human Consequences,* New York: Columbia University Press.

Bender, B. (1999) *Stonehenge: Making Space,* Oxford: Berg.

Benjamin, W. (1999) *Illuminations,* London: Pimlico.

Bevan, R. (2006) *The Destruction of Memory, Architecture at War,* London: Reaktion Books.

Bhandari, C.M. (1995) *Saving Angkor,* Bangkok: White Orchid Press.

Bishop, R. and Clancey, G. (2003) 'The city as target, or perpetuation and death' in R. Bishop, J. Phillips and W.W. Yeo (eds) *Postcolonial Urbanism: Southeast Asian Cities and Global Processes,* London: Routledge, pp. 63–86.

Brown, F. and Timberman, D. (1998) 'Introduction: peace, development, and democracy in Cambodia - shattered hopes' in F. Brown and D. Timberman (eds) *Cambodia and the International Community: The Quest for Peace, Development and Democracy,* Singapore: Asia Society, pp. 13–31.

Brown, K. (1998) 'Contests of heritage and the politics of preservation in the former Yugoslav Republic of Macedonia' in L. Meskell, (ed.) *Archaeology Under Fire: Nationalism, Politics and Heritage in the Eastern Mediterranean and Middle East,* London: Routledge, pp. 68–86.

Buckley, J. (1999) 'Perfect ruin, after a long period of isolation, Cambodia's Angkor Wat is more accessible than ever. Go now before everybody catches on', *Washington Post Sunday,* p. EO1

Calavan, M., Briquets, S. and O'Brien, J. (2004) *Cambodian Corruption Assessment,* Phnom Penh: USAID.

Calvert, B. (2001) 'Bangkok Airways looks to promote Cambodian tourism', 31 May, *Cambodia Daily,* p. 14.

Cambodia Daily (1997) 'Direct Siem Reap flights begin Friday', 19 December, p. 18.

— (2001) 'Angkor's future in fine hands, ex-official says', 20 June, pp. 1, 13.

— (2004) 'Rebuilding a bygone era', *Cambodia Daily Weekend, July 3-4,* pp. 8–9.

Cambodia Today (2002) *Monks, Pagodas near Cambodia's Angkor Wat Can Stay, Official Says.* Associated Press Release, Phnom Penh, Distributed by Cambodia Daily, 22 June 2002. Available online at: http://go.to/CambodiaToday (accessed 2 September 2004).

Canclini, N. (2001) *Consumers and Citizens: Globalization and Multicultural Conflicts,* Minnesota: University of Minnesota Press.

Cartier, C. (2005) 'Introduction: touristed landscapes/seductions of place' in C. Cartier and A. Lew (eds) *Seductions of Place; Geographical Perspectives on Globalization and Touristed Landscapes*, London: Routledge, pp. 1–22.

Casey, E. (1996) 'How to get from space to place in a fairly short stretch of time: phenomenological prolegomena' in S. Feld and K. Basso (eds) *Senses of Place*, Santa Fe: School of American Research Press, pp. 13–52.

Castells, M. (1996) *The Rise of the Network Society*, Oxford: Blackwell.

Castells, M. (2000) *End of Millennium*, Oxford: Blackwell.

CDC (1999) *Cambodia: Economic Developments in 1999 and Outlook for 2000*, Phnom Penh: Cambodian Development Council.

Chandler, D. (1996a) *Facing the Cambodian Past: Selected Essays, 1971-1994*, Chiang Mai: Silkworm Books.

— (1996b) *A History of Cambodia*, Colorado, USA: Westview Press.

— (1998) 'The burden of Cambodia's past' in F. Brown and D. Timberman (eds) *Cambodia and the International Community: the Quest for Peace, Development and Democracy*, Singapore: Asia Society, pp. 33–47.

— (2000) *Voices from S-21: Terror and History in Pol Pot's Secret Prison*, Chiang Mai: Silkworm Books.

Chau, K.S. (2000) *The APSARA Authority Plan for Tourism*, Siem Reap: APSARA.

Chen, K.A.C.G. (eds) (1998) *Trajectories: Inter-Asian Cultural Studies*, London: Routledge.

Clarke, J. (1997) *Oriental Enlightenment: the Encounter Between Asian and Western Thought*, London: Routledge.

Coedès, G. (1944) *Histoire ancienne des états hindouisés d'Extrême-Orient*, Hanoi: Imprimerie d'Extrême-Orient.

— (1963) *Angkor: an Introduction*, London: Oxford University Press.

— (1968) *Inscriptions du Cambodge*, 8 Volume, Hanoi: EFEO, EFEO, *Textes et Documents sur l'Indochine, III, 1937-1966*, Paris: EFEO.

Coleman, S. and Crang, M. (eds) (2002) *Tourism, Between Place and Performance*, New York: Berghahn Books.

Colet, J. and Eliot, J. (1997) *Cambodia Handbook*, Bath, England: Footprint Handbooks Ltd.

Connerton, P. (1995) *How Societies Remember*, Cambridge: Cambridge University Press.

Cooper, N. (2001) *France in Indochina: Colonial Encounters*, Oxford: Berg.

Crouch, D. (1999) 'The intimacy and expansion of space' in D. Crouch (ed.) *Leisure/Tourism Geographies: Practices and Geographical Knowledge*, London: Routledge, pp. 257–76.

— (2005) 'Flirting with Space: tourism geographies as sensous/expressive practice' in C. Cartier and A. Lew (eds) *Seductions of Place; Geographical Perspectives on Globalization and Touristed Landscapes*, London: Routledge, pp. 23–35.

Curtis, G. (1998) *Cambodia Reborn?: The Transition to Democracy and Development*, Washington, D.C.: Brookings Institution.

Dagens, B. (1995) *Angkor: Heart of an Asian Empire*, London: Thames and Hudson.

Dahles, H. (2001) *Tourism, Heritage and National Culture in Java: Dilemmas of a Local Community*, Richmond: Curzon.

Dahles, H. and ter Horst, J. (2006) 'Weaving into Cambodia: negotiated ethnicity in the (post)colonial silk industry' in L. Ollier and T. Winter (eds) *Expressions of Cambodia: the Politics of Tradition, Identity and Change*, London: Routledge, pp. 119–32.

De Certeau, M. (1984) *The Practice of Everyday Life*, London: University of California Press.

De Kadt, E. (1979) *Tourism: Passport to Development?*, Oxford: Oxford University Press.

Diethelm Travel (2002) *Mekong World Heritage Tour*. Available online at: www.diethelm-travel.com/8mwh_home.html (accessed 20 April 2003).

Dieulefils, P. (2001) *Ruins of Angkor, Cambodia in 1909 (Facsimile Edition)*, Bangkok: River Books.

Dixon, C. and Smith, D. (1997) *Uneven Development in Southeast Asia*, Aldershot: Ashgate.

Domínguez, V. (1992) 'Invoking culture: the messy side of cultural politics', *South Atlantic Quarterly*, Vol. 91, No. 1, pp. 19–42.

Donovan, D. (1993) 'The Cambodian legal system: an overview' in F. Brown (ed.) *Rebuilding Cambodia; Human Resources, Human Rights and Law*, Washington: The John Hopkins Foreign Policy Institute, pp. 69–107.

Dumarcay, J. and Groslier, B.P. (1973) *Le Bayon, EFEO Mémoires Archéologiques, III-2*, Paris: EFEO.

Dwyer, D. (1990) 'Southeast Asia in the world today' in D. Dwyer (ed.) *Southeast Asian Development: Geographical Perspectives*, New York: Wiley, pp. 1–14.

Edensor, T. (1998) *Tourists at the Taj: Performance and Meaning at a Symbolic Site*, London: Routledge.

— (2001) 'Performing tourism, staging tourism: (re)producing tourist space and practice', *Tourist Studies*, Vol. 1, No. 1, pp. 59–77.

Edwards, P. (1999) 'Cambodge: the cultivation of a nation 1860-1945', Unpublished PhD thesis, Monash University.

— (2005) 'Taj Angkor: enshrining L'Inde in le Cambodge' in K. Robson and J. Yee (eds) *France and "Indochina"; Cultural Representations*, Lanham: Lexington Books, pp. 13–27.

— (2006) 'The tyranny of proximity: power and mobility in colonial Cambodia (1863-1954)', *Journal of Southeast Asian Studies*, Vol. 37, No. 3, pp. 421–43.

— (2007) *Cambodge: the cultivation of a nation 1860-1945*, Honolulu: University of Hawaii Press.

Edwards, P. and Winter, T. (2004) 'Ephemeral Angkor: a sign of different times', *Phnom Penh Post, December 17-31*, p. 18.

Etchison, C. (2005) *After the Killing Fields; Lessons from the Cambodian Genocide*, Connecticut: Praeger.

Evans, S. and Spaul, M. (2004) 'Straight ways and loss: the tourist encounter with woodlands and forests' in N. Lubbren and D. Crouch (eds) *Visual Culture and Tourism: A Reader*, London: Berg, pp. 205–22.

Forbes, D. (1999) 'Imaginative geography and postcolonial spaces of Pacific Asia' in T.-C. Wong and M. Singh (eds) *Development and Change: Southeast Asia in the New Millennium*, London: Times Academy Press, pp. 1–22.

Forty, A. and Küchler, S. (eds) (2001) *The Art of Forgetting*, Oxford: Berg.

Foucault, M. (1980) 'Two Lectures' in C. Gordan (ed.) *Power/Knowledge: Selected Interviews and Other Writings 1972-1977*, New York: Pantheon Books, pp. 78–108.

Franklin, A. and Crang, M. (2001) 'The trouble with tourism and travel theory?', *Tourist Studies*, Vol. 1, No. 1, pp. 5–22.

Fryer, D. (1970) *Emerging South East Asia: A Study in Growth and Stagnation*, London: Philip.

Gamboni, D. (1997) *The Destruction of Art: Iconoclasm and Vandalism Since the French Revolution*, London: Reaktion Books.

Giteau, M., Gueret, D. and Renaut, T. (1998) *Khmer Art: Civilisations of Angkor*, Paris: ASA Editions.

Goffman, E. (1990) *The Presentation of Self in Everyday Life*, London: Penguin.

Golden, J. (2004) 'Targeting heritage: the abuse of symbolic sites in modern conflicts' in Y. Rowan and U. Baram (eds) *Marketing Heritage: Archaeology and the Consumption of the Past*, Walnut Creek, California: Altamira Press, pp. 183–202.

Gottesman, E. (2003) *Cambodia After the Khmer Rouge: Inside the Politics of Nation Building*, New Haven: Yale University Press.

Graham, B., Ashworth, G. and Tunbridge, J. (2000) *A Geography of Heritage: Power, Culture, and Economy*, London: Oxford University Press.

Green, N. (1990) *The Spectacle of Nature*, Manchester: Manchester University Press.

Greenhalgh, P. (2000) *Ephemeral Vistas: the Expositions Universelles, Great Exhibitions and World Fairs, 1851 - 1939*, Manchester: Manchester University Press.

Gregory, D. (2001) 'Colonial nostalgia and cultures of travel: spaces of constructed visibility in Egypt' in N. AlSayyad (ed.) *Consuming Tradition, Manufacturing Heritage: Global Norms and Urban Forms in the Age of Tourism*, New York: Routledge, pp. 111–51.

Groslier, B.-P. and Arthaud, J. (1966) *Angkor, Art and Civilization*, London: Thames and Hudson.

Guha-Thakurta, T. (2003) 'Archaeology and the monument: an embattled site of history and memory in contemporary India' in R. Helson and M. Olin (eds) *Monuments and Memory, Made and Unmade*, Chicago: University of Chicago Press, pp. 233–58.

Gupta, A. and Ferguson, J. (1997) 'Beyond "culture": space, identity and the politics of difference' in A. Gupta and J. Ferguson (eds) *Culture, Power, Place: Explorations in Critical Anthropology*, Durham: Duke University Press, pp. 33–51.

Hall, M. and Page, S. (2000) 'Introduction: tourism in South and Southeast Asia - region and context' in M. Hall and S. Page (eds) *Tourism in South and Southeast Asia: Issues and Cases*, Oxford: Butterworth Heinemann, pp. 3–27.

Hall, M. and Tucker, H. (2004) 'Tourism and postcolonialism: an introduction' in M. Hall and H. Tucker (eds) *Tourism and Postcolonialism: Contested Discourses, Identities and Representations*, London: Routledge, pp. 1–24.

Harley, J. (1988) 'Maps, knowledge and power' in D.E. Cosgrove and S. Daniels (eds) *The Iconography of Landscape: Essays on the Symbolic Representation, Design and Use of Past Environments*, Cambridge: Cambridge University Press, pp. 277–305.

Harris, I. (2005) *Cambodian Buddhism; History and Practice*, Honolulu: University of Hawaii.

Harrison, D. (ed.) (1992) *Tourism and the Less Developed Countries*, London: Belhaven.

Higham, C. (2001) *The Civilization of Angkor*, London: Weidenfeld & Nicolson.

Hitchcock, M. (2005) 'Afterword' in D. Harrison and M. Hitchcock (eds) *The Politics of World Heritage; Negotiating Tourism and Conservation*, Clevedon: Channel View Publications, pp. 181–86.

Hodder, I. (1992) *Theory and Practice in Archaeology*, London: Routledge.

— (1998) 'The past as passion and play: Çatalhöyük as a site of conflict in the construction of multiple pasts' in L. Meskell (ed.) *Archaeology Under Fire: Nationalism, Politics and Heritage in the Eastern Mediterranean and Middle East*, London: Routledge, pp. 124–39.

Hughes, C. (2003) *The Political Economy of Cambodia's Transition 1991-2001*, London: Routledge.

Hun Sen (2001) *Address to the Closing Ceremony of the Ministry of Tourism Annual Meeting, 17th May 2001*.

ICC (1995) *International Co-ordinating Committee for the Safeguarding and Development of the Historic Site of Angkor; Report of Activities 1994,* Phnom Penh: ICC.
— (1996) *International Co-ordinating Committee for the Safeguarding and Development of the Historic Site of Angkor; Report of Activities 1995,* Phnom Penh: ICC.
— (1997) *International Co-ordinating Committee for the Safeguarding and Development of the Historic Site of Angkor; Report of Activities 1996,* Phnom Penh: ICC.
— (1998) *International Co-ordinating Committee for the Safeguarding and Development of the Historic Site of Angkor; Report of Activities 1997,* Phnom Penh: ICC.
— (1999) *International Co-ordinating Committee for the Safeguarding and Development of the Historic Site of Angkor; Report of Activities 1998,* Phnom Penh: ICC.
Ito, N. (1995) '"Authenticity" inherent in cultural heritage in Asia and Japan' in K.E. Larson (ed.) *Nara Conference on Authenticity*, Japan: UNESCO World Heritage Affairs/Agency for Cultural Affairs Japan, pp. 35–45.
Jackson, P. (2004) 'Local consumption cultures in a globalizing world', *Transactions of the Institute of British Geographers,* Vol. 29, No. 2, pp. 165–78.
Jacques, C. and Freeman, M. (1997) *Angkor: Cities and Temples*, London: Thames & Hudson.
Jokilehto, J. (1995) 'Authenticity: a general framework for the concept' in K.E. Larson, (ed.) *Nara Conference on Authenticity*, Japan: UNESCO World Heritage Affairs/Agency for Cultural Affairs Japan, pp. 17–34.
Kamm, H. (1998) *Cambodia; Report from a Stricken Land*, New York: Arcade Publishing.
Kato, T., Kaplan, J., Chan, S. and Real, S. (2000) *Cambodia: Enhancing Governance for Sustainable Development*, Manila, Philippines: Asian Development Bank.
Kiernan, B. (1996) *The Pol Pot Regime: Race, Power and Genocide in Cambodia Under the Khmer Rouge, 1975-79*, New Haven: Yale University Press.
— (2004) *How Pol Pot Came to Power; Colonialism, Nationalism and Communism in Cambodia, 1930-1975*, 2nd edition, New Haven: Yale University Press.
Kim, K. (2002) 'Tourism group: Thais undercut Cambodian travel industry', 22 February, *Cambodia Daily*, p. 14.
Kirshenblatt-Gimblett, B. (1998) *Destination Culture: Tourism, Museums and Heritage*, London: University of California Press.
Kohl, P. and Fawcett, C. (eds) (1995) *Nationalism, Politics and the Practice of Archaeology*, Cambridge: Cambridge University Press.
Lasansky, D. and McLaren, B. (eds) (2004) *Architecture and Tourism; Perception, Performance and Place*, Oxford: Berg.
Layton, R. and Thomas, J. (2001) 'Introduction: the destruction and conservation of cultural property' in R. Layton, P. Stone and J. Thomas (eds) *Destructions and Conservation of Cultural Property*, London: Routledge, pp. 1–21.
Ledgerwood, J. (1998) 'Rural Development in Cambodia: the View from the Village' in F. Brown and D. Timbermaned (eds) *Cambodia and the International Community: the Quest for Peace, Development and Democracy*, Singapore: Asia Society.
Lennon, J. and Foley, M. (2000) *Dark Tourism: the Attraction of Death and Disaster*, London: Continuum.
Leone, M., Potter, P.J. and Shackel, P. (1987) 'Toward a critical archaeology', *Current Anthropology*, Vol. 28, No. 3, pp. 283–302.
Logan, W. (2001) 'Globalising heritage: world heritage as a manifestation of modernism and challenges from the periphery, Proceedings of the Australia ICOMOS National Conference 2001', 20th Century Heritage Our Recent Cultural Legacy, Adelaide, 28 November–1 December 2001. ICOMOS Australia.

Loti, P. (1996) *A Pilgrimage to Angkor*, Bangkok: Silkworm Books.

Low, L. and Toh, M. (1997) 'Singapore: development of gateway tourism' in F. Go and C. Jenkins (eds) *Tourism and Economic Development in Asia and Australasia*, London: Cassell, pp. 237–54.

Luco, F. (2006) 'The people of Angkor: between tradition and development' in J. Chermayeff (ed.) *Phnom Penh Workshop on Public Interpretation*, Phnom Penh: APSARA, World Monuments Fund, pp. 118–30.

Mabbett, I. and Chandler, D. (1995) *The Khmers*, Oxford: Blackwell.

Macdonald, S. (2006) 'Undesirable heritage: fascist material culture and historical consciousness in Nuremberg', *International Journal of Heritage Studies*, Vol. 12, No. 1, pp. 9–28.

Macnaghten, P. and Urry, J. (1998) *Contested Natures*, London: Sage.

Malraux, A. (1930) *La Voie Royale*, Paris: Bernard Grasset.

McCrone, D. (1998) *The Sociology of Nationalism*, London: Routledge.

McManamon, F. and Hatton, A. (eds) (2000) *Cultural Resource Management in Contemporary Society*, London: Routledge.

McPhillips, J. and Van Roeun (2000) 'UNESCO Urges Halt to Angkor Karaoke Club, 5 December', *Cambodia Daily*, p. 12.

Meethan, K. (2001) *Tourism in Global Society*, Basingstoke, England: Palgrave.

Mehta, H. and Mehta, J. (1999) *Hun Sen: Strongman of Cambodia*, Singapore: Graham Brash.

Meskell, L. (1998) 'Introduction: archaeology matters' in L. Meskell (ed.) *Archaeology Under Fire: Nationalism, Politics and Heritage in the Eastern Mediterranean and Middle East*, London: Routledge, pp. 1–12.

Ministry of External Affairs (2005) *India-Cambodia Relations, Statement by Ministry of External Affairs, India, March 2005*. Available online at: http://meaindia.nic.in/foreignrelation/cambodia.htm (accessed 15 March 2006).

Ministry of Planning (1996) *First Socioeconomic Development Plan 1996-2000*, Phnom Penh: Ministry of Planning, Royal Government of Cambodia.

— (2003) *Cambodia Millennium Development Goals Report 2003*, Phnom Penh: Ministry of Planning, Royal Government of Cambodia.

Ministry of Tourism (2000) *Cambodia Tourism Statistical Report 2000*, Phnom Penh: Ministry of Tourism, Cambodia.

Ministry of Tourism/UNDP/WTO (1996) *National Tourism Development Plan for Cambodia*, Phnom Penh: Ministry of Tourism.

Miskell, B. and Thomas, F. (1998) *Angkor Forest Rehabilitation and Landscape Enhancement Project*, Phnom Penh: APSARA & Royal Government of Cambodia.

Miura, K. (2004) 'Contested heritage: people of Angkor', Unpublished PhD dissertation, London: School of Oriental and African Studies.

Mouhot, H. (1864a) *Travels in the Central Parts of Indo-China, Cambodia and Laos. Vol. 1*, London: John Murray.

— (1864b) *Travels in the Central Parts of Indo-China, Cambodia and Laos. Vol. 2*, London: John Murray.

Muan, I. (2001) *Citing Angkor: the 'Cambodian Arts' in the Age of Restoration 1918-2000*, Unpublished PhD thesis, Columbia University.

Myrdal, J. and Kessle, G. (1970) *Angkor: An Essay on Art and Imperialism*, New York: Pantheon Books.

Nora, P. (1998) 'Introduction' in P. Nora and L. Kritzman (eds) *Realms of Memory: The Construction of the French Past*, New York: Columbia University Press, pp. ix–2.

Norindr, P. (1995) 'Representing Indochina: the French colonial fantasmatic and the Exposition Coloniale de Paris', *French Cultural Studies*, Vol. vi, February, pp. 35–60.
— (1996) *Phantasmatic Indochina: French Colonial Ideology in Architecture, Film, and Literature*, London: Duke University Press.
— (2006) 'The fascination for the Angkor Wat and the ideology of the visible' in L. Ollier and T. Winter (eds) *Expressions of Cambodia: the Politics of Tradition, Identity and Change*, London: Routledge, pp. 54–70.
O'Connor, K. (1995) 'Airport development in Southeast Asia', *Journal of Transport Geography*, Vol. 3, No. 4, pp. 269–79.
Ong, A. (2006) *Neoliberalism as Exception: Mutations in Citizenship and Sovereignty*, Durham: Duke University Press.
Page, S. (2001) 'Gateways, hubs and transport interconnections in Southeast Asia: implications for tourism development in the twenty first century' in Peggy Teo, T. Chang and K. Ho (eds) *Interconnected Worlds: Tourism in Southeast Asia*, London: Pergamon, pp. 84–99.
Parmentier, H. (1959) *Henri Parmentier's Guide to Angkor*, Phnom Penh: E.K.L.I.P.
— (1939) *L'Art Khmer Classique*, Paris: Les Éditions d'art et d'histoire.
Peleggi, M. (1996) 'National heritage and global tourism', *Annals of Tourism Research*, Vol. 23, No. 2, pp. 432–48.
Peou, S. (2000) *Intervention & Change in Cambodia*, Chiang Mai: Silkworm Books.
Picard, M. and Wood, R. (eds) (1997) *Tourism, Ethnicity and the State in Asian and Pacific Societies*, Honolulu: University of Hawaii Press.
Pottier, C. (1999) *Carte Archéologique de la Région d'Angkor. Zone Sud.*, Paris: Universite Paris III - Sorbonne Nouvelle (UFR Orient et Monde Arabe).
Quintyn, M. and Zamaróczy, M. (1998) *Cambodia: Recent Economic Developments*, Phnom Penh: International Monetary Fund.
Raffles Hotels and Resorts (2003) *Fables of the Exotic East Volume 1*, Singapore: Raffles Hotels and Resorts.
Reid, A. (1993) *Southeast Asia in the Age of Commerce 1450-1680, Volume Two: Expansion and Crisis*, New Haven: Yale University Press.
Reyum Publishing (2001) *Cultures of Independence*, Phnom Penh: Reyum Publishing.
Richter, L. (1993) 'Tourism policy making in South-East Asia' in M. Hitchcock, V. King and M. Parnwell (eds) *Tourism in South East Asia*, London: Routledge, pp. 179–99.
Rigg, J. (1997) *Southeast Asia: The Human Landscape of Modernization and Development*, London: Routledge.
Roberts, D. (2001) *Political Transition in Cambodia 1991-1999: Power, Elitism and Democracy*, Richmond: Curzon.
Robinson, D. and Wheeler, T. (1992) *Cambodia; a Travel Survival Kit*, Australia: Lonely Planet Publications.
Robison, R., Rodan, G. and Hewison, K. (1999) 'Introduction' in R. Robison, G. Rodan and K. Hewison (eds) *Political Economy of Southeast Asia*, Oxford: Oxford University Press, pp. 1–28.
Robson, K. and Yee, J. (2005) 'Introduction' in K. Robson and J. Yee (eds) *France and "Indochina": Cultural Representations*, Lanham: Lexington Books, pp. 1–11.
Rooney, D. (2001) *Angkor Observed*, Thailand: Orchid Press.
Rose, P. (2002) 'Anticipating Angkor, a dream deferred, 21 July', *New York Times*. Available online at: http://query.nytimes.com/gst/fullpage.html?sec=travel&res=9800E5DD1739F932A15754C0A9649C8B63 (accessed 10 April 2007).

Rowley, K. (1996) 'The making of the Royal Government of Cambodia' in V. Selochan and C. Thayer (eds) *Bringing Democracy to Cambodia*, Canberra: Australian Defence Studies Centre, pp. 2–44.

Roy, A. (2004) 'Nostalgias of the modern' in N. AlSayyaded (ed.) *The End of Tradition?*, London: Routledge, pp. 63–86.

Said, E. (1995) *Orientalism*, Harmondsworth: Penguin.

Sanday, J. (2001) *A Summary Report on the Activities at the World Monuments Fund Conservation Program in Angkor, December 2001*, Siem Reap, New York: World Monuments Fund.

Sassen, S. (ed.) (2002) *Global Networks, Linked Cities*, London: Routledge.

Schama, S. (1995) *Landscape and Memory*, London: HarperCollins Publishers.

Shaftel, D. (2002) 'Asian tourism ministers to promote regional "branding"', 3 February, *Cambodia Daily*, p. 3.

Shanks, M. and Tilley, C. (1987) *Social Theory and Archaeology*, Cambridge: Polity Press.

Shawcross, W. (1993) *Sideshow*, London: Hogarth Press.

Shawcross, W. (1994) *Cambodia's New Deal; a report by William Shawcross*, Washington: Carnegie Endowment for International Peace.

Shepherd, R. (2006) 'UNESCO and the politics of cultural heritage in Tibet', *Journal of Contemporary Asia*, Vol. 36, No. 2, pp. 243–57.

Singh, T. (2004) 'Tourism Searching for New Horizons: an Overview' in T. Singh (ed.) *New Horizons in Tourism: Strange Experiences and Stranger Practices*, Wallingford, Oxfordshire: CAB International, pp. 1–10.

Smith, L. (2004) *Archaeological Theory and the Politics of Cultural Heritage*, London: Routledge.

Sofield, T. (2001) 'Globalisation, tourism and culture in Southeast Asia' in Peggy Teo, T. Chang and K. Ho (eds) *Interconnected Worlds: Tourism in Southeast Asia*, London: Pergamon.

Soja, E. (2000) *Thirdspace: Journeys to Los Angeles and Other Real and Imagined Places*, Oxford: Blackwell.

Souknilundon, S. (2001) 'Smoother Driving in Siem Reap Next Year, 27 June', *Cambodia Daily*, p. 8.

Stark, M. and Griffin, B. (2004) 'Archaeological research and cultural heritage management in Cambodia's Mekong Delta: the search for the "Cradle of Khmer Civilization"' in Y. Rowan and U. Baram (eds) *Marketing Heritage: Archaeology and the Consumption of the Past*, Walnut Creek, California: Altamira Press, pp. 117–41.

Steinberg, D. (1959) *Cambodia; its People, its Society, its Culture*, New Haven: Hraf Press.

Stierlin, H. (1997) *Angkor and Khmer Art*, Paudex, Switzerland: Parkstone.

Taylor, K. (2004) 'Cultural heritage management: a possible role for charters and principles in Asia', *International Journal of Heritage Studies*, Vol. 10, No. 5, pp. 417–33.

Teo, P., Chang, T. and Ho, K. (2001) 'Introduction: globalisation and interconnectedness in Southeast Asian tourism' in P. Teo, T. Chang and K. Ho (eds) *Interconnected Worlds: Tourism in Southeast Asia*, London: Pergamon.

Terkenli, T. (2002) 'Landscapes of tourism: towards a global cultural economy of space?', *Tourism Geographies*, Vol. 4, No. 3, pp. 227–54.

Thai Air (2004) *Fah Thai, In-flight Magazine, September-October, p. 12*, Bangkok: Thai Air.

The Hindu (2002) 'India to help restore temple at Angkor Wat', *The Hindu*, 11 February 2002. Available online at: www.hinduonnet.com/2002/04/11/stories/2002041102831100.htm (accessed 15 March 2006).

The Tribune (2002) 'India offers $ 10m loan to Cambodia', *The Tribune*, 11 November 2002. Available online at: http://www.tribuneindia.com/2002/20021107/main8.htm (accessed 15 March 2006).

Thibault, C. (1998) *Siem Reap-Angkor: Une région du Nord - Cambodge en voie de mutation*, Paris: Prodig.

Thomas, J. (1996) *Time, Culture and Identity*, London: Routledge.

Thompson, A. (2004) 'Pilgrims to Angkor: a Buddhist "Cosmpolis" in Southeast Asia?', *Bulletin of the Students of the Department of Archaeology, Department of Archaeology Royal University of Fine Arts, Phnom Penh*, Vol. 3, pp. 88–119.

Tilley, C. (1999) *Metaphor and Material Culture*, Oxford: Blackwell.

Tith, N. (1998) 'The challenge of sustainable economic growth and development in Cambodia' in F. Brown and D. Timberman (eds) *Cambodia and the International Community: the Quest for Peace, Development and Democracy*, Singapore: Asia Society.

Trail of Indochina (2002) *Trail of Indochina*. Available online at: www.onetravelworld.com/vietnam.cfm?do=NOT-TOI-01 (accessed 12 December 2002).

Tully, J. (2002) *France on the Mekong: a History of the Protectorate in Cambodia, 1863-1953*, Lanham: University Press of America.

Tunbridge, J. and Ashworth, G. (1996) *Dissonant Heritage: the Management of the Past as a Resource in Conflict*, Chichester: Wiley.

Turnbull, R. (2004) 'Conservation at twenty paces: the politics of Angkor restoration', *Sarika*, Vol. 3, No. 4, pp. 32–9.

— (2006) 'A burned out theater: the state of Cambodia's performing arts' in L. Ollier and T. Winter (eds) *Expressions of Cambodia: the Politics of Tradition, Identity and Change*, London: Routledge, pp. 133–49.

Turner, V. (1995) *The Ritual Process: Structure and Anti-Structure*, New York: Aldine de Gruyter.

Turtinen, J. (2000) 'Globalising heritage - On UNESCO and the transnational construction of a world heritage', *SCORE Working Paper Series*. Available online at: www.score.su.se/workingpapers.html (accessed 10 June 2006).

UNESCO (1993) *Safeguarding and Development of Angkor*, Tokyo: UNESCO.

— (1996) *Angkor - Past, Present and Future*, Phnom Penh: APSARA.

— (1997) *World Heritage and the Prevention of Illicit Traffic of Cultural Property: World Heritage Committee, Twenty First Session*, France: UNESCO.

— (1999) *Report by the Intergovernmental Committee for Promoting the Return of Cultural Property to its Countries of Origin or its Restitution in Case of Illicit Appropriation on its Activities (1998-1999)*, Paris: UNESCO.

— (2003) *Paris Declaration: Adopted at Second Intergovernmental Conference for the Safeguarding and Sustainable Development of Angkor and its Region*, 14 & 15 November, Paris: UNESCO.

UNESCO and Ministry of Culture and Fine Arts (2004) *Inventory of Intangible Cultural Heritage of Cambodia*, Phnom Penh: UNESCO/Ministry of Culture and Fine Arts.

Urry, J. (1990) *The Tourist Gaze: Leisure and Travel in Contemporary Societies*, London: Sage Publications.

— (1995) *Consuming Places*, London: Routledge.

— (1997) 'Sociology of time and space' in B. Turner (ed.) *The Blackwell Companion to Social Theory*, Cambridge, MA: Blackwell.

— (2000) *Sociology Beyond Societies*, London: Routledge.

— (2003) *Global Complexity*, Cambridge: Polity.

Vann Molyvann (2003) *Modern Khmer Cities*, Phnom Penh: Reyum Publishing.

Vickery, M. (1998) *Society, Economics, and Politics in Pre-Angkor Cambodia: the 7th-8th Centuries*, Tokyo: The Centre for East Asian Cultural Studies for UNESCO.

Vickery, M. (1999) *Cambodia 1975 - 1982*, Chiang Mai: Silkworm Books.

Wager, J. (1995a) 'Developing a strategy for the Angkor world heritage site', *Tourism Management*, Vol. 16, No. 7, pp. 515–23.

— (1995b) 'Environmental planning for a world heritage site: case study of Angkor Wat, Cambodia', *Environmental Planning and Management*, Vol. 38, No. 3, pp. 419–34.

Waterton, E. (2005) 'Whose sense of place? Reconciling archaeological perspectives with community values: cultural landscapes in Britain', *International Journal of Heritage Studies,* Vol. 11, No. 4, pp. 309–25.

Winter, T. (2003) 'Tomb raiding Angkor: a clash of cultures', *Indonesia and the Malay World*, Vol. 31, No. 89, pp. 58–9.

— (2004) 'Landscape, memory and heritage: New Year celebrations at Angkor, Cambodia', *Current Issues in Tourism*, Vol. 7, Nos. 4 & 5, pp. 330–45.

— (2006) 'When ancient 'glory' meets modern 'tragedy': Angkor and the Khmer Rouge in contemporary tourism' in L. Ollier and T. Winter (eds) *Expressions of Cambodia: the Politics of Tradition, Identity and Change*, London: Routledge, pp. 37–53.

— (2007) 'Rethinking tourism in Asia', *Annals of Tourism Research*, Vol. 34, No. 1, pp. 27–44.

Wolters, O. (1999) *History, Culture, and Region in Southeast Asian Perspectives*, Ithaca: Cornell Southeast Asia Program Publications.

Wong, G. (2001) 'Angkor Wat, Cambodia', *Time Traveler: Access Asia,* pp. 82–3.

Wood, R. (1993) 'Tourism, culture and the sociology of development' in M. Hitchcock, V. King and M. Parnwell (eds) *Tourism in Southeast Asia*, London: Routledge, pp. 49–70.

Wood, T. (2006) 'Touring memories of the Khmer Rouge' in L. Ollier and T. Winter (eds) *Expressions of Cambodia: the Politics of Tradition, Identity and Change*, London: Routledge.

Woodward, C. (2001) *In Ruins*, London: Chatto and Windus.

Wright, G. (1991) *The Politics of Design in French Colonial Urbanism*, London: University of Chicago Press.

WTO (1999) *Tourism: 2020 Vision (Executive Summary)*, Madrid: World Tourism Organization.

Yalouri, E. (2001) *The Acropolis*, Oxford: Berg.

Yogerst, J. (2001) *Legends of Indochina*, London: The Illustrated London News Group.

Young, J. (1994) *The Art of Memory: Holocaust Memorials in History*, New York: Presto.

Yúdice, G. (2003) *The Expediency of Culture; Uses of Culture in the Global Era*, Durham: Duke University Press.

Yunis, E. (2000) *Cultural Heritage, Tourism and Sustainable Development*, Madrid: World Tourism Organization.

Index

Aid *see* Reconstruction
    Cultural heritage 22–3, 63–6, 133
    UNTAC 6
Airports 86
Air Space 86
Ancestral Spirits, animism 128, 132
Ang Choulean 59, 73
Angkor
    Archaeological Park 35, 147
    Conservation office 31, 51
    Mapping 48–51
    Period 10, 33
Anlong Veng 21
Anthropology 60
Apocalypse Now 103
APSARA Authority 51–4, 59, 136–7
    Restructure 71
Apsara dance 145
Archaeological Survey of India 65, 133–8
Asian Development Bank 69–70, 77
Asian Tourism 138, 148

Bangkok 18
Baray 11
Bender, B 13
Buddhism 5, 8, 33, 60, 142–3
    Monasteries 114–5
    Monks 59
    Pilgrims 26

Capacity building 59, 140–2
Cartier, C 19
Castells, M 17
Ceramics 34–5
Circuits, grand et petit 40, 124
Civil war 3–8, 113
Chandler, D 3, 45, 71, 143
Charters 13–14, 55, 136
Coedès, G 33, 64

Colonialism 143–7
    Arts 41–2
    Expositions 32–9
    Nation Building 35–6
    Restoration 31–3, 39
    Territories 30–1
    Tourism 38–42
Commaille, J 39
Commodification 38–9, 43, 45
Communitas 113
Communities *see* villages
Conservation 54–8
    Positivism 56, 140–2
Crouch, D 19
Cruise Ships 88
Cultural Resource Management 14, 140
Cultural tourism 73–80
Culture
    High/low 64, 144
    Relativism 140–2

Dagens, B 31
Dahles, H 16
Danger 106–8, 148
De Certeau, M 121
Delaporte, L 29
Democratic Kampuchea *see* Khmer Rouge
Development
    and Culture 22
    ignored 58–60, 142–3
    Socio-economic 68–77, 147–9
    Southeast Asia 82–4
    Sustainable 77–9
    tourism industry 80–1
Discovery 27–9, 92–109, 133

École française d'Extrême Orient 31–3,
    55, 135–8, 141
Edensor, T 19

Edwards, P 27, 32, 35
Elections, *see* UNTAC (1998) 69
Epigraphy 33
Ethnicity *see* Khmer identity
Eurocentrism 13, 130–8, 141
Extended Metropolitan Region 84–6

Forest *see* jungle
Foucault, M 115

Genocide *see* Khmer Rouge
Glaize, M 32
Grand Hotel d'Angkor 40, 44
Grenade attack 69
Groslier, BP 44
Groslier, G 41
Guidebooks *see* Lonely Planet
Guides 129

Hall of Dancers 131
Higham, C 10
Historiography 33–5, 55–6, 143, 144
Hotel Zone 61, 74–5, 78
Hun Sen 69–71

ICC 8, 51–8, 63, 68–80, 130–142
Independence 42–3
India 65, 133–8
Indiana Jones 121
Indianization 32
Indochina 28–33, 98–103
Inequality *see* poverty, 79, 147–8
Infrastructure 80–2
Intangible Heritage 145
International Monetary Fund 6

Japan 65
Jayavarman VII 34, 117, 132
Jungle *see* ruin, 25–30, 31–6, 97–103,
    117–25, 130–38, 143

Khmer
    Identity 5–9, 109–114, 126, 128, 143
    New Year 111–14, 143–5
Khmer Rouge 3–4, 44–5, 112, 130

Landmines 7, 57, 105, 130
Logan, B 14
Lonely Planet 1, 68, 107, 125
Lon Nol 44, 113
Loti, P 29

Malraux, A 30, 102
Meethan, K 139
Mekong World Heritage Tour 93–6
Memory 19–20, 110, 114, 134
Meskell, L 140
Ministry of Culture 145
Ministry of Tourism 70, 80, 148
Mise en Valeur 35, 41
Mission Civilisatrice 35–6
Modernity 43–4, 139–41
monastery *see* Buddhism
Mouhot, H 26–30, 101
Muan, I 41

Nagarra Vatta 36
Nara Declaration *see* Charters, 136
National Anthem 42
Nationalism/Nation Building 16, 35–6,
    42–6, 66, 72, 109–14, 142, 146
Neo-colonialism 63–6
Networks 17–18, 80–8
Norindr, P 28, 30, 38, 144

Open skies policy 69, 80

Paris Peace Accords 5
Peoples Republic of Kampuchea 3–4
Phnom Penh 6, 145
Pilgrimage 26
Political reform 70
Pol Pot 3–4, 44–5
Pottier, C 11
Poverty 8, 78–9, 147–9
Preah Khan 116–38

Reconciliation 8, 21, 112
Reproductions *see* expositions, 37–8, 41, 45
Restoration *see* conservation, 11–15, 20–2,
    125–30, 133–8
    Colonial era 31–5
    Post-war 139, 140–9
    World heritage 54–8
Revival *see* restoration
Romance 32, 97–103, 137, 141, 145
Romanticism 28–9
Rooney, D 101, 118
Roy, A 145
Royal University of Fine Arts 44
Ruins *see* Preah Khan and Ta Prohm
    French discovery 26, 29
    Painting 43
    Representations of 97–103, 117–25
    Restoration 31, 125

Schama, S 121
Sculpture 33, 41, 56
Shawcross, W 4, 6
Siem Reap 58–62, 72–9 147–8
Sihanouk, N 42–4, 71
Smith, LJ 14, 139
Sok An 76
Space, representations of 47–54,
    58–63
Structural Adjustment Program 68
Supreme Council for National
    Culture 5–52
Sustainable development 77–9

Taliban 21
Ta Prohm 116–38
Thai Air 86–8
Tilley, C 14
Tonle Sap 3, 148
Tourism *see* development
    Arrivals 8, 68, 86, 111
    Cultural economy 91–105
    Facilities 72–80
    Hubs 86–8
    Networks 18, 84–6, 97, 148
    Regional 80–81
    Threat 72–3
Tourist, narratives
    Domestic 109–14, 125–30
    International 91–109, 118–25
Touristscape 78, 148
Touristscapes 88, 148
Trees *see* jungle, 135
Tully, J 35

Turnbull, R 145
Tuol Sleng 21

UNESCO 13, 54–8, 130–8, 140
United Nations *see* UNTAC
UNTAC 5–6, 63, 69
Urban
    Migration 78
    Development 72–80
Urry, J 17, 124

Vann Molyvann 44, 71
Vegetation *see* ruin
Vickery, M 10
Vietnam War 3–4, 103–9
Villages 15, 142
    Removed 32, 40
    Neglected 58–63

Wager, J 48
World Bank 69–70, 77
World heritage *see* charters, restoration,
    UNESCO
    Listing 8, 47–8
    Narratives of 91–7
World Monuments Fund 57, 130–7
World Tourism Organization 73
Wright, G 34

Yúdice, G 22

ZEMP 48–54, 78, 147–8
Zhou Daguan 9